THE

# FOUR LEADING DOCTRINES

OF

THE NEW CHURCH.

THE

# FOUR LEADING DOCTRINES

OF

# THE NEW CHURCH,

SIGNIFIED BY THE NEW JERUSALEM IN THE REVELATION:

BEING THOSE CONCERNING

THE LORD; THE SACRED SCRIPTURE; FAITH; AND LIFE.

---

BY EMANUEL SWEDENBORG,

*Servant of the Lord Jesus Christ.*

---

NEW YORK:

AMERICAN SWEDENBORG PRINTING AND PUBLISHING SOCIETY.

1873.

*Published by* The American Swedenborg Printing and Publishing Society, *organized for the purpose of Stereotyping, Printing, and Publishing Uniform Editions of the Theological Writings of* Emanuel Swedenborg, *and incorporated in the State of New York,* A. D. 1850.

# CONTENTS.

## THE DOCTRINE OF THE NEW JERUSALEM CONCERNING THE LORD.

## DOCTRINE OF THE SACRED SCRIPTURE.

## DOCTRINE OF FAITH.



## DOCTRINE OF LIFE.

# THE DOCTRINE OF THE NEW JERUSALEM RESPECTING THE LORD.

---

BY EMANUEL SWEDENBORG,

*Servant of the Lord Jesus Christ.*

---

BEING A TRANSLATION OF HIS WORK ENTITLED

"DOCTRINA NOVÆ HIEROSOLYMÆ DE DOMINO." Amstelodami, 1763.

TO WHICH ARE ADDED,

ANSWERS TO QUESTIONS ON THE TRINITY,

PROPOSED BY THE LATE REV. T. HARTLEY, A. M.

NEW YORK:

AMERICAN SWEDENBORG PRINTING AND PUBLISHING SOCIETY.

1873.

THE DOCTRINE

OF

# THE NEW JERUSALEM

CONCERNING

# THE LORD.

---

### THE WHOLE SACRED SCRIPTURE TREATS OF THE LORD, AND THE LORD IS THE WORD.

1. We read in John, "In the beginning was the Word, and the Word was with God, and God was the Word. The same was in the beginning with God. All things were made by him; and without him was not any thing made that was made. In him was life, and the life was the light of men: and the light shineth in darkness; but the darkness comprehended it not." Moreover, "The Word was made flesh, and dwelt among us, and we beheld his glory, the glory as of the Only-begotten of the Father, full of grace and truth" (chap. i. 1—5, 14). The same Evangelist further adds, "Light is come into the world, and men loved darkness rather than light, because their deeds were evil" (chap. iii. 19). And in another place, "While ye have light believe in the light, that ye may be the children of light. I am come a light into the world, that whosoever believeth on me should not abide in darkness" (chap. xii. 36, 46). From these passages it is evident, that the Lord is God from eternity, and that this God is himself the Lord who was born in the world; for it is said, that the Word was with God, and God was the Word: as, also, that without him was not any thing made that was made: and again, that the Word was made flesh, and they beheld him. Why the Lord is called THE WORD, is but little understood in the church: he is however called the Word, because THE WORD, signifies Divine Truth, or Divine Wisdom; and the Lord is Divine Truth itself, or Divine Wisdom itself; for which reason he is likewise called the Light, which also is said to have come into the world. Divine Wisdom and Divine Love, constitute a one, and were from eternity a one in

the Lord, wherefore it is said, "In him was life, and the life was the light of men:"—Life is Divine Love, and Light is Divine Wisdom. This oneness is what is meant by these words: "In the beginning—the Word was with God, and God was the Word:"—with God, means to be in him; for wisdom is in love, and love in wisdom. So also in another place in John: "And now, O Father, glorify thou me with thine own self, with the glory which I had with thee, before the world was" (chap. xvii. 5). With thy own self, means, in thyself: wherefore it is also said, and God was the Word: and elsewhere, that the Lord is in the Father, and the Father in him, as well as, that the Father and he are one. Now as the Word is the Divine Wisdom of the Divine Love, it follows, that it is Jehovah himself, thus the Lord, by whom all things were made that are made, for all things were created from the Divine Love by the Divine Wisdom.

2. That the Word which is here specifically meant is the same that was manifested by Moses, and the Prophets, and by the Evangelists, may evidently appear from this consideration; that this is Divine Truth Itself, from which is derived all the wisdom that exists with angels, and all spiritual intelligence with men. For angels have in the heavens the very same Word that men have in the world, save only that with men it is natural, whereas, in the heavens it is spiritual. And since the Word is Divine Truth, it is also the Divine Proceeding, and this is not only from the Lord but is also the Lord Himself. As this Word is thus the Lord Himself, each and all [things] of the Word are written in reference to him alone: from Isaiah even to Malachi, there is nothing given which is not concerning the Lord, or, in the opposite sense, contrary to the Lord. That this is the case, has not heretofore been seen by any one; but yet every one may see it, provided he is apprised of it, and thinks of it whilst he is reading; and is informed further, that in the word there is not only a natural but also a spiritual sense; and that in this sense, by the names of persons and of places, is signified something of the Lord, and thence something of heaven and the church from him, or something opposite thereto. Now as each and all things of the Word have reference to the Lord; and as the Word, because it is Divine Truth, is the Lord; it clearly appears why it is said, "and the Word was made flesh, and dwelt among us, and we beheld his glory;" and also why it is said, "While ye have light, believe in the light, that ye may be the children of light. I am come a light into the world, that whosoever believeth on me should not abide in darkness." Light is the Divine Truth,—thus the Word: wherefore every one, even at the present day, who, when reading the Word, approaches the Lord alone, and prays to him, is enlightened by it.

3. We will here state, in a few words, what is declared concerning the Lord, both in general and in particular, in all the Prophets of the Old Testament, from *Isaiah* unto *Malachi*. I. That the Lord would come into the world in the fulness of time, which was, when he was no longer known by the Jews, and when, consequently, there was nothing which constitutes a church remaining; and that unless he should then come into the world and reveal himself, mankind would perish in eternal death: as he himself says in John: "If ye believe not that I am [he], ye shall die in your sins" (viii. 24). II. That the Lord would come into the world to accomplish a last judgment, and thereby to subjugate the then prevailing power of the hells; which was to be effected by combats or by temptations admitted to assault the Human derived from the mother, and by continual victories then obtained; and that unless the hells should be so subjugated, no man could possibly be saved. III. That the Lord would come into the world to glorify his Human, that is, to unite it to the Divine which was in him by conception. IV. That the Lord would come into the world to establish a New Church, which should acknowledge him as the Redeemer and Saviour, and by love and faith towards him be redeemed and saved. V. That he would then also arrange heaven in order, so that it, with the church, should constitute a one. VI. That the passion of the cross would be the last combat or temptation, by which he would fully conquer the hells, and fully glorify his Human.—That the Word treats of no other subjects, may be seen in the small treatise concerning the *Sacred Scriptures*.

4. In confirmation of this, I shall merely, in the first article, adduce such passages from the Word, as mention *that day*, *in that day*, and *in that time*; in which, by *day* and *time*, are meant the coming of the Lord. Thus in Isaiah: "And it shall come to pass in the *last days* that the mountain of the house of Jehovah shall be established in the top of the mountains." "Jehovah alone shall be exalted *in that day*." "*The day* of Jehovah of hosts shall be upon every one that is proud and lofty." "*In that day* a man shall cast his idols of silver and his idols of gold" (chap. ii. 2, 11, 12, 20). "*In that day* Jehovah will take away the bravery of their tinkling ornaments" (chap. iii. 18). "*In that day* shall the Branch of Jehovah be beautiful and glorious" (chap. iv. 2). "*In that day* they shall roar against them like the roaring of the sea, and if one look unto the land behold darkness and sorrow, and the light is darkened in the heavens thereof" (chap. v. 30). "And it shall come to pass *in that day* that Jehovah shall hiss for the fly that is in the uttermost part of the rivers of Egypt." "*In the same day* shall Jehovah shave with a razor that is hired." "It shall come to pass *in that day* that a man shall nourish a young cow and two

sheep." "*In that day* it shall even be for briers and thorns" (chap. vii. 18, 20, 21, 23). "And what will ye do *in the day* of visitation, and in the desolation which shall come from far?" "*In that day* the remnant of Israel, and such as are escaped of the house of Jacob, shall no more again stay upon him that smote them, but shall stay upon Jehovah" (chap. x. 3, 20). "*In that day* there shall be a root of Jesse which shall stand for an ensign of the people; to it shall the Gentiles seek, and his rest shall be glorious." "*In that day*—Jehovah shall set his hand again the second time to recover the remnant of his people" (chap. xi. 10, 11). "*In that day* thou shalt say, O Jehovah, I will praise thee." "*In that day* shall ye say, Praise Jehovah, call upon his name" (chap. xii. 1, 4). "Howl ye, for *the day* of Jehovah is at hand, it shall come as a destruction from the Almighty." "Behold, *the day* of Jehovah cometh, cruel both with wrath and fierce anger." "I will shake the heavens, and the earth shall remove out of her place, in the wrath of Jehovah of hosts, and *in the day* of his fierce anger." "Her *time* is near to come, and her *days* shall not be prolonged" (chap. xiii. 6, 9, 13, 22). "*In that day* it shall come to pass that the glory of Jacob shall be made thin." "*At that day* shall a man look to his Maker, and his eyes shall have respect to the Holy One of Israel." "*In that day* shall his strong cities be as a forsaken bough" (chap. xvii. 4, 7, 9). "And the inhabitants of this isle shall say *in that day*, Behold, such is our expectation" (chap. xx. 6). "*In that day* shall five cities in the land of Egypt speak the language of Canaan." "*In that* day shall there be an altar to Jehovah in the midst of the land of Egypt." "*In that day* shall there be a highway out of Egypt to Assyria." "*In that day* shall Israel be the third with Egypt and with Assyria, even a blessing in the midst of the land" (chap. xix. 18, 19, 23, 24). "For it is *a day* of trouble, and of treading down, and of perplexity by the Lord Jehovah of hosts" (chap. xxii. 5). "*In that day* Jehovah shall punish the host of the high ones that are on high, and the kings of the earth upon the earth." "And they shall be gathered together as prisoners are gathered in the pit, and shall be shut up in the prison, and after many *days* shall they be visited; then the moon shall be confounded, and the sun ashamed" (chap. xxiv. 21—23). "It shall be said *in that day* Lo, this is our God, we have waited for him, and he will save us" (chap. xxv. 9). "*In that day* shall this song be sung in the land of Judah, We have a strong city" (chap. xxvi. 1). "*In that day* Jehovah, with his sore, and great, and strong sword, shall punish." "*In that day* sing ye unto her, A vineyard of red wine." "And it shall come to pass in *that day* that the great trumpet shall be blown" (chap. xxvii. 1, 2, 13). "*In that day* shall Jehovah of hosts be for a crown of glory, and for a diadem of beauty" (chap. xxviii. 5). "*In that day* shall the deaf hear the words of the book, and the eyes of the blind shall see out of obscurity, and out of darkness" (chap. xxix. 18). "And there shall be upon every high mountain and upon every high hill, rivers, and streams of waters, *in the day* of the great slaughter, when the towers fall: moreover, the light of the moon shall be as the light of the sun, &c., *in the day* that Jehovah bindeth up the breach of his people" (chap. xxx. 25, 26). "*In that day* every man shall cast away his idols of silver, and his idols of gold" (chap. xxxi. 7). "For it is *the day* of Jehovah's vengeance, the year of his recompences" (chap. xxxiv. 8). "These two things shall come to thee in a moment, *in one day;* the loss of children and widowhood" (chap. xlvii. 9). "Therefore my people shall know my name; therefore they shall know *in that day*, that I am he that doth speak, behold it is I" (chap. lii. 6). "Jehovah hath anointed me to preach good tidings unto the meek;—to proclaim the acceptable year of Jehovah, to comfort all that mourn" (chap. lxi. 1, 2). "For *the day* of vengeance is in my heart, and *the year* of my redeemed is come" (chap. lxiii. 4).

So in Jeremiah. "*In those days*, saith Jehovah, they shall say no more, The ark of the covenant of Jehovah." "*At that time* they shall call Jerusalem the throne of Jehovah." "*In those days* the house of Judah shall walk with the house of Israel" (chap. iii. 16—18). "*At that day*, saith Jehovah, the heart of the king shall perish, and the heart of the princes; and the priests shall be astonished, and the prophets shall wonder" (chap. iv. 9). "Therefore, behold *the days come*, saith Jehovah, that it shall no more be called Tophet:—for the land shall be desolate" (chap. vii. 32, 34). "Therefore shall they fall among them that fall, *in the time* of their visitation" (chap. viii. 12). "Behold, *the days come*, saith Jehovah, that I will punish all them which are circumcised with the uncircumcised" (chap. ix. 25). "*In the time* of their visitation they shall perish" (chap. x. 15). "And there shall be no remnant of them, for I will bring evil upon the men of Anathoth, even *the year* of their visitation" (chap. xi. 23). "Behold, *the days come*, saith Jehovah, that it shall no more be said," &c. (chap. xvi. 14). "I will shew them the back and not the face *in the day* of their calamity" (chap. xviii. 17). "Behold, *the days come*, saith Jehovah, that this place shall be no more called Tophet, nor the valley of the son of Hinnom, but the valley of slaughter" (chap. xix. 6). "Behold, *the days come*, saith Jehovah, that I will raise unto David a righteous branch, and a king shall reign and prosper." "*In his days* Judah shall be saved, and Israel shall dwell safely." "Therefore, behold, *the days come*, saith Jehovah, that they shall no more say," &c. "I will bring evil upon them, even *the year* of their visitation, saith Jehovah." "In *the latter days* ye shall consider it perfectly" (chap. xxiii. 5—7,

12, 20). "For lo, *the days come*, saith Jehovah, that I will bring again the captivity of my people Israel and Judah." "Alas, for *that day* is great, so that none is like it." "For it shall come to pass *in that day*, saith Jehovah of hosts, that I will break his yoke from off thy neck, and will burst thy bonds" (chap. xxx. 3, 7, 8). "For there shall be *a day* that the watchmen upon the mount Ephraim shall cry, Arise ye, and let us go up to Zion, unto Jehovah our God." "Behold, *the days come*, saith Jehovah, that I will make a new covenant." "Behold, *the days come*, saith Jehovah, that the city shall be built to Jehovah" (chap. xxxi. 6, 31, 38). "Behold, *the days come*, saith Jehovah, that I will perform that good thing." "*In those days*, and *at that time*, will I cause the branch of righteousness to grow up unto David." "*In those days* shall Judah be saved" (chap. xxxiii. 14—16). "I will bring my words upon this city for evil, and not for good, and they shall be accomplished *in that day* before thee. But I will deliver thee *in that day*" (chap. xxxix. 16, 17). "For this is *the day* of the Lord Jehovah of hosts, a day of vengeance, that he may avenge him of his adversaries." "*The day* of their calamity was come upon them, and *the time* of their visitation" (chap. xlvi. 10, 21). "Because of *the day* that cometh to spoil," &c. (chap. xlvii. 4). "I will bring upon it, even upon Moab, *the year* of their visitation, saith Jehovah. Yet will I bring again the captivity of Moab *in the latter days*, saith Jehovah" (chap. xlviii. 41, 47). "I will bring the calamity of Esau upon him, *the time* that I will visit him." "Her young men shall fall in her streets, and all the men of war shall be cut off *in that day*." "*In the latter days*, I will bring again the captivity of Elam" (chap. xlix. 8, 26, 39). "*In those days*, and *in that time*, saith Jehovah, the children of Israel shall come, they and the children of Judah together, going and weeping: they shall go, and seek Jehovah their God." "*In those days*, and *in that time*, saith Jehovah, the iniquity of Israel shall be sought for, and there shall be none." "Woe unto them, for *their day* is come, *the time* of their visitation." "Thy *day* is come, *the time* that I will visit thee" (chap. l. 4, 20, 27, 31). "They are vanity, the work of errors; *in the time* of their visitation they shall perish" (chap. li. 18).

So in Ezekiel. "*An end* is come, *the end* is come." "The morning is come upon thee, O thou that dwellest in the land; *the time* is come, *the day* of trouble is near." "Behold *the day*, behold, it is come: the morning is gone forth; the rod had blossomed; pride hath budded." "*The time* is come, *the day* draweth near;—wrath is upon the multitude thereof." "Their silver and their gold shall not be able to deliver them *in the day* of the wrath of Jehovah" (chap. vii. 6, 7, 10, 12, 19). "They of the house of Israel say, The vision that he seeth is for many *days to come*, and he prophesieth of the *times that are far off*" (chap. xii. 72). "Ye have not gone up into the gaps, neither made up the hedge for the house of Israel, to stand in the battle *in the day* of Jehovah" (chap. xiii. 5). "And thou profane wicked prince of Israel, whose *day is come* when iniquity shall have an end" (chap. xxi. 25). "Then say thou, Thus saith the Lord Jehovah: The city sheddeth blood in the midst of it, that her *time* may come." "Thou hast caused *thy days* to draw near, and art come even unto *thy years*" (chap. xxii. 3,4). "Shall it not be *in the day* when I take from them their strength?" "He that escapeth *in that day* shall come unto thee, to cause thee to hear it with thine ears." "*In that day* shall thy mouth be opened to him which is escaped" (chap. xxiv. 25–27). "*In that day* will I cause the horn of the house of Israel to bud forth" (chap. xxix. 21). "Howl ye, Woe worth the day! For *the day* is near, even *the day* of Jehovah is near, a cloudy *day* it shall be *the time* of the heathen." "*In that day* shall messengers go forth from me" (chap. xxx. 2, 3, 9). "*In the day* when he went down to the grave" (chap. xxxi. 15). "As a shepherd seeketh out his flock *in the day* that he is among his sheep that are scattered; so will I seek out my sheep, and will deliver them out of all places, where they have been scattered in the cloudy and dark *day*" (chap. xxxiv. 12). "*In the day* that I shall have cleansed you from all your iniquities" (chap. xxxvi. 33). "Prophesy and say, *In that day* when my people of Israel dwelleth safely, shalt thou not know it?" "It shall be *in the latter days*, and I will bring thee against my land." "And it shall come to pass *at the same time*, when Gog shall come against the land of Israel, fury shall come up in my face." "For in my jealousy, and in the fire of my wrath, have I spoken: Surely *in that day* there shall be a great shaking in the land of Israel" (chap. xxxviii. 14, 16, 18, 19). "Behold, it is come:— this is *the day* whereof I have spoken." "And it shall come to pass *in that day*, that I will give unto Gog a place there of graves in Israel." "So the house of Israel shall know that I am Jehovah their God, from *that day* and forward" (chap. xxxix. 8, 11, 22).

So in DANIEL. "There is a God in heaven that revealeth secrets, and maketh known what shall be *in the latter days*" (chap. ii. 28). "Until—*the time* came that the saints possessed the kingdom" (chap. vii. 22). "Understand, O Son of man: for *at the time of the end* shall be the vision." "And he said, Behold, I will make thee know what shall be *in the last end* of the indignation; for at the *time appointed the end* shall be." "And the vision of the evening and the morning, which was told, is true; wherefore shut thou up the vision, for it shall be for *many days*" (chap. viii. 17, 19, 26). "I am come to make thee understand what shall befall thy people in *the latter days*: for yet the vision is for *many days*" (chap. x. 14). "And some of them of understanding shall fall, to try them, and to purge, and to make them white, even to *the time of the end;* because it is yet for a *time* appointed" (chap. xi. 35). "*At that time* shall Michael stand up, the great prince which standeth for the children of thy people; and there shall be a *time* of trouble, such as there never was since there was a nation, even to *that same time;* and *at that time* thy people shall be delivered, every one that shall be found written in the book" (chap. xii. 1). "But thou, O Daniel, shut up the words, and seal the book, even to *the time of the end.*" "From *the time* that the daily sacrifice shall be taken away, and the abomination that maketh desolate set up, there shall be a thousand two hundred and ninety days." "Thou shalt rest and stand in thy lot at *the end of the days*" (chap. xii. 4, 11, 13).

So in Hosea. "Yet a *little while*, and I will avenge the blood of Jezreel upon the house of Jehu, and will cause to cease the kingdom of the house of Israel." "*At that day* I will break the bow of Israel." "Great shall be *the day* of Jezreel" (chap. i. 4, 5, 11). "And it shall be *at that day*, saith Jehovah, that thou shalt call me Ishi." "*In that day* will I make a covenant for them." "*In that day* I will hear" (chap. ii. 16, 18, 21). "Afterwards shall the children of Israel return, and seek Jehovah their God, and David their king, and shall fear Jehovah and his goodness *in the latter days*" (chap. iii. 5). "Come and let us return unto Jehovah; for he hath torn, and he will heal us; after two days will he revive us; *in the third day* he will raise us up, and we shall live in his sight" (chap. vi. 1, 2). "*The days* of visitation are come; *the days* of recompense are come" (chap. ix. 7).

So in Joel. "Alas, for *the day*, for *the day* of Jehovah is at hand, and as a destruction from the Almighty shall it come" (chap. i. 15). "*The day* of Jehovah cometh, for it is nigh at hand; *a day* of darkness and of gloominess; *a day* of clouds and of thick darkness." "*The day* of Jehovah is great and very terrible; and who can abide it?" (chap. ii. 1, 2, 11). "And it shall come to pass afterwards, that I will pour out my spirit upon all flesh:—and also upon the servants and upon the handmaids in *those days* will I pour out my spirit." "The sun shall be turned into darkness, and the moon into blood, before the great and terrible *day* of Jehovah come" (chap. ii. 28, 29, 31). "*In those days*, and in *that time*, when I shall bring again the captivity of Judah and Jerusalem, I will also gather all nations." "For *the day* of Jehovah is near." "*In that day* the mountains shall drop down new wine" (chap. iii. 1, 2, 14, 18).

So in Obadiah. "Shall I not *in that day*, saith Jehovah, even destroy the wise men out of Edom?" "Neither shouldst thou have rejoiced over the children of Judah *in the day* of their destruction; neither shouldst thou have spoken proudly *in the day* of distress." "*For the day* of Jehovah is near upon all the heathen" (verses 8, 12, 15).

So in Amos. "He that is courageous among the mighty, shall flee away naked *in that day*" (chap. ii. 16). "*In the day* that I shall visit the transgressions of Israel upon him" (chap. iii. 14). "Wo unto you that desire *the day* of Jehovah: to what end is it for you? *the day* of Jehovah is darkness and not light." "Shall not *the day* of Jehovah be darkness and not light? even very dark and no brightness in it" (chap. v. 18, 20). "The songs of the temple shall be howlings *in that day.*" "*In that day*, saith Jehovah God, I will cause the sun to go down at noon, and I will darken the earth in the clear day." "*In that day* shall the fair virgins and young men faint for thirst" (chap. viii. 3, 9, 13). "*In that day* I will raise up the tabernacle of David that is fallen." "Behold, *the days come* that the mountains shall drop sweet wine" (chap. ix. 11, 13).

So in Micah. "*In that day* shall one take up a parable against you, and lament with a doleful lamentation, and say, We be utterly spoiled" (chap. ii. 4). "*In the last days* the mountain of the house of Jehovah shall be established in the top of the mountains." "*In that day*, saith Jehovah, will I assemble her that halteth" (chap. iv. 1, 6). "*In that day* I will cut off thy horses out of the midst of thee, and I will destroy thy chariots" (chap. v. 10). "*The day* of thy watchmen and thy visitation cometh." "*In the day* that thy walls are to be built, *in that day* shall the decree be far removed." "*In that day* also, he shall come even to thee" (chap. vii. 4, 11, 12).

So in Habakkuk. "The vision is yet for *an appointed time*, but at the end it shall speak and not lie: though it tarry, wait for it; because it will surely come, it will not tarry" (chap. ii. 3). "O Jehovah, revive the work *in the midst of the years, in the midst of the years* make known; in wrath remember mercy" (chap. iii. 2).

So in Zephaniah. "*The day* of Jehovah is at hand." "*In the day* of Jehovah's sacrifice, I will punish the princes, and the king's children." "*In that day* there shall be the noise of a cry." "*At that time* I will search Jerusalem with candles." "*The great day* of Jehovah is near." "*That day* is a *day* of wrath, a *day* of trouble and distress, a *day* of wasteness and desolation, a *day* of darkness and gloominess, a *day* of clouds and thick darkness, a *day* of the trumpet and alarm against the fenced cities and against the high towers." "*In the day* of Jehovah's wrath, the whole land shall be devoured by the fire of his jealousy; for he shall make even a speedy riddance of all them that dwell in the land" (chap. i. 7, 8, 10, 12, 14—16, 18). "Before *the day* of Jehovah's anger came upon you." "It may be ye shall be hid *in the day* of Jehovah's anger" (chap. ii. 2, 3). "Wait ye upon me until *the day* that I rise up to the prey." "*In that day* shalt thou not be ashamed for all thy doings?" "*In that day* it shall be said to Jerusalem, Fear thou not." "*At that time* I will undo all that afflict thee." "*At that time* will I bring you again, even in *the time* that I gather you; for I will make you a name" (chap. iii. 8, 11, 16, 19, 20).

So in ZECHARIAH. "I will remove the iniquity of that land *in one day.*" "And many nations shall be joined to Jehovah *in that day*" (chap. ii. 11). "*In that day* shall ye call every man his neighbour under the vine and under the fig-tree" (chap. iii. 9, 10). "*In those days* ten men shall take hold of the skirt of him that is a Jew" (chap. viii. 23). "And Jehovah their God shall save them *in that day*, as the flock of his people" (chap. ix. 16). "My covenant was broken *in that day*" (chap. xi. 11). "*In that day* will I make Jerusalem a burdensome stone for all people." "*In that day*, saith Jehovah, I will smite every horse with astonishment." "*In that day* will I make the governors of Judah like a hearth of fire among the wood." "*In that day* shall Jehovah defend the inhabitants of Jerusalem." "*In that day* I will seek to destroy all nations that come against Jerusalem." "*In that day* shall there be a great mourning in Jerusalem" (chap. xii. 3, 4, 6, 8, 9, 11). "*In that day* there shall be a fountain opened to the house of David, and to the inhabitants of Jerusalem." "*In that day* I will cut off the names of the idols out of the land." "*In that day* the prophets shall be ashamed" (chap. xiii. 1, 2, 4). "Behold, *the day* of Jehovah cometh." "His feet shall stand *in that day* upon the mount of Olives." "*In that day* the light shall not be clear nor dark; but it shall be *one day* which shall be known to Jehovah, not day nor night; but it shall come to pass that at evening-time it shall be light." "*In that day* living waters shall go out from Jerusalem." "*In that day* there shall be one Jehovah, and his name one." "*In that day* a great tumult from Jehovah shall be among them." "*In that day* shall there be upon the bells of the horses, Holiness unto Jehovah." "*In that day* there shall be no more Canaanite in the house of Jehovah" (chap. xiv. 1, 4, 6—9, 13, 20, 21).

So in MALACHI. "But who may abide *the day* of his coming, and who shall stand when he appeareth?" "And they shall be mine, saith Jehovah of hosts, *in that day* when I make up my jewels." "Behold, *the day cometh* that shall burn as an oven." "Behold, I will send you Elijah the prophet before the coming of the great and dreadful *day of Jehovah*" (chap. iii. 2, 17, and iv. 1, 5).

And in the PSALMS OF DAVID. "*In his days* shall the righteous flourish, and abundance of peace;—he shall have dominion also from sea to sea, and from the river unto the ends of the earth" (Psalm lxxii. 7, 8); besides other places.

5. By *day* and *time*, in these places, is meant the coming of the Lord. By *a day* or *time* of darkness, of thick darkness, of gloominess, of no light, of desolation, of the end of iniquity, and of destruction, is meant the coming of the Lord when he is no longer known, and consequently when there is nothing which constitutes a church remaining. By *a day* cruel and terrible, *a day* of wrath, of anger, of tumult, of visitation, of sacrifice, of recompense, of trouble, of battle, and of mourning, is meant the coming of the Lord to judgment. His coming for the purpose of establishing a new church, which should acknowledge him as the Redeemer and Saviour, is meant by *the day* in which Jehovah alone should be exalted; in which he should be one, and his name one; in which the branch of Jehovah should be beautiful and glorious; in which the righteous should flourish; in which he should revive, seek his sheep, and make a new covenant; in which the mountains shall drop new wine, and living waters go out from Jerusalem; in which they should look unto the God of Israel; besides many similar expressions.

6. To the above passages, shall here be added some others which speak more openly of the coming of the Lord; as these: "The Lord himself shall give you a sign: Behold, a virgin shall conceive and bear a Son, and shall call his name Immanuel [*God with us*]" (Isaiah vii. 14; Matt. i. 22, 23). "Unto us a Child is born, unto us a Son is given; and the Government shall be upon his shoulder; and his name shall be called Wonderful, Counsellor, the mighty God, the *everlasting Father*, the Prince of Peace. Of the increase of his government and peace there shall be no end, upon the throne of David, and upon his kingdom,—to establish it with judgment and with justice, from henceforth, even for ever" (Isaiah ix. 6, 7). "There shall come forth a rod out of the stem of Jesse, and a branch shall grow out of his roots: and the spirit of Jehovah shall rest upon him, the spirit of wisdom and understanding, the spirit of counsel and might." "Righteousness shall be the girdle of his loins, and truth the girdle of his reins." "And in that day there shall be a root of Jesse which shall stand for an ensign of the people: to it shall the Gentiles seek: and his rest shall be glorious" (Isaiah xi. 1, 2, 5, 10). "Send ye the lamb to the ruler of the land, from Sela to the wilderness, unto the mount of the daughter of Zion." "And in mercy shall the throne be established: and he shall sit upon it in truth, in the tabernacle of David, judging, and seeking judgment, and hasting righteousness" (Isaiah xvi. 1, 5). "It shall be said in that day, Lo! *This is our God;* we have waited for him, and he will save us: *this is Jehovah;* we have waited for him, we will be glad and rejoice in his salvation" (Isaiah xxv. 9). "The voice of him that crieth in the wilderness, Prepare ye the way of *Jehovah*, make straight

in the desert a highway *for our God.*" "The glory of *Jehovah* shall be revealed, and all flesh shall see it together." "Behold, the *Lord Jehovah* will come with a strong hand, and his arm shall rule for him." "He shall feed his flock like a shepherd" (Isaiah xl. 3, 5, 10, 11). "Behold—my elect in whom my soul delighteth." "I *Jehovah* have called thee in righteousness,—and will give thee for a covenant of the people, for a light of the Gentiles; to open the blind eyes, to bring out the prisoners from the prison, and them that sit in darkness out of the prison-house. I am *Jehovah*, that is my name, and my glory will I not give to another" (Isaiah xliii. 1, 6—8). "Who hath believed our report, and to whom is the arm of Jehovah revealed?" "He hath no form nor comeliness; and when we shall see him there is no beauty—." "He hath borne our griefs, and carried our sorrows" (Isaiah liii. 1, 2, 4). "Who is this that cometh from Edom, with dyed garments from Bozrah—travelling in the greatness of his strength? I that speak in righteousness, mighty to save." "For the day of vengeance is in my heart, and the year of my redeemed is come." "So he was their Saviour" (Isaiah lxiii. 1, 4, 8). "Behold, the days come, saith Jehovah, that I will raise unto David a righteous branch, and a king shall reign and prosper, and shall execute judgment and justice in the earth; and this is his name whereby he shall be called: *Jehovah our righteousness*" (Jer. xxiii. 5, 6, and xxxiii. 15, 16). "Rejoice greatly, O daughter of Zion; shout, O daughter of Jerusalem: behold, thy king cometh unto thee: he is just, and having salvation." "He shall speak peace unto the heathen: and his dominion shall be from sea even to sea, and from the river even to the ends of the earth" (Zechariah ix. 9, 10). "Sing and rejoice, O daughter of Zion, for lo! I come, and I will dwell in the midst of thee.—And many nations shall be joined to *Jehovah* in that day, and shall be my people" (ii. 10, 11). But thou, Bethlehem Ephratah, though thou be little among the thousands of Judah; yet out of thee shall he come forth unto me, that is to be Ruler in Israel, whose goings forth have been from of old, from everlasting." "He shall stand and feed in the strength of *Jehovah*" (Micah v. 2, 4). "Behold, I will send my messenger, and he shall prepare the way before me; and Jehovah whom ye seek shall suddenly come to his temple, even the messenger of the covenant, whom ye delight in; behold, he shall come.—But who may abide the day of his coming?" "Behold, I will send unto you Elijah the prophet, before the coming of the great and dreadful day of *Jehovah*" (Malachi iii. 1, 2, and iv. 5). "I saw, and behold, one like the Son of Man came with the clouds of heaven;—and there was given him dominion, glory and a kingdom, that all people, and nations, and languages, should serve him. His dominion is an everlasting dominion, which shall not pass awa·

and his kingdom that which shall not be destroyed." "And all dominions shall serve and obey him" (Dan. vii. 13, 14, 27). "Seventy weeks are determined upon thy people, and upon thy holy city, to finish the transgression,—and to seal up the vision and prophecy, and to anoint the most holy. Know, therefore, and understand, that from the going-forth of the commandment to restore and to build Jerusalem, unto the Messiah the prince, shall be seven weeks" (Dan. ix. 24, 25). "I will set his hand also in the sea, and his right hand in the rivers. He shall cry unto me, Thou art my Father, my God, and the rock of my salvation. Also I will make him my First-born, higher than the kings of the earth." "His seed also will I make to endure forever, and his throne as the days of heaven" (Psalm lxxxix. 25—27, 29). "*Jehovah* said unto my Lord, Sit thou at my right hand, until I make thine enemies thy footstool. *Jehovah* shall send the rod of thy strength out of Zion; rule thou in the midst of thine enemies. Thou art a priest for ever after the order of Melchizedeck" (Psalm cx. 1, 2, 4; see Matt. xxii. 44, Luke xx. 42). "I have set my king upon my holy hill of Zion. I will declare the decree:—*Jehovah* hath said unto me, Thou art my Son; this day have I begotten thee.—I shall give thee the heathen for thy inheritance, and the uttermost parts of the earth for thy possession." "Kiss the Son, lest he be angry, and ye perish from the way.—Blessed are all they that put their trust in him" (Psalm ii. 6—8, 12). "Thou hast made him a little lower than the angels; and hast crowned him with glory and honour. Thou madest him to have dominion over the works of thy hands: thou hast put all things under his feet" (Psalm viii. 5, 6). "*Jehovah*, remember David —how he sware unto *Jehovah*, and vowed unto the mighty God of Jacob: Surely I will not come into the tabernacle of my house, nor go up into my bed; I will not give sleep to mine eyes,—until I find out a place for *Jehovah*, a habitation for the mighty God of Jacob. Lo, we heard of it at Ephratah, we found it in the fields of the wood. We will go into his tabernacles: we will worship at his footstool.—Let thy priests be clothed with righteousness, and let thy saints shout for joy" (Psalm cxxxii. 1, 7, 9). But these passages are but few compared to what might be adduced.

7. That the whole Sacred Scripture treats solely concerning the Lord, will more fully appear from what follows, and is more particularly shewn in *The Treatise on the Sacred Scripture.* In this circumstance alone the sanctity of the Word is grounded. This is also signified by these words in the Apocalypse: "*The testimony of Jesus is the spirit of prophecy*" (xix. 10).

BY THE LORD'S FULFILLING ALL THE CONTENTS OF THE LAW, IS MEANT, THAT HE FULFILLED ALL THE CONTENTS OF THE WORD.

8. IT is supposed by many at this day, that when it is said of the Lord, that he fulfilled the law, the meaning of his expression is, that he fulfilled all the commandments of the Decalogue, and that thus he became righteousness; and it is further supposed that by the belief of this on the part of mankind, he justifies them, that is, makes them righteous also. Nevertheless, that is not the meaning of that expression; but its real signification is, that he fulfilled all things which are written concerning him in the law and the prophets, that is, in the whole sacred Scripture, because this treats of him alone, as was observed in the foregoing section. The reason why many have entertained a different belief is, because they have not searched the Scriptures and seen what is there meant by *the law*. By the law are therein signified, in a strict sense, the ten commandments of the Decalogue; in a more extensive sense, all things that are written in the five books of Moses; and in the most extensive sense, all things that are contained in the Word.

I. *That by the law, in a strict sense, are meant the Ten Commandments of the Decalogue*, is a thing generally acknowledged.

9. II. *That by the law, in a more extensive sense, are meant all things that are written in the five books of Moses*, will appear from the following passages: In Luke: "Abraham said unto him, [the rich man in hell] They have *Moses and the prophets*, let them hear them. If they hear not *Moses and the prophets*, neither will they be persuaded, though one rose from the dead" (xvi. 29, 31). In John: Philip said unto Nathaniel, "We have found him of whom *Moses in the law and the prophets* did write" (i. 45). In Matthew: "Think not that I am come to destroy *the law or the prophets:* I am not come to destroy, but to *fulfil*" (v. 17). In the same: "For all the *prophets and the law* prophesied unto John" (xi. 13). In Luke: "*The law and the prophets* were until John; since that time the kingdom of God is preached" (xvi. 16). In Matthew: "All things whatsoever ye would that men should do unto you, do ye even so to them; for this is *the law and the prophets*" (vii. 12). In the same: "Thou shalt love the Lord thy God with all thy heart, and with all thy soul."—And—"Thou shalt love thy neighbour as thyself. On these two commandments hang all *the law and the prophets*" (xxii. 37, 39, 40). In these places, by Moses and the prophets, as also by the law and the prophets, are signified all things that are written in the books of Moses and in those of the prophets. That by the law in particular are signified all things that were written by Moses, will further appear from

the following passages: In Luke: "And when the days of her purification, according to *the law of Moses*, were accomplished, they brought him to Jerusalem, to present him to the Lord: (as it is written in *the law of the Lord*, Every male that openeth the womb shall be called holy to the Lord;) and to offer a sacrifice, according to that which is said in *the law of the Lord*, a pair of turtle doves, or two young pigeons." "And the parents brought in the child Jesus, to do for him after the custom of *the law*." "And when they had performed all things according to *the law of the Lord*" (ii. 22—24, 27, 39). In John: "Moses in *the law* commanded us, that such should be stoned" (viii. 5). In the same: "*The law* was given *by Moses*" (i. 17). From whence it appears, that sometimes the law is named, and sometimes Moses, where such things are treated of as are contained in the books written by him; as is also done in Matthew viii. 4; Mark x. 2—4; xii. 19; Luke xx. 28, 37; John iii. 14; vii. 19, 51; viii. 17; xix. 7. Many things commanded to be performed, are also called, by Moses himself, *the law:* as in relation to the burnt offerings, Levit. vi. 9; vii. 1, 11; to the meat offering, Levit. vi. 14; to the leprosy, Levit. xiv. 2; to jealousy, Numb. v. 29; and to the Nazariteship, Numb. vi. 13, 21. Moses himself also called his book *the law:* "Moses wrote this *law*, and delivered it unto the priests, the sons of Levi, who bare the ark of the covenant of Jehovah." And he said unto them, "Take *this book of the law*, and put it in the side of the ark of the covenant of Jehovah." (Deut. xxxi. 9, 26). It was put in the side of the ark, because within the ark were the tables of stone, which, in a strict sense, are called the law. The books of Moses are afterwards, also, called the law: "And Hilkiah the high priest said unto Shaphan the scribe, I have found *the book of the law* in the house of Jehovah." "And when the king had heard the words of the *book of the law*, he rent his clothes" (2 Kings xxii. 8, 11).

10. III. *That by the law, in the most extensive sense, are meant all things that are contained in the Word*, may appear from the following passages. "Jesus answered them, Is it not written in *your law*, I said ye are gods" (John x. 34)? This is written in Psalm lxxxii. 6. "The people answered him, We have heard out of *the law*, that Christ abideth for ever" (John xii. 34). This is written in Psalm lxxxix. 29; cx. 4; and in Daniel vii. 14. "That the word might be fulfilled that is written in *their law*, They hated me without a cause" (John xv. 25). This is written in Psalm xxxv. 19. "The Pharisees answered, Have any of the rulers—believed on him? but this people who knoweth not *the law* are cursed" (John vii. 48, 49). "It is easier for heaven and earth to pass, than one tittle of *the law* to fail" (Luke xvi. 17); where, by *the law*, is signified the whole of the Sacred Scripture.

11. That by the Lord's fulfilling all the contents of the law, is meant, that he fulfilled all the contents of the Word, will farther appear from those passages where it is said, that the Scripture was fulfilled by him, and that all things were finished; as from the following: Jesus "went into the synagogue,—and stood up to read. And there was delivered unto him the book of the prophet Esaias. And when he had opened the book, he found the place where it was written, the spirit of the Lord is upon me, because he hath anointed me to preach the gospel to the poor; he hath sent me to heal the broken-hearted, to preach deliverance to the captives, and recovering of sight to the blind;—to preach the acceptable year of the Lord. And he closed the book,—and began to say, *This day is this Scripture fulfilled* in your ears" (Luke iv. 16, 21). "Search *the Scriptures* for they—testify of me" (John v. 39). "*That the Scripture may be fulfilled*, He that eateth bread with me hath lifted up his heel against me" (John xiii. 18). "None of them is lost, but the son of perdition, *that the Scripture might be fulfilled*" (John xvii. 12). "*That the saying might be fulfilled* which he spake; Of them which thou gavest me have I lost none" (John xviii. 9). "Then said Jesus unto him [Peter], Put up again thy sword into his place;—*how then shall the Scriptures be fulfilled*, that thus it must be?" "But all this was done, *that the Scriptures of the prophets might be fulfilled*" (Matt. xxvi. 52, 54, 56). "The Son of Man indeed goeth, as *it is written of him.*" "But *the Scriptures must be fulfilled*" (Mark xiv. 21, 49). "And *the Scripture was fulfilled* which saith, and he was numbered with the transgressors" (Mark xv. 28; Luke xxii. 37). "*That the Scripture might be fulfilled* which said, They parted my raiment amongst them, and for my vesture did they cast lots" (John xix. 24). "After this, Jesus, knowing that all things were now accomplished, that *the Scripture might be fulfilled*, saith, I thirst" (John xix. 28). "When Jesus received the vinegar, he said, *It is finished*," that is, *It is fulfilled* (John xix. 30). "These things were done *that the Scripture should be fulfilled*, A bone of him shall not be broken: And again, *another Scripture saith*, They shall look on him whom they pierced" (John. xix. 36, 37): besides other places, where passages are adduced from the prophets, without its being said, at the same time, that the law, or the Scripture, was fulfilled. That the whole of the World treats of the Lord, and that he came into the world to fulfil it, he also taught his disciples before his departure, in these words: "Jesus said unto them, O fools, and slow of heart to believe all that the prophets have spoken! Ought not Christ to have suffered these things, and to enter into his glory? And beginning at *Moses and all the prophets*, he expounded unto them in *all the Scriptures the things concerning himself*" (Luke xxiv. 25—27). And further: Jesus said unto his disciples, "These are

the words which I spake unto you whilst I was yet with you, *that all things must be fulfilled which were written in the law of Moses, and in the prophets, and in the Psalms concerning me*" (Luke xxiv. 44). That the Lord whilst in the world, fulfilled all the contents of the Word, even to its minutest particulars, is evident from these his own words: "Verily I say unto you, till heaven and earth pass, *one jot, or one tittle shall in no wise pass from the law, till all be fulfilled*" (Matt. v. 18.)

Hence then may be clearly seen, that when it is said that the Lord fulfilled all the contents of the law, the meaning is, not merely that he fulfilled all the commandments of the Decalogue, but all the contents of the Word.

---

## THE LORD CAME INTO THE WORLD TO SUBJUGATE THE HELLS AND TO GLORIFY HIS HUMAN; AND THE PASSION OF THE CROSS WAS THE LAST COMBAT, BY WHICH HE FULLY CONQUERED THE HELLS, AND FULLY GLORIFIED HIS HUMAN.

12. It is known in the church, that the Lord conquered death, by which is meant hell, and that he afterwards ascended in glory into heaven; but it is not yet known that the Lord conquered death or hell by combats, which are temptations, and at the same time, by these means, glorified his Human; and that the passion of the cross was the last combat or temptation, by which he conquered the one and glorified the other. These [combats] are frequently treated of in the prophets and in David, but not so frequently in the evangelists; for by these the temptations which he sustained from his childhood are briefly described by his temptations in the wilderness, and afterwards by the devil, and finally by his sufferings in Gethsemane and on the cross. His temptations in the wilderness, and afterwards by the devil, are related in Matthew iv. 1—11; in Mark i. 12, 13; and in Luke iv. 1—13. But by these are signified all the temptations that he suffered even to the last. He did not reveal more concerning them to his disciples, for it is said in Isaiah, "He was oppressed, and he was afflicted, yet he opened not his mouth: he is brought as a lamb to the slaughter, and as a sheep before her shearers is dumb, so he openeth not his mouth" (liii. 7). His temptations in Gethsemane are related in Matthew xxvi. 36—44; in Mark xiv. 32—42; and in Luke xxii. 39—46: and these on the cross, in Matthew xxvii. 33—50; in Mark xv. 22—37; in Luke xxiii. 33—39; and in John xix. 17—34. Temptations are nothing else than combats against the hells. Concerning the temptations or spiritual conflicts of the Lord, see the treatise on *the New Jerusalem and its Heavenly Doctrine*, n. 201 and 302; and concerning temptations in general, n. 189—200 of the same work.

13. That the Lord, by the passion of the cross, fully conquered the hells, he himself teaches in John: "Now is the judgment of this world; *now shall the prince of this world be cast out*" (xii. 31). This the Lord spoke, when the passion of the cross was about to take place. So again: "*The prince of this world* is judged" (xvi. 11). Also: "Be of good cheer, *I have overcome the world*" (xvi. 33). And in Luke: "He [Jesus] said,—I beheld *Satan as lightning fall from heaven*" (x. 18.) In these passages, by the world, the prince of the world, Satan, and the devil, is meant hell.

That the Lord, also, by the passion of the cross, fully glorified his Human, he teaches in John: "When he [Judas] was gone out, Jesus said, Now *is the Son of Man glorified*, and *God is glorified in him.* If God be *glorified* in him, God *will also glorify* him in himself, *and will straightway glorify him*" (xiii. 31, 32). In the same: "Father, the hour is come: *glorify* thy Son, that thy Son also *may glorify* thee" (xvii. 1). And again: "Now is my soul troubled." And he said: "Father, *glorify* thy name. Then came there a voice from heaven, saying, *I have both glorified it, and will glorify it* again" (xii. 27, 28). In Luke: "Ought not Christ to have suffered these things, and to enter into *his glory?*" (xxiv. 26). All this is said in reference to his passion. The glorifying here spoken of, is the uniting of the Divine and the Human; wherefore it is said, "and God will glorify him in himself."

14. That the Lord came into the world to reduce to order all things in heaven and thence on earth; that this was effected by combats against the hells, which at that time infested every man on his entrance into and departure out of the world; and that hereby he became righteousness and saved mankind, who otherwise could not have been saved; is evident from many predictions of the prophets, of which only a few shall be here adduced. In Isaiah: "Who is this that cometh from Edom, with dyed garments from Bozrah? this that is glorious in his apparel, travelling in the greatness of his strength? I that speak in righteousness, mighty to save. Wherefore art thou red in thine apparel, and thy garments like him that treadeth in the wine-fat? I have trodden the wine-press alone, and of the people there was none with me; for I will tread them in mine anger, and trample them in my fury; and their blood shall be sprinkled upon my garments;—for the day of vengeance is in my heart, and the year of my redeemed is come.—Mine own arm brought salvation unto me.—I will bring down their strength to the earth.—He said, Surely they are my people, children that will not lie: so he was their Saviour.—In his love and in his pity he redeemed them" (lxiii. 1, 6, 8, 9). These words are spoken of the Lord's combats against the hells. By the apparel in which he was glorious, and which was red, is

signified the Word, which suffered violence from the Jewish people. His combats against the hells, and his victories over them, are described by his treading them in his anger, and trampling them in his wrath. His combating alone, and by his own proper power, is described by these words: "Of the people there was none with me;—therefore mine own arm brought salvation unto me;—I will bring down their strength to the earth." That he thereby became a Saviour and a Redeemer, is described by these words: "So he was their Saviour; —in his love and in his pity he redeemed them." And that this was the cause of his coming is described by these words: "The day of vengeance is in my heart, and the year of my redeemed is come." Again, in Isaiah: "He saw that there was no man, and wondered that there was no intercessor: therefore his arm brought salvation unto him, and his righteousness it sustained him. For he put on righteousness as a breast-plate, and a helmet of salvation upon his head; and he put on the garments of vengeance for clothing, and was clad with zeal as a cloak." "And the Redeemer shall come to Zion" (lix. 16, 17, 20). These words are also spoken in reference to the combats of the Lord against the hells during his abode in the world. That he fought against them from his own proper power, is signified by this: "He saw that there was no man;—therefore his arm brought salvation unto him." That thereby he became righteousness itself, is thus described: "His righteousness it sustained him: for he put on righteousness as a breast-plate." And that thus he redeemed mankind, by this: "And the Redeemer shall come to Zion." So in Jeremiah: "Wherefore have I seen them dismayed?—and their mighty ones are beaten down, and are fled apace, and look not back." "For this is the day of the Lord Jehovah of hosts, a day of vengeance, that he may avenge him of his adversaries: and the sword shall devour and it shall be satiate" (xlvi. 5, 10). Here also, the combats of the Lord with the hells, and his victories over them, are described when it is said, "Wherefore have I seen them dismayed? and their mighty ones are beaten down; and are fled apace, and look not back:" by their mighty ones, and the Lord's enemies, are here meant the hells, for all therein entertain hatred against the Lord. His coming into the world for this purpose, is signified by these words: "It is the day of the Lord Jehovah of hosts, a day of vengeance, that he may avenge him of his adversaries." Again, in the same prophet: "Her young men shall fall in her streets, and all the men of war shall be cut off in that day" (xlix. 26). So in Joel: "Jehovah shall utter his voice before his army:—the day of Jehovah is great and very terrible; and who can abide it?" (ii. 11). In Zephaniah: "In the day of the sacrifice of Jehovah, I will punish the princes, and the king's children, and all such as are clothed with strange apparel." "That day is a day of trouble, —a day of the trumpet and alarm against the fenced cities" (i. 8, 15, 16). In Zechariah: "Then shall Jehovah go forth and fight against those nations, as when he fought in the day of battle: and his feet shall stand in that day upon the mount of Olives, which is before Jerusalem.—And ye shall flee to the valley of the mountains.—In that day the light shall not be clear nor dark." "And Jehovah shall be king over all the earth; in that day there shall be one Jehovah, and his name one" (xiv. 3—6, 9). In these places, also, the Lord's combats are the subject treated of: by "that day," is meant his coming. The mount of Olives, which was before Jerusalem, was also the place where the Lord was wont to abide; see Mark xiii. 3; xiv. 26; Luke xxi. 37; xxii. 39; John viii. 1; besides other places. So in David: "The sorrows of hell compassed me about, the snares of death prevented me." "He sent out his arrows and scattered them, and he shot out lightnings and discomfited them." "I have pursued mine enemies and overtaken them, neither did I turn again till they were consumed. I have wounded them that they were not able to rise.—Thou hast girded me with strength unto the battle: thou hast subdued under me those that rose up against me. Thou hast also given me the necks of mine enemies.—Then did I beat them small as the dust before the wind, I did cast them out as the dirt in the street" (Psalm xviii. 5, 14, 37—40, 42). The cords and snares of death that compassed and prevented, signify temptations, which, being from hell, are also called the cords of hell. These verses, with the whole of this Psalm, treat of the combats and victories of the Lord; it is therefore said, "Thou hast made me the head of the heathen; a people whom I have not known shall serve me" (verse 43). Again: "Gird thy sword upon thy thigh, O most mighty.—Thine arrows are sharp in the heart of the king's enemies; whereby the people fall under thee. Thy throne, O God, is for ever and ever.—Thou lovest righteousness, —therefore God, thy God, hath anointed thee" (Psalm xlv. 3, 5—7). These words also relate to the combats with the hells, and their subjugation; the whole Psalm treats of the Lord, of his combats, his glorification, and of the salvation of the faithful by him. Again, in David: "A fire goeth before him, and burneth up his enemies round about. The earth saw and trembled; the hills melted like wax—at the presence of the Lord of the whole earth. The heavens declare his righteousness, and all the people see his glory" (Psalm xcvii. 3—6). This Psalm likewise treats of the Lord, and of the same things as the former. So again: "Jehovah said unto my Lord, Sit thou at my right hand until I make thine enemies my footstool.—Rule thou in the midst of thine enemies." "The Lord at thy right hand shall strike through kings in the day of his wrath;—he shall fill the places with the dead bodies; he shall wound the heads over many countries" (Psalm cx. 1, 2, 5, 6). That this relates to the Lord, appears from his own words in Matthew xxii. 44; in Mark xii. 36; and in Luke xx. 42. By sitting on the right hand is signified omnipotence; by his enemies are signified the hells; by kings, those who are principled in falsities grounded in evil; to make them a footstool, to strike them through in the day of his wrath, and to fill the places with dead bodies, is to destroy their power; and to wound the head over many countries, is to destroy the whole. Since the Lord conquered the hells alone, without the aid of any angel, he is therefore called *a mighty man and a man of war* (Isaiah xlii. 13): *the king of glory, Jehovah strong and mighty, Jehovah mighty in battle* (Psalm xxiv. 8, 10): *the mighty God of Jacob* (Psalm cxxxii. 2); and, in many places, *Jehovah Zebaoth*, that is, Jehovah of the hosts or armies of war. His coming also, which is meant by the *day of Jehovah*, is called a terrible day, a cruel day, a day of indignation, of anger, of wrath, of vengeance, of destruction, of war, of the trumpet and alarm, and of tumult; as may be seen in the places adduced above.* And because by means of such combats with the hells, and their subjugation, a last judgment was accomplished by the Lord whilst he was in the world, therefore this also is spoken of in many places: as in David: Jehovah "cometh to judge the earth: he shall judge the world with righteousness, and the people with his truth" (Psalm xcvi. 13). So likewise in many other places. These quotations have been taken from the prophetical parts of the Word; but, in the historical parts, the same things are represented by the wars of the children of Israel with various nations: for whatever is written in the Word, either in its prophetical or historical parts, has reference to the Lord; and hence the Word is divine. Many arcana relating to the Lord's glorification are contained in the rituals of the Israelitish Church; as in its burnt offerings and sacrifices, in its sabbaths and feasts, and in the priesthood of Aaron and the Levites: so also in the other ordinances of Moses, which are called laws, judgments, and statutes: and this is meant by the Lord's words when he said to the disciples, "All things must be fulfilled which were written in the law of Moses —concerning me" (Luke xxiv. 44); and when he said of Moses to the Jews, "He wrote of me" (John v. 46).

From all this then it is evident, that the Lord came into the world to subjugate the hells, and to glorify his human; and that the passion of the cross was the final conflict, by which he fully conquered the hells, and fully glorified his human. The passages in the prophetical part of the Word which treat of the Lord's combats with the hells and victories over them; or,

* No. 4.

what is the same thing, which treat of the last judgment executed by him when in the world; as also of his passion, and the glorification of his human; are so numerous, that were they all adduced, they would fill many pages.

---

### THE LORD, BY THE PASSION OF THE CROSS, DID NOT TAKE AWAY SINS, BUT BORE THEM.

15. There are some within the church, who believe that the Lord by the passion of the cross took away sins, and made satisfaction to the father, and thus redeemed mankind: some also imagine that he transferred to himself the sins of those who have faith in him, bore them, and cast them into the depth of the sea, that is, into hell: in which opinion they confirm themselves by the words of John concerning Jesus: "Behold, the Lamb of God, which taketh away the sin of the world" (John i. 29): and by these words of the Lord in Isaiah: "He hath borne our griefs, and carried our sorrows.—He was wounded for our transgressions, he was bruised for our iniquities; the chastisement of our peace was upon him; and with his stripes we are healed.—Jehovah hath made the iniquities of us all to meet on him. He was oppressed, and he was afflicted, yet he opened not his mouth; he is brought as a lamb to the slaughter.—He was cut off out of the land of the living: for the transgression of my people was he stricken: and he made his grave with the wicked, and with the rich in his death.—He shall see of the travail of his soul, and shall be satisfied: by his knowledge shall my righteous servant justify many; for he shall bear their iniquities.—He hath poured out his soul unto death; and he was numbered with the transgressors: and he bare the sin of many, and made intercession for the transgressors" (liii. 4, to the end). Both these passages relate to the temptations and passion of the Lord; and by his taking away sins, and by the iniquities of us all meeting on him, the same is meant as by carrying sorrows and iniquities. It shall therefore be shewn, in the first place, what is implied by bearing iniquities, and afterwards, what by taking them away. By the Lord's bearing iniquities, nothing else is meant than his sustaining dire temptations; also, his suffering the Jews to treat him as they had treated the word; which they did, because he was the Word. For the church, which at that time existed with the Jewish nation, was then in a state of utter devastation, in consequence of having perverted every thing contained in the Word, so that there was not a single truth left; which also was the reason that they did not acknowledge the Lord. This is meant, and was signified, by all the circumstances that attended the

Lord's passion. The prophets were also treated in a similar manner, because they represented the Lord with respect to the Word, and thence with respect to the church; and the Lord was pre-eminently THE PROPHET.

That the Lord was THE PROPHET, may appear from these passages: Jesus said, "a *prophet* is not without honour, save in his own country, and in his own house" (Matt. xiii. 57; Mark vi. 4; Luke iv. 24). Jesus said, "it cannot be that a *prophet* perish out of Jerusalem" (Luke xiii. 33). "And the multitude said, This is Jesus the *prophet* of Nazareth" (Matt. xxi. 11; John vii. 40). "And there came a fear on all; and they glorified God, saying that a great *prophet* is risen up among us" (Luke vii. 16). So it is declared by Moses, that a *prophet* should be raised out of the midst of their brethren, "whose words they shall obey" (Deut. xviii. 15—19).

That the prophets also represented the state of the church, and were commanded to do certain things with that view, may appear from the following instances; The prophet Isaiah was for that purpose enjoined to loose the sackcloth from off his loins, and to put off the shoe from his foot, and to walk naked and bare-foot three years, for a sign and a wonder (Isaiah xx. 2, 3). The prophet Jeremiah, in order that he might represent the state of the church, was commanded to get for himself a linen girdle, and put it upon his loins, and not put it in water, and that he should hide it in the hole of a rock near the river Euphrates: and after many days he found it rotten (Jerem. xiii. 1—7). The same prophet was commanded, for the same purpose, not to take a wife in that place, nor to enter into the house of mourning, neither go to lament, nor enter into the house of feasting (Jerem. xvi. 2, 5, 8). The prophet Ezekiel, that he might represent the state of the church, was commanded to take unto him a barber's razor, and cause it to pass upon his head, and upon his beard; and afterwards to divide it, and to burn with fire the third part of it in the midst of the city, to smite a third part of it with a knife, and to scatter a third part in the wind; and that he should take a few in number and bind them in his skirts, then take of them again, and cast them into the midst of the fire, and burn them (Ezek. v. 1—4). He was also commanded, for the same purpose, to prepare for himself stuff for removing, and to remove into another place in the sight of the children of Israel; and that he should bring forth his stuff by day, and should go forth in the evening through a hole made in the wall, covering his face so that he might not see the ground; and that so he should be a *sign* unto the house of Israel, and should say, I *am your sign:* like as I have done, so shall it be done unto you (Ezek. xii. 3—7, 11). The prophet Hosea, that he might represent the state of the church, was commanded to take to himself a harlot for a wife: and it is written that he did so, and that she bare him three children, one of whom was called *Jezreel* [Dropping of the friendship of God], the second, *She that hath not obtained mercy*, and the third, *Not my people* (see Hosea i. 2—9). And, again, he was commanded to go and love a woman beloved of her friend, yet an adultress; whom also he bought for fifteen pieces of silver (Hosea iii. 1, 2). The prophet Ezekiel, that he might represent the state of the church, was also commanded to take a tile, and to portray upon it the city Jerusalem, and to lay siege against it, and build a fort against it, and cast a mount against it, and to put an iron pan between him and the city, and to lie on his left side three hundred and ninety days, and afterwards on his right side forty days: Also to take wheat, barley, beans, lentiles, millet, and fitches, and make bread thereof, which he should then eat by measure; and also, that he should eat it as barley cakes, and bake it with the dung of man: and because he prayed that it might not be so, he was allowed to bake it with cows' dung (Ezek. iv. 1—15). Other prophets also represented other things; as Zedekiah, by the horns of iron that he made (1 Kings xxii. 11): And another prophet, by causing himself to be smitten and wounded, and putting ashes on his face (1 Kings xx. 35—38). In general, the prophets represented the Word in its ultimate sense, which is that of the letter, by wearing a garment of hair (see Zech. xiii. 4): thus Elijah was clothed with such a coat, and was girt about his loins with a leathern girdle (2 Kings i. 8): so also John the Baptist had his raiment of camels' hair, a leathern girdle about his loins, and ate locusts and wild honey (Matt. iii. 4). From all these circumstances it appears, that the prophets represented the state of the church, and the Word; for whosoever represents the one, represents also the other, because the church has its existence from the Word, and its quality is according to its reception of the Word in life and faith. Hence by prophets, wherever they are mentioned in both Testaments, is signified the doctrine of the church derived from the Word: but by the Lord, considered as the greatest prophet, is signified the church itself, and the Word itself.

16. The state of the church, from the Word, thus represented in the Prophets, is what is meant when mention is made of their bearing the iniquities and sins of the people. This is evident from its being related of the prophet Isaiah, that he went naked and bare-foot three years, for a sign and a wonder (Isaiah xx. 2, 3): and of Ezekiel the prophet, that he carried out stuff for removing through the hole he had dug in the wall, covering his face, so as not to see the earth: and that thus he was for a sign unto the house of Israel; and also said, *I am your sign* (Ezek. xii. 3—11). That this was to bear iniquities, manifestly appears from what is said, when Ezekiel

was commanded to lie three hundred and ninety days on his left side, and forty days on his right side, against Jerusalem, and to eat barley cakes made with cows' dung; where we read thus: "Lie thou also upon thy left side, and lay *the iniquity of the house of Israel upon it:* according to the number of the days that thou shalt lie upon it, *thou shalt bear their iniquity.* For I have laid upon thee the years of their iniquity, according to the number of the days, three hundred and ninety days: *so shalt thou bear the iniquity of the house of Israel.* And when thou hast accomplished them, lie again on thy right side, and *thou shalt bear the iniquity of the house of Judah* forty days" (Ezek. iv. 4—6). That the prophet by thus bearing the iniquities of the house of Israel and the house of Judah, did not thereby take them away, and thus expiate them, but only represented and pointed them out, is evident from what follows in the same chapter: "And Jehovah said, even thus shall the children of Israel eat their defiled bread among the gentiles, whither I will drive them." "Behold, I will break the staff of bread in Jerusalem,—that they may want bread and water, and be astonished one with another, and consume away for their iniquity" (verses 13, 16, 17). So when the same prophet showed himself, and said, "I am your sign," it is also added, "as I have done, so shall it be done unto them" (Ezek. xii. 11). The meaning is similar when it is said of the Lord, "He hath borne our griefs, and carried our sorrows;—Jehovah hath laid on him the iniquity of us all;—by his knowledge shall my righteous servant justify many, for he shall bear their iniquities" (Isaiah liii.); the whole of which chapter treats of the passion of the Lord. That the Lord himself, as the Greatest Prophet, represented the state of the church as to the Word, appears from the circumstances attending his passion: as, that he was betrayed by Judas; that he was taken and condemned by the chief priests and elders; that they buffeted him; that they smote him on the head with a reed; that they put a crown of thorns on his head; that they divided his garments, and cast lots for his vesture; that they crucified him; that they gave him vinegar to drink; that they pierced his side; that he was buried and rose again on the third day. His being betrayed by Judas, signified that he was betrayed by the Jewish nation, who at that time were the depositaries of the Word; for Judas represented that nation; his being taken and condemned by the chief priests and elders, signified that he was taken and condemned by the whole Jewish Church: their scourging him, spitting in his face, buffeting him, and smiting him on the head with a reed, signified that they treated in a similar manner the Word, with respect to its divine truths, all of which relate to the Lord: their putting a crown of thorns on his head, signified that they had falsified and adulterated those truths: thei dividing his garments and casting lots for his vesture, signified that they had divided and dispersed all the truths of the Word, but not its spiritual sense, which his vesture or inner garment represented: their crucifying him, signified that they had destroyed and profaned the whole Word: their giving him vinegar to drink, signified that all was falsified and false; and therefore he did not drink it, but said, It is finished; their piercing his side, signified that they had entirely extinguished every truth and every good of the Word: his being buried, signified the rejection of the residue of the Human taken from the mother; and his rising again on the third day, signified his glorification. Where these circumstances are predicted in the Prophets and Psalms, their signification is similar. On this account also, after he had been scourged, when he was led out bearing the crown of thorns, and arrayed in a purple robe put on him by the soldiers, he said, "Behold the man!" (John xix. 1, 5). This he said, because by the term *man* is signified the church; for by *the Son of Man* is meant the truth of the church, consequently the Word. Hence then it appears, that by bearing iniquities is meant to represent, and to display in effigy, sins against the divine truths of the word. That the Lord underwent and suffered such treatment as the Son of Man, and not as the Son of God, will be shown in the following pages; for *Son of Man*, signifies the Lord as to the Word.

17. Something shall be now said a to what is meant by taking away sins. To take away sins is much the same as to redeem man, and save him. For the Lord came into the world to render salvation possible to man. Had he not come, no one could have been reformed and regenerated, nor, of course, saved: but this became possible after the Lord had deprived the devil, that is, hell, of all his power, and had glorified his Human, that is, united it to the Divine of the Father. If these things had not been done, no man would have been capable of permanently receiving any divine truth, still less any divine good: for the devil, whose power before was the stronger, would have plucked it out of his heart.

From these statements, it is manifest, that the Lord did not take away sins by the passion of the cross, but that he takes them away, that is, removes them, in such as believe in him, and live according to his commandments; as the Lord also teaches in Matthew: "Think not that I have come to destroy the law and the prophets." "Whosoever shall break one of these least commandments, and shall teach men so, he shall be called the least in the kingdom of heaven; but whosoever shall do and teach them, the same shall be called great in the kingdom of heaven" (v. 17, 19). Reason alone may teach every one, if he be at all enlightened, that sins cannot be taken away from man, except by actual repentance; which consists in man's seeing his sins, imploring help of the Lord, and desisting from them. To see, believe, and teach otherwise, does not originate in the Word, nor in sound reason, but in evil lust, and a depraved will, which constitutes man's *proprium*, or selfhood, by which his intelligence is debased into folly.

---

THE IMPUTATION OF THE LORD'S MERIT PROPERLY MEANS NOTHING ELSE THAN THE REMISSION OF SINS AFTER REPENTANCE.

18. It is believed in the church, that the Lord was sent by the Father to make an atonement for the human race, and that this was effected by his fulfilling the law, and suffering the passion of the cross; by which it is conceived that he took away the damnation incurred by man, and made satisfaction for his sins. It is further believed, that without such atonement, satisfaction, and propitiation, the human race would have perished in eternal death; and this because justice, or vindictive justice, as it is styled by some, demanded such a penalty. It is certainly true, that if the Lord had not come into the world all mankind would have perished: but how it is to be understood that the Lord fulfilled the whole of the law; and also why he suffered the death of the cross, may be seen above in their respective chapters: from which also it may appear, that he did not fulfil the law, and suffer the cross, on account of any vindictive justice in God, since there can be no such divine attribute as this. The divine attributes are justice [or righteousness], love, mercy, and goodness; and God is justice itself, love itself, mercy itself, and goodness itself; and where these are, there can be nothing of vengeance, consequently, no vindictive justice. The Lord's fulfilling of the law, and his passion on the cross, have, however, been heretofore understood by many, only as a satisfaction made by him for the human race, whereby he delivered them from the damnation otherwise foreseen or appointed: and from viewing these two things (commonly called his active and passive obedience), in which the Lord's merit is believed to consist, in the light of a satisfaction, and combining therewith the principle that man is saved solely by the faith that it is so, has followed by natural connexion, the received tenet of the imputation of the Lord's merit. But this tenet falls to the ground when the Lord's fulfilling of the law, and his passion on the cross, as explained above, are rightly understood. It may then be seen, that imputation of merit are words without meaning, unless they imply the remission of sins after repentance: for no act or attribute of the Lord can possibly be imputed to man; but salvation may be awarded him

by the Lord when he has done the work of repentance, that is, when after he has seen and acknowledged his sins, he desists from them by virtue of a power given him from the Lord. Then is salvation awarded to him: not that he is saved by his own merit or righteousness, but by the Lord, who alone hath fought and conquered the hells, and who alone still fights for every individual, and conquers the hells for him. These combats and conquests are what properly constitute the merit and righteousness of the Lord; and these cannot possibly be imputed to man: if they could, the merit and righteousness of the Lord must be appropriated to man as his own; which they never were, nor ever can be. Supposing such imputation possible, any impenitent and wicked person might impute to himself the merit of the Lord, and so imagine himself justified; whereas this would be to defile what is holy by what is profane, and to profane the name of the Lord; since in so doing he would keep his thoughts fixed on the Lord, whilst his will remained in hell; although it is the will that constitutes the man. There is a faith which is of God, and a faith which is of man: those have the faith which is of God, who do the work of repentance; but those who neglect repentance, and yet think of imputation, have only the faith which is of man: and the faith which is of God, is a living faith, but the faith which is of man is a dead faith. That the Lord himself, and his disciples, preached repentance for the remission of sins, is evident from the following passages: "Jesus began to preach, and to say, *Repent*, for the kingdom of heaven is at hand" (Matt. iv. 17). John said, "Bring forth fruits worthy of *repentance*." "And now also the axe is laid unto the root of the trees; every tree therefore which bringeth not forth good fruit, is hewn down and cast into the fire" (Luke iii. 8, 9). Jesus said, "Except ye *repent*, ye shall all likewise perish" (Luke xiii. 5). "Jesus came—preaching the gospel of the kingdom of God, and saying, The time is fulfilled, and the kingdom of God is at hand; *repent ye*, and believe the gospel" (Mark i. 14, 15). Jesus sent the disciples, who "went out, and preached that men should *repent*" (Mark vi. 12). Jesus said to the apostles, "that *repentance and remission of sins* should be preached in his name among all nations, beginning at Jerusalem" (Luke xxiv. 47). John preached the baptism of *repentance* for the *remission of sins*" (Luke iii. 3; Mark i. 4). By baptism is signified spiritual washing, which is a washing from sins, and is called regeneration. Repentance and the remission of sins are thus described by the Lord in John: "He came unto his own, and his own received him not; but as many as received him, to them gave he power to become the sons of God, even to them that believed on his name; who were born, not of blood, nor of the will of the flesh, nor of the will of man, but of God" (i. 11—

40

13). By his own are here signified the members of the church which was in the possession of the Word; by the children of God, and them that believe in his name, are meant those who believe in the Lord, and who believe in the Word: by blood are signified falsifications of the word, and confirmations by means of it of what is false: the will of the flesh is man's voluntary *proprium* [selfhood], which in itself is nothing but evil; the will of man is man's intellectual *proprium*, which in itself is mere falsity: those who are born of God are such as are regenerated by the Lord. The whole passage demonstrates, that those are saved who are in the good of love and in the truths of faith from the Lord; but not such as abide in their *proprium*.

---

## THE LORD, AS TO HIS DIVINE HUMAN, IS CALLED THE SON OF GOD; AND, AS TO THE WORD, THE SON OF MAN.

19. No other idea is at present entertained in the church, than that the Son of God is a second person of the Godhead, distinct from the person of the Father; whence has arisen the belief, that the Son of God was born from eternity. In consequence of the general prevalence of this notion, and of its relating to God, no liberty is allowed, in thinking about it, to make any use of the understanding, not even so far as to ask, What can be meant by being born from eternity? For whosoever, when he thinks of it, at all exercises his understanding, must be led to say within himself, It is quite above my comprehension; but still I say it because others say it, and I believe it because others believe it. Be it known, then, that there is no Son from eternity, and yet that the Lord is from eternity. But when it is known what is implied by the term *Lord*, and what by the term *Son*, it will then be possible, and not before, to think with understanding of a Triune God.

That the Human of the Lord, conceived of Jehovah the Father, and born of the Virgin Mary, is what is called the Son of God, manifestly appears from the following passages: "The angel Gabriel was sent from God unto a city of Galilee named Nazareth, to a virgin espoused to a man whose name was Joseph of the house of David; and the virgin's name was Mary. And the angel came in unto her, and said, Hail, thou that art highly favoured! The Lord is with thee: blessed art thou among women. And when she saw him, she was troubled at his saying, and cast in her mind what manner of salutation this should be. And the angel said unto her, Fear not, Mary: for thou hast found favour with God. And behold, thou shalt conceive in thy womb, and bring forth a Son, and shall call his name Jesus. He shall be great, and shall be called THE SON OF THE HIGHEST." "Then said Mary unto the angel, How shall this be, seeing I know not a man? And the angel answered and said unto her, *The Holy Spirit shall come upon thee, and the Power of the Highest shall overshadow thee;* therefore also that HOLY THING which shall be born of thee shall be called THE SON OF GOD" (Luke i. 26, 32—35). It is here said, "Thou shalt conceive and bring forth a son; he shall be great, and shall be called THE SON OF THE HIGHEST:" and again, "That Holy Thing which shall be born of thee shall be called THE SON OF GOD:" whence it is evident that the Human conceived of God, and born of the Virgin Mary, is what is called the son of God. So in Isaiah: "Jehovah himself shall give you a sign: Behold a virgin shall conceive and bear *a Son*, and shall call his name IMMANUEL" (that is, GOD WITH US—vii. 14): where also it clearly appears, that the Son conceived of God, and born of the virgin, is what was to be called "GOD WITH US," consequently what is termed the Son of God; as is again further confirmed by Matthew (i. 22, 23). Again, in Isaiah: "Unto us a child is born, unto us a Son is given; and the government shall be upon his shoulder: and his name shall be called Wonderful, Counsellor, the Mighty God, the EVERLASTING FATHER, the Prince of Peace" (ix. 6). Here the same doctrine is taught; for it is said, "Unto us a child is born, unto us a son is given," who consequently is not a Son from eternity, but the Son born in the world; as also appears from the words of the prophet in the next verse, which are similar to those of the angel Gabriel to Mary (Luke i. 32, 33). So in David: "I will declare the decree: Jehovah hath said unto me, THOU ART MY SON, this day have I begotten thee. KISS THE SON, lest he be angry, and ye perish from the way" (Psalm ii. 7, 12). Here no Son from eternity is meant, but a Son that was to be born in the world; for the passage contains a prophecy concerning the coming of the Lord, and therefore it is called a decree, which Jehovah declared unto David: *this day*, denoting in time, cannot mean from eternity. Again, in David: "I will set his hand also in the sea.—He shall cry unto me, thou art my father.—I will make him my *First-Born*" (Psalm lxxxix. 25—27). The whole of this Psalm treats of the coming of the Lord; of course, it is he that should call Jehovah his father, and that should be the first-born, consequently, who is the Son of God. So, also, in other passages; as where he is said to be "A rod out of the stem of Jesse" (Isaiah xi. 1): A branch of David (Jerem. xxiii. 5): The seed of the woman (Gen. iii. 15): "The Only-Begotten" (John i. 18): "A Priest for ever" and "The Lord" (Psalm cx. 4, 5).

The Jewish Church understood, by the Son of God, their expected Messiah, of whom they knew that he should be born in Bethlehem. That, by the Son of God, they understood the Messiah, appears from these passages: in John: Peter said, "We believe and are sure, that thou art THE CHRIST, THE SON OF THE LIVING GOD" (vi. 69). In the same: "Thou art THE CHRIST, THE SON OF GOD, who should come into the world" (xi. 27). In Matthew: The high priest asked Jesus, whether he was "THE CHRIST, THE SON OF GOD? Jesus saith unto him Thou sayest" (xxvi. 63, 64). In John: "These are written, that ye might believe that Jesus is THE CHRIST, THE SON OF GOD" (xx. 31). So also Mark i. 1. Christ is a Greek word which signifies Anointed, the same as Messiah does in Hebrew: wherefore it is said in John: "We have found the Messias, which is, being interpreted, THE CHRIST" (i. 41). And in another place: "The woman said, I know that MESSIAS cometh, who is called Christ" (iv. 25). It has been shewn in the first section, that the Law and the Prophets, or the whole Word of the Old Testament, treat of the Lord; consequently by the Son of God, whose future advent was predicted, nothing can be meant but the Human which the Lord assumed in the world. Hence, too, it follows, that the Human was what was meant, when Jesus, at his baptism, was called by Jehovah, in a voice from heaven, his son: "This is MY BELOVED SON, in whom I am well pleased" (Matt. iii. 17; Mark i. 11; Luke iii. 22); for it was his Human that was baptized. The same appellation was given him when he was transfigured: "This is MY BELOVED SON, in whom I am well pleased: hear ye him" (Matt. xvii. 5; Mark ix. 7; Luke ix. 35). And so in other passages, as Matt. viii. 29; xiv. 33; Mark iii. 11; xv. 39; John i. 34, 49; iii. 18; v. 25; x. 36; xi. 4.

20. Since by the phrase, *Son of God*, is signified the Lord as to the human which he assumed in the world, which is the Divine Human, we may discover what the Lord means by saying repeatedly, "*That he was sent by the Father into the world*," and that "*He came forth from the Father;*" namely, that he was conceived of Jehovah the Father. That no other meaning belongs to the expression, *sent of the Father*, appears from all those passages where it is said, that he came to do the will and works of his Father. These works consisted in conquering the hells, glorifying his human, teaching the Word, and instituting a new church; and these could not possibly be accomplished but by a Human conceived of Jehovah, and born of a virgin; thus, they never could have been effected, had not God become man. Examine the passages where the term *sent* is used in reference to the Lord, and you will see the truth of what is here asserted: as Matt. x. 40; xv. 24; Mark ix. 37; Luke iv. 43; ix. 48, x. 16; John iii. 17, 34; iv. 34; v. 23, 24, 36—38; vi. 29, 39, 40, 44, 57; vii. 16, 18, 28, 29; viii. 16, 18, 29, 42; ix. 4; xi. 42; xii. 44, 45, 49; xiii. 20; xiv. 24; xv. 21; xvi.

5; xvii. 3, 8, 21, 23, 25; xx. 21. Examine, also, the passages where the Lord calls Jehovah, Father.

21. Many at this day think of the Lord only as of an ordinary man, like themselves; the reason is, because they only think of his Human, and not at the same time of his Divine, although his Divine and his Human cannot be separated: For the Lord is God and man, and God and man in the Lord are not two but one person, yea, altogether one, even "as the reasonable soul and flesh are one man;" as is taught in the doctrine received throughout the whole Christian world, called the Athanasian Creed, which has been confirmed by several councils. Let me, therefore, entreat the reader, that he may not henceforward separate in his thoughts the Lord's Human from his Divine, to peruse the passages quoted above from Luke, as also the following from Matthew: "The birth of Jesus Christ was on this wise. When as his mother Mary was espoused to Joseph, before they came together, she was found with child of THE HOLY SPIRIT. Then Joseph, her husband, being a just man, and not willing to make her a public example, was minded to put her away privily. But while he thought on these things, behold, the angel of the Lord appeared unto him in a dream, saying, Joseph, thou son of David, fear not to take unto thee Mary thy wife; for that which is conceived in her is of THE HOLY SPIRIT: and she shall bring forth a son, and thou shalt call his name Jesus: for he shall save his people from their sins. Then Joseph, being raised from sleep, did as the angel of the Lord had bidden him, and took unto him his wife. *And he knew her not* till she had brought forth her first-born son; and he called his name Jesus" (i. 18—25). From these words, as well as from the relation of the nativity given in Luke, and from the other passages adduced above, it is evident, that Jesus, who was conceived of Jehovah the Father, and born of the Virgin Mary, is the Son of God, of whom all "the prophets and the law prophesied until John."

22. He who knows in what respect the Lord is called the Son of God, and in what the Son of Man, possesses a key to many arcana of the word; for the Lord at one time calls himself the *Son*, at another, the *Son of God*, and again, at another, the *Son of Man;* always using the epithet which is appropriate to the subject of his discourse. When his Divinity, his unity with the Father, his divine power, faith in him, and life from him, are treated of, he then calls himself *the Son*, and *the Son of God;* as in John v. 17—26, and elsewhere: but where his passion, the judgment, his coming, and, in general, redemption, salvation, reformation and regeneration, are treated of, he calls himself *the Son of Man;* the reason is, because he is then spoken of as the Word. The Lord is designated by various names in the Word of the Old Testament, being there named Jehovah, Jah,

the Lord, God, the Lord Jehovih, Zebaoth, the God of Israel, the Holy One of Israel, the Mighty One of Jacob, Shaddai,* the Rock; as also the Creator, Former, Saviour, and Redeemer; that name being always applied which is appropriate to the occasions on which it is used. Similar distinctions are made in the Word of the New Testament, where the Lord is called Jesus Christ, the Lord, God, the Son of God, the Son of Man, the Prophet, and the Lamb, with other names: which are never applied indiscriminately, but that is adopted which is suitable to the subject.

23. Having shown in what respect the Lord is called the *Son of God*, we will now explain in what respect he is called the *Son of Man*. He is called the Son of Man, when his passion, the judgment, or his coming is treated of; and, in general, where it relates to redemption, salvation, reformation, or regeneration: the reason is, because the Lord is the Son of Man as to the Word; and it is as the Word that he suffers, judges, comes into the world, redeems, saves, reforms, and regenerates. This shall be now shewn in what follows.

24. I. THAT THE LORD IS CALLED THE SON OF MAN WHEN THE PASSION IS TREATED OF, is evident from the following passages: Jesus said unto his disciples, "Behold, we go up to Jerusalem, and THE SON OF MAN shall be delivered unto the chief priests and unto the scribes, and they shall condemn him to death, and shall deliver him to the Gentiles, and they shall mock him, and shall scourge him, and shall spit upon him, and shall kill him; and the third day he shall rise again" (Mark x. 33, 34). So, likewise, in other places where he foretels his passion, as Matthew xx. 18, 19; Mark viii. 31; Luke ix. 22. Jesus said, "Behold, the hour is at hand, and THE SON OF MAN is betrayed into the hands of sinners" (Matt. xxvi. 45). The angel said unto the women that came unto the sepulchre, "Remember how he spake unto you,—saying, THE SON OF MAN must be delivered into the hands of sinful men, and be crucified and the third day rise again" (Luke xxiv. 6, 7). The reason why the Lord then called himself the Son of Man, is, because he suffered himself to be treated after the same manner as they had treated the Word; as has been shewn at large above.

25. II. THAT THE LORD IS CALLED THE SON OF MAN WHEN JUDGMENT IS TREATED OF, is clear from these passages: "When THE SON OF MAN shall come in his glory,—then shall he sit on the throne of his glory, and he shall set the sheep on his right-hand, but the goats on the left" (Matt. xxv. 31, 33). "When the SON OF MAN shall sit on the throne of his glory ye also shall sit upon twelve thrones, judging the twelve tribes of Israel" (Matt. xix. 28). "THE SON OF MAN

* The name does not occur in the authorized version of the English Bible, being there always translated *the Almighty;* the learned, however, are much divided about its exact meaning.

shall come in the glory of his father,—and he shall reward every man according to his works" (Matt. xvi. 27). "Watch ye, therefore,—that ye may be accounted worthy,—to stand before THE SON OF MAN" (Luke xxi. 36). "In such an hour as ye think not, THE SON OF MAN cometh" (Matt. xxiv. 44; Luke xii. 40). "For the Father judgeth no man, but hath committed all judgment unto the Son,—because he is THE SON OF MAN" (John v. 22, 27). The reason why the Lord thus calls himself the Son of Man when judgment is treated of, is, because all judgment is executed according to the Divine Truth, which is in the Word. That it is this which judges every one, the Lord himself declares in John: "If any man hear my words, and believe not, I judge him not; for I came not to judge the world:—*the Word that I have spoken*, the same shall judge him in the last day" (xii. 47, 48). And in another place: "God sent not his Son into the world to condemn the world; but that the world through him might be saved: he that believeth on him is not condemned; but he that believeth not is condemned already, because he hath not believed in the name of the only-begotten Son of God" (iii. 17, 18). That the Lord does not sentence any one to hell, nor cast any one down to hell, but that evil spirits do so themselves, may be seen in the treatise concerning *Heaven and Hell*. N. 245–550, 574. By THE NAME of Jehovah, of the Lord, and of the Son of God, is also meant the Divine Truth, consequently, the Word, which is from Him, of Him, and thus Himself.

26. III. THAT THE LORD IS CALLED THE SON OF MAN WHERE HIS COMING IS TREATED OF, is plain from the following passages: The disciples said unto Jesus, "What shall be the sign of thy coming, and the consummation of the age?" in answer to which inquiry, the Lord foretold the successive states of the church down to the period of its end; of which he saith, "Then shall appear the sign of the SON OF MAN.—And they shall see the SON OF MAN coming in the clouds of Heaven, with power and great glory" (Matt. xxiv. 3, 30; Mark xiii. 26; Luke xxi. 27). By the consummation of the age, is meant the last time of the church; by the coming of the Son of Man in the clouds of Heaven with glory, is signified the opening of the Word, with a manifestation that it treats of the Lord alone. So in Daniel: "I saw—and behold, one like THE SON OF MAN came with the clouds of Heaven" (vii. 13). And in the Revelation: "Behold he cometh with clouds, and every eye shall see him" (i. 7): This is spoken concerning the SON OF MAN, as appears from verse 13 of the same chapter. It is also said in another part of the same book, "I looked and behold, a white cloud, and upon the cloud one sat like unto the SON OF MAN" (xiv. 14). That the Lord himself understood one thing by the Son of God, and another by the Son of Man,

but both in himself, appears from his answer to the high priest: The high priest said unto Jesus, "I adjure thee by the living God, that thou tell us whether thou be the Christ, THE SON OF GOD: Jesus saith unto him, Thou hast said: nevertheless, I say unto you, Hereafter shall ye see THE SON OF MAN sitting on the right hand of power, and coming in the clouds of heaven" (Matt. xxvi. 63, 64). Here he first confessed that he was THE SON OF GOD, and afterwards said that they should see THE SON OF MAN sitting on the right hand of power, and coming in the clouds of heaven: by which is signified that, after the passion of the cross, he should possess the divine power of opening the Word, and establishing his church; which could not be effected before, because he had not before completed the conquest of hell, and the glorification of his Human. What is signified by sitting on the clouds of heaven, and coming in glory is explained in the treatise on *Heaven and Hell.* N. 1.

27. IV. THAT THE LORD IS CALLED THE SON OF MAN WHERE REDEMPTION, SALVATION, REFORMATION, AND REGENERATION ARE TREATED OF, appears from the following passages: "THE SON OF MAN came—to give his life a ransom for many" (Matt. xx. 28; Mark x. 45). "THE SON OF MAN is not come to destroy men's lives but to save them" (Luke ix. 56). "THE SON OF MAN is come to seek and to save that which was lost" (Luke xix. 10). "He that soweth the good seed is the SON OF MAN" (Matt. xiii. 37). Salvation and Redemption are here treated of, and, as the Lord effects these by means of the Word, therefore he here calls himself the Son of Man. The Lord saith, that "THE SON OF MAN hath power to forgive sins" (Mark ii. 10; Luke v. 24);—that is, to save. Also, that "The SON OF MAN is Lord even of the sabbath" (Matt. xii. 8; Mark ii. 28; Luke vi. 5): because he is the Word, which is what he there teaches. He also says in John, "Labour not for the meat which perisheth, but for that meat which endureth unto everlasting life, which THE SON OF MAN shall give unto you" (vi. 27). By meat is here signified every good and truth of doctrine from the Word, consequently, from the Lord: this is also signified by the manna and bread that came down from heaven, mentioned on the same occasion; and likewise by the following words in the subsequent part of the chapter: "Except ye eat the flesh of THE SON OF MAN, and drink his blood, ye have no life in you" (verse 53). Flesh or bread is the good of love from the Word; blood or wine, the good of faith from the same; and both from the Lord.

*The same is meant by* THE SON OF MAN, *when spoken of on other occasions;* as in the following passages: "The foxes have holes, and the birds of the air have nests, but THE SON OF MAN hath not where to lay his head." (Matt. viii. 20; Luke ix. 58); by which is signified that the Word had no place with the Jews;

as the Lord also expressly says (John viii. 37); and also, that they had it not abiding in them, because they did not believe in him (v. 38). In the Revelation, likewise by THE SON OF MAN is signified the Lord with respect to the Word: "In the midst of the seven candlesticks" I saw "one like unto THE SON OF MAN, clothed with a garment down to the foot, and girt about the paps with a golden girdle" (i. 13, and following verses); where the Lord is described as the Word by various representatives, which is the reason that he is called THE SON OF MAN. So in David: "Let thy hand be upon the man of thy right hand, upon THE SON OF MAN whom thou madest strong for thyself. So will not we go back from thee: quicken us" (Psalm lxxx. 17, 18). By the man of the right hand is here meant the Lord with respect to the Word: and the same also is signified by THE SON OF MAN. He is called "the man of the right hand," because the Lord has power by virtue of his Divine Truth, which, likewise, is the Word; thus, also, when he had fulfilled the whole Word, he had Divine Power; hence he said, that "they should see THE SON OF MAN sitting on the right hand of power" (Mark xiv. 62).

28. THAT BECAUSE THE SON OF MAN SIGNIFIES THE LORD AS TO THE WORD, THE SAME TITLE WAS ALSO GIVEN TO THE PROPHETS. The title, SON OF MAN, was given to the prophets, because they represented the Lord as to the Word, and thence signified the doctrine of the church derived from the Word. This is what is constantly understood in heaven, wherever prophets are named in the Word; for the spiritual signification of the term *Prophet*, as also of the term SON OF MAN, is *the Doctrine of the Church derived from the Word*, and, when applied to the Lord, *the Word itself*. That the prophet Daniel is called the SON OF MAN, may be seen in the book of Daniel, viii. 17. And that the prophet Ezekiel was so called, may be seen in Ezek. ii. 1, 3, 6, 8; iii. 1, 3, 4, 10, 17, 25; iv. 1, 16; v. 1; vi. 2; vii. 2; viii. 5, 6, 8, 12, 15; xi. 2, 4, 15; xii. 2, 3, 9, 18, 22, 27; xiii. 2, 17; xiv. 3, 13; xv. 2; xvi. 2; xvii. 2; xx. 3, 4, 27, 46; xxi. 2, 6, 9, 12, 14, 19, 28; xxii. 18, 24; xxiii. 2, 36; xxiv. 2, 16, 25; xxv. 2; xxvi. 2; xxvii. 2; xxviii. 2, 12, 21; xxix. 2, 18; xxx. 2; xxxi. 2; xxxii. 2, 18; xxxiii. 2, 7, 10, 12, 24, 30; xxxiv. 2; xxxv. 2; xxxvi. 1, 17; xxxvii. 3, 9, 11, 16; xxxviii. 2, 14; xxxix. 1, 17; xl. 4; xliii. 7, 10, 18; xlv. 5.

From all that has been advanced, then, it is evident that the Lord is called the Son of God with respect to the Divine Human, and the Son of Man with respect to the Word.

---

THE LORD MADE HIS HUMAN DIVINE FROM THE DIVINE WHICH WAS IN HIM, AND THUS BECAME ONE WITH THE FATHER.

29. It is affirmed in that *Doctrine of the Church* which is received throughout the Christian world, that "our Lord Jesus Christ, the Son of God, is God and Man, who, although he is God and Man, yet he is not two, but one Christ; one, by the taking of the manhood into God; one altogether, by unity of person: for as the reasonable soul and flesh is one man, so God and man is one Christ." These words are taken from the Athanasian Creed, and they contain what it delivers, as the essential articles of faith, on the subject of the union of the Divine and Human in the Lord: what is further said in the same creed concerning the Lord, will be explained in a subsequent article. From these words it clearly appears, that it is *an article of faith in the Christian Church*, that the Divine and Human in the Lord, are not two, but a one, as the soul and body are one man; and that the Divine in him assumed, or took to itself, the Human. Hence it follows, that the Divine cannot possibly be separated from the Human, nor the Human from the Divine; for this would be like separating the soul from the body. The truth of this must also be acknowledged by every one who reads what is cited above (n. 19—21), from two of the evangelists (Luke i. 26—35, and Matt. i. 18—25), concerning the nativity of the Lord; from which it is manifest, that Jesus was conceived of Jehovah God, and born of the virgin Mary; so that the Divine was in him, and was his soul. Since, then, his soul was the very Divine of the Father, it follows, that his body, or Human, must have been made Divine also; for where the one is Divine, the other must necessarily be so too; thus, and no otherwise, can the passages be true which say, that the Father and the Son are one; that the Father is in the Son, and the Son in the Father; that all things belonging to the Son are the Father's, and all things belonging to the Father are the Son's: as the Lord himself teaches. But how the union was accomplished shall be explained in the following order: I. That the Lord from eternity is Jehovah. II. That the Lord from eternity, or Jehovah, assumed the Human, to save mankind. III. That he made the Human Divine, from the Divine in himself. IV. That he made the Human Divine, by temptations admitted therein. V. That the complete union of the Divine and Human in him was effected by the passion of the cross, which was the last temptation. VI. That he successively put off the Human taken from the mother, and put on a Human from the Divine within him, which is a Divine-Human, and is the Son of God. VII. That thus God became Man, as in first principles, so also in ultimates

30. I. THAT THE LORD FROM ETERNITY IS JEHOVAH, is known from the Word; for the Lord said unto the Jews,

"Verily, verily, I say unto you, before Abraham was, I am" (John viii. 58): and elsewhere: "O Father, glorify thou me,—with the glory which I had with thee before the world was" (John xvii. 5): by which is meant, the Lord from eternity, and not a Son from eternity: for as has already been demonstrated, what is called *the Son*, is his Human, conceived of Jehovah the Father, and born of the Virgin Mary in time. That the Lord from eternity is Jehovah himself, appears from many passages in the Word, of which we will here only adduce these few: "It shall be said in that day, Lo, *this is our God;* we have waited for him, and he will save us: this is JEHOVAH; we have waited for him, we will be glad and rejoice in his salvation" (Isaiah xxv. 9); from which words it is evident, that he who was to be waited for was God himself, even Jehovah. "The voice of him that crieth in the wilderness, Prepare ye the way of JEHOVAH, make straight in the desert a highway *for our God.*—The glory of JEHOVAH shall be revealed, and all flesh shall see it together. Behold, the LORD JEHOVIH will come with a strong hand" (Isaiah xl. 3, 5, 10; Matt. iii. 3; Mark i. 3; Luke iii. 4): Here, also, the Lord, who was to come, is called Jehovah. "I, JEHOVAH—will give—thee for a covenant of the people, for a light of the Gentiles: I am JEHOVAH, *that is my name, and my glory will I not give to another*" (Isaiah xlii. 6, 8). The covenant of the people, and the light of the gentiles, is the Lord with respect to the Human; and because this was from Jehovah, and was made a one with him, it is said, "I am Jehovah; that is my name, and my glory will I not give to another;" that is, to no other than himself: to give glory is to glorify, or to unite to himself. "JEHOVAH, whom ye seek, shall suddenly come to his temple" (Malachi iii. 1); where the temple is the temple of his body; as in John ii. 19, 21. "The *Day-spring from on high* hath visited us" (Luke i. 78). The Day-spring from on high, also, is Jehovah, or the Lord from eternity. Hence it appears, that, by the Lord from eternity, we are to understand his all-originating Divine [*Divinum a quo*], which, in the Word, is Jehovah: but from the passages which will be adduced presently, it will appear, that by the term *Lord*, as also by *Jehovah*, after his Human was glorified, we are to understand the Divine and Human together, as a one; and by *the Son*, alone, the Divine Human.

31. II. THAT THE LORD FROM ETERNITY, OR JEHOVAH, ASSUMED THE HUMAN TO SAVE MANKIND, has been confirmed from the Word in the preceding sections; that mankind could not have been saved in any other manner, will be shewn elsewhere. That the Lord from eternity, or Jehovah, assumed the Human, appears, also, from those passages in the Word, where it is said of Jesus that he came forth from God, that he came down from heaven, and that he was sent into the world; as from the

following: "*I came forth* from the Father, and am come into the world" (John xvi. 28): "*I proceeded forth and came from God;* neither came I of myself, but he sent me" (John viii. 42). "The Father himself loveth you, because ye have believed that *I came out from God*" (John xvi. 27). "No man hath ascended up to heaven, but he *that came down from heaven*" (John iii. 13). "The bread of God is he *which cometh down from heaven*, and giveth life unto the world" (John vi. 33, 35, 41, 50, 51). "He that *cometh from above*, is above all" (John iii. 31). "I know him [the Father], for *I am from him*, and *he hath sent me*" (John vii. 29). That by being sent from the Father into the world is understood the assumption of the Human, may be seen above. N. 20.

32. III. THAT THE LORD MADE HIS HUMAN DIVINE FROM THE DIVINE IN HIMSELF, may appear from many passages in the Word, of which those shall be here adduced which prove, 1. *That it was done by successive steps;* which are these: "The child [Jesus] grew and waxed strong in spirit, filled with wisdom; and the grace of God was upon him" (Luke ii. 40). "Jesus increased in wisdom and stature, and in favour with God and man" (verse 52). 2. *That the Divine operated by the Human, as the soul does by the body*, from these: "The Son can do nothing of himself, but what he seeth the Father do" (John v. 19). "I do nothing of myself, but as my Father hath taught me, I speak these things: and he that sent me is with me; the Father hath not left me alone" (John viii. 28, 29, v. 30). "I have not spoken of myself, but the Father who sent me, he gave me a commandment, what I should say, and what I should speak" (xii. 49). "The words that I speak unto you, I speak not of myself: but the Father that dwelleth in me, he doeth the works" (John xiv. 10). "I am not alone because the Father is with me" (John xvi. 32). 3. *That the Divine and Human operated unanimously.* From these: "What things soever the Father doeth, these also doeth the Son likewise" (John v. 19). "For, as the Father raiseth up the dead and quickeneth them, even so the Son quickeneth whom he will" (John v. 21). "As the Father hath life in himself, so hath he given to the Son to have life in himself" (John v. 26). "Now they have known that all things whatsoever thou hast given me, are of thee" (John xvii. 7). 4. *That the Divine is united to the Human, and the Human to the Divine.* From these: "If ye had known me, ye would have known my Father also; and from henceforth ye know him, and have seen him." "He [Jesus] saith unto Philip [who desired to see the Father], Have I been so long time with you, and yet hast thou not known me, Philip? He that hath seen me, hath seen the Father:—Believest thou not that I am in the Father, and the Father in me?" (John xiv. 7, 9, 10). "If I do not the works of my Father, believe me not;

but if I do,—believe the works; that ye may know and believe that the Father is in me, and I in him" (John x. 37, 38). "That they all may be one, as thou, Father, art in me, and I in thee" (John xvii. 21). "At that day ye shall know that I am in my Father" (John xiv. 20). "No one is able to pluck them [my sheep] out of my Father's hand. I and my Father are one" (x. 29, 30). "The Father loveth the Son, and hath given all things into his hand" (John iii. 35). "All things that the Father hath are mine" (John xvi. 15). "All mine are thine, and thine are mine" (John xvii. 10). "Thou hast given him [the Son] power over all flesh" (John xvii. 2). "All power is given unto me in heaven and earth" (Matt. xxviii. 18). 5. *That the Divine Human is to be worshipped*, appears from the following passages: "That all men should honour the Son, even as they honour the Father" (John v. 23). "If ye had known me, ye would have known my Father also" (John viii. 19). "He that seeth me, seeth him that sent me" (John xii. 45). "If ye had known me, ye would have known my Father also, and from henceforth ye know him, and have seen him" (John xiv. 7). "He that receiveth me, receiveth him that sent me" (John xiii. 20). The reason of this is, because no one can see the Essential Divine, which is called the Father, but he may see the Divine Human; for the Lord says, "No man hath seen God at any time; the Only-begotten Son, which is in the bosom of the Father, he hath declared him" (John i. 18). "Not that any man hath seen the Father, save he who is of God; he hath seen the Father" (John vi. 46). "Ye have neither heard his [the Father's] voice at any time, nor seen his shape" (John v. 37). 6. *That since the Lord made his Human Divine from the Divine in Himself; and since the Human is to be approached in worship, and is the Son of God; it is therefore necessary to believe in the Lord, who is both the Father and the Son*, appears from the following passages: "As many as received him to them gave he power to become the sons of God, *even to them that believe on his name*" (John i. 12). "That whosoever *believeth in him* should not perish, but have eternal life" (John iii. 15). "God so loved the world, that he gave his only-begotten Son, that whosoever *believeth in him* should not perish, but have everlasting life" (John iii. 16). "He that *believeth on him* [*the Son*] is not condemned; but he that *believeth not*, is condemned already, because *he hath not believed in the name of the only-begotten Son of God*" (John iii. 18). "He *that believeth on the Son*, hath everlasting life; and *he that believeth not the Son*, shall not see life, but the wrath of God abideth on him" (John iii. 36). "The bread of God is he that cometh down from heaven, and giveth life unto the world. He that cometh to me shall never hunger, and he *that believeth on me*, shall never thirst" (John vi. 33, 35). "This is the will of him that sent me, that every one who seeth the Son, and *believeth on him*, may have everlasting life; and I will raise him up at the last day" (John vi. 40). "Then said they unto him [Jesus], What shall we do that we might work the works of God? Jesus answered,—This is the work of God, that *ye believe on him whom he hath sent*" (John vi. 28, 29). "Verily, verily, I say unto you, he *that believeth on me* hath everlasting life" (John vi. 47). "Jesus cried, saying, If any man thirst, let him come unto me and drink; he *that believeth on me*, as the Scripture hath said, out of his belly shall flow rivers of living water" (John vii. 37, 38). "*If ye believe not* that I am he, ye shall die in your sins" (John viii. 24). "Jesus said, I am the resurrection and the life; he *that believeth in me*, though he were dead, yet shall he live; and whosoever liveth *and believeth in me*, shall never die" (John xi. 25, 26). Jesus said, "I am come a light into the world, that *whosoever believeth on me* should not abide in darkness" (John xii. 46; viii. 12). "While ye have the light, *believe in the light*, that ye may be the children of light" (John xii. 36). "Verily, verily, I say unto you,—the dead shall hear the voice of the Son of God, and they that hear shall live" (John v. 25). "Abide in me, and I in you; I am the vine, ye are the branches; he that abideth in me, and I in him, the same bringeth forth much fruit; for without me ye can do nothing" (John xv. 4, 5). I am in the Father, and ye in me, and I in you" (John xiv. 20; see also xvii. 23). "I am the way, and the truth, and the life: no man cometh unto the Father, but by me" (John xiv. 6). In these, and in all other places, where the Father is mentioned, is meant the Divine that was in the Lord from conception, and which, according to the Athanasian Creed, which forms the standard of faith for the Christian world, was to him what the soul of man is to his body: the Human from the Divine is the Son of God. Now since this also was made Divine, therefore, lest man should approach the Father alone, and so in thought, faith, and thence worship, should separate the Father from the Lord, in whom he exists; after teaching that the Father and he are one; that the Father is in him, and he in the Father; that all should abide in him; and that no one cometh to the Father but by him; the Lord instructs us further, that we must believe in him, and that man is saved by a faith directed to him. That the Human was made Divine in the Lord, is a truth of which many in Christendom can form no conception; the chief reason is, because, in thinking concerning man, they take their ideas from his material body, and not from his spiritual; when, nevertheless, all angels, who are spiritual beings, are also men in perfect human form; nay, further, every divine proceeding from Jehovah God, from its first beginnings in heaven to its ultimate in the world, tends to the human form. That angels are in the human form, and that everything divine tends to that form, may be seen in the treatise on *Heaven and Hell*, n. 73—77, and n. 453—460; and still more fully in *The Angelic Wisdom concerning the Divine Love.*

33. IV. That the Lord made his Human Divine by Temptations admitted therein, and by continual Victories in those conflicts, has been already shewn above, n. 12—14, to which only this shall be added. Temptations are nothing else but combats against evils and falses; and since these are from hell, they are also combats against hell. Evil spirits from hell are moreover with the men who undergo spiritual temptations, which are occasioned by their agency; and, although man is not aware of this, it is a certain fact, which has been made known to me by much experience. Hence it is, that when a man, by the divine assistance of the Lord, conquers in temptations, he is drawn out of hell, and elevated into heaven; which is the reason that by temptations, or combats against evils, he is made spiritual,—thus an angel. But the Lord fought, by his own power against all the hells, and wholly quelled and subdued them; and as he, at the same time, glorified his Human, he holds them in a state of subjection to eternity. For, before the coming of the Lord, the hells had risen to such a height, that they began to infest the very angels of heaven themselves; and, in like manner, every man that came into and went out of the world. The cause of the hells having risen to such a height, was, because the church was in a state of utter devastation, and the inhabitants of the world, being devoted to idolatry, were in mere falses and evils; and it is from men that the hells are filled with inhabitants: hence it had come to pass, that unless the Lord had come into the world, no man could have been saved. Of these combats of the Lord much is said in the Psalms of David, and in the Prophets, but little in the Evangelists. These combats are what are meant by the temptations which the Lord endured, the last of which was the passion of the cross; and it is on account of his victories in them that he is called a Saviour and Redeemer. This is so far known in the church as to have given occasion to the general confession, that the Lord conquered death or the devil, that is, hell, and arose victorious; as, also, that without the Lord there is no salvation. That the Lord also glorified his Human, and thereby became a Saviour, Redeemer, Reformer, and Regenerator, unto eternity, will be subsequently shewn. That the Lord became a Saviour by his combats or temptations, is evident from the numerous passages adduced from the Word above; n. 12—14, and from the following in Isaiah: "The day of vengeance is in my heart, and *the year of my redeemed is* come." "And I will tread down the people in my anger,—I will bring down their strength to the earth;—*so he was their Saviour*" (lxiii. 4, 6, 8); in which chapter the Lord's combats are treated of. And in David: "Lift up your heads,

O ye gates, and be ye lift up, ye everlasting doors, and the *King of glory* shall come in. Who is *the King of glory? Jehovah strong and mighty, Jehovah mighty in battle*" (Psalm xxiv. 7, 8); which words are also spoken in reference to the Lord.

34. V. THAT THE FULL UNION OF THE DIVINE AND HUMAN IN THE LORD, WAS EFFECTED BY THE PASSION OF THE CROSS, WHICH WAS HIS LAST TEMPTATION. This was confirmed above, in its proper section, where it was shewn that the Lord came into the world to subdue the hells, and glorify his Human; and that the passion of the cross was the last combat, by which he fully conquered the hells, and fully glorified his Human. Since, then, the Lord, by the passion of the cross, fully glorified his Human, that is, united it to his Divine, and thus made his Human also Divine, it follows that he is Jehovah and God with respect to both. Hence, in many passages of the Word, he is called Jehovah, God, and the Holy One of Israel, the Redeemer, Saviour, and Former; as in the following: "Mary said, My soul doth magnify the LORD, and my spirit hath rejoiced in GOD my SAVIOUR" (Luke i. 46, 47). And the angel said unto the shepherds, "Behold, I bring you good tidings of great joy, which shall be to all people, for unto you is born this day, in the city of David, a SAVIOUR, who is Christ the LORD" (Luke ii. 10, 11). And they said, "This is indeed the Christ the SAVIOUR of the world" (John iv. 42). "I will help thee, saith JEHOVAH, and thy REDEEMER, the HOLY ONE OF ISRAEL" (Isaiah xli. 14). "Thus saith JEHOVAH that *created* thee, O Jacob, and He that *formed* thee, O Israel:—I have *redeemed* thee:—I am JEHOVAH thy GOD, THE HOLY ONE OF ISRAEL, THY SAVIOUR" (Isaiah xliii. 1, 3). "Thus saith JEHOVAH YOUR REDEEMER, the HOLY ONE OF ISRAEL.—I am JEHOVAH YOUR HOLY ONE, the CREATOR OF ISRAEL, your KING" (Isaiah xliii. 14, 15). "Thus saith JEHOVAH the HOLY ONE OF ISRAEL, and his MAKER" (Isaiah xlv. 11). "Thus saith JEHOVAH THY REDEEMER, the HOLY ONE OF ISRAEL" (Isaiah xlviii. 17). "All flesh shall know that I JEHOVAH am thy SAVIOUR and thy REDEEMER, the MIGHTY ONE OF JACOB" (Isaiah xlix. 26). "And the REDEEMER shall come to Zion" (Isaiah lix. 20). "And thou shalt know that I JEHOVAH am thy SAVIOUR and thy REDEEMER, the MIGHTY ONE OF JACOB" (Isaiah lx. 16). "And now saith JEHOVAH that *formed* me from the womb" (Isaiah xlix. 5). "JEHOVAH, my strength and my REDEEMER" (Psalm xix. 14). "And they remembered that GOD was their rock, and the HIGH GOD their REDEEMER" (Psalm lxxviii. 35). "Thus saith JEHOVAH thy REDEEMER, and he that *formed* thee from the womb" (Isaiah xliv. 24). "As for our REDEEMER, JEHOVAH OF HOSTS is his name, the HOLY ONE OF ISRAEL" (Isaiah xlvii. 4). "With everlasting kindness will I have mercy on thee, saith JEHOVAH THY REDEEMER" (Isaiah liv. 8). "Their

REDEEMER is strong, JEHOVAH OF HOSTS is his name" (Jerem iv. 34). "Let Israel hope in JEHOVAH, for with JEHOVAH there is mercy, and with him is plenteous *redemption*. He shall redeem Israel from all his iniquities" (Psalm cxxx. 7, 8). "JEHOVAH is my rock, and my fortress,—and the horn of my salvation,—my SAVIOUR" (2 Sam. xxii. 2, 3). "Thus saith JEHOVAH the REDEEMER OF ISRAEL, his HOLY ONE :—Kings shall see and arise—because of the Lord that is faithful, and the HOLY ONE OF ISRAEL : and he shall choose thee" (Isaiah xlix. 7). "Surely GOD is in thee, and there is none else.—Verily thou art a God that hidest thyself, O GOD of Israel, the SAVIOUR" (Isaiah xlv. 14, 15). "Thus saith JEHOVAH the King of Israel, and his REDEEMER, JEHOVAH OF HOSTS :—*Beside* ME *there is no God*" (Isaiah xliv. 6). "I am JEHOVAH, and *beside* ME *there is no* SAVIOUR" (Isaiah xliii. 11). "Have not I JEHOVAH, and *there is no God else beside* ME,—and a SAVIOUR, *there is none beside* ME" (Isaiah xlv. 21). I am JEHOVAH thy GOD, and thou shalt know no GOD but ME, for *there is. no* SAVIOUR *beside* Me" Hosea xiii. 4). "Look unto ME and be ye *saved*, all the ends of the earth, for I am GOD, and *there is none else*" (Isaiah xlv.22). "JEHOVAH OF HOSTS is his name, and thy REDEEMER the HOLY ONE OF ISRAEL : the GOD of the whole earth shall he be called" (Isaiah liv. 5). From these passages it may be seen that the Divine of the Lord, which is called the Father, and, here, Jehovah and God, and the Divine-Human, which is called the Son, and, here, the Redeemer and Saviour, as also the Former, that is, the Reformer and Regenerator; are not two, but one; for not only is mention made of Jehovah, God, and the Holy One of Israel, and of a Redeemer and Saviour, but it is said, that Jehovah is the Redeemer and Saviour; nay farther, that Jehovah is the Saviour, and there is none beside. Hence, it manifestly appears, that the Divine and Human in the Lord are One Person, and that the Human also is Divine; for the Redeemer and Saviour of the World is no other than the Lord as to the Divine-Human, which is what is called the Son. Redemption and salvation also constitute the attribute proper to his Human, which is called merit and righteousness; for it was his Human that endured temptations and the passion of the cross; thus by his Human he saved and redeemed mankind. Now whereas, after the union [unitio] of the Human with the Divine within it, which was like that of the soul and body in man, they were no longer two, but one person,—agreeably to the doctrine of the Christian world,—it follows that the Lord is Jehovah and God in respect to both; wherefore we sometimes read of Jehovah and the Holy One of Israel, the Redeemer and Saviour, and, at others, of Jehovah the Redeemer and Saviour; as may be seen in the passages cited. Thus Christ is called the Saviour (Luke

ii. 11; John iv. 42). God, and the God of Israel, are called the Saviour and Redeemer (Luke i. 47; Isaiah xlv. 15; liv. 5; Psalm lxxviii. 35). Jehovah, the Holy One of Israel, is called the Saviour and Redeemer (Isaiah xli. 14; xliii. 3, 11, 14, 15; xlviii. 17; xlix. 7; liv. 5). Jehovah is called the Saviour, Redeemer, and Former (Isaiah xliv. 6; xlvii. 4; xlix. 26; liv. 5; lxiii. 16; Jerem. l. 34; Psalm lxxviii. 35; Psalm cxxx. 7, 8; 2 Sam. xxii. 2, 3). Jehovah God is called the Redeemer and Saviour, and it is said that beside him there is no other (Isaiah xliii. 11; xliv. 6; xlv. 14, 15, 21, 22; Hosea xiii. 4).

35. VI. THAT THE LORD PUT OFF, BY SUCCESSIVE STEPS, THE HUMAN FROM THE MOTHER, AND PUT ON A HUMAN FROM THE DIVINE IN HIMSELF, WHICH IS THE DIVINE-HUMAN AND THE SON OF God. That the Lord was Divine and Human, Divine from Jehovah the Father, and Human from the virgin Mary, is well known. Hence he was both God and man, having a Divine Essence and a human nature, a Divine Essence from the Father, and a human nature from the mother; and hence was equal to the Father, as to the Divine, and inferior to the Father, as to the Human: and further, that this human nature from the mother was not transmuted into the Divine Essence, neither commingled with it, is taught by the doctrine of faith, called the Athanasian Creed. Indeed, the human nature cannot be transmuted into the Divine Essence, nor commingled therewith. And moreover from the same creed is our doctrine, that the Divine took, that is, united, to itself the Human as the soul is united to its body, so that they were not two, but one person. From this, it follows, that the Lord put off the Human from the mother, which, in itself, was like the human of another man, and thus material, and put on a Human from the Father, which, in itself, was like his Divine, and thus substantial: so that the Human also was made Divine. Hence it is, that in the prophets, the Lord is called, even with respect to the Human, Jehovah and God; and in the Evangelists, the Lord, God, the Messiah or Christ, and the Son of God, in whom we must believe, and by whom we are to be saved.

Now as the Lord had from the first a Human from the mother, which he put off by successive steps, therefore, he was, during his abode in this world, in two states; the one a state of humiliation, or exinanition, and the other a state of glorification, or union with the Divine, which is called the Father. He was in the state of humiliation at the time, and in the degree, that he was in the human from the mother; and he was in the state of glorification, at the time, and in the degree, that he was in the Human from the Father. In the state of Humiliation he prayed to the Father, as to a being distinct from himself; but in the state of glorification he spoke with the Father as with himself. In this latter state he said, that the Father was in him, and he in the Father, and that the Father and he were One; but in the other state he underwent temptations, and suffered the cross, and prayed to the father not to forsake him; for the Divine could not be tempted, much less could it suffer the cross. Hence it further appears, that, by temptations followed by continual victories, and by the passion of the cross, which was the last of those temptations, he fully conquered the hells, and fully glorified the Human, as was shown above.

That the Lord put off the human from the mother, and put on a Human from the Divine in himself, which is called the Father, may also be concluded from this circumstance, that whenever he spoke to or of her, he did not give her the title of mother. There are but three occasions recorded in the Evangelists, on which the Lord addressed her or mentioned her; and on two of these he called her woman, and the third time he declined to acknowledge her as his mother. That he twice called her woman, we read in John: "The mother of Jesus saith unto him, They have no wine: Jesus saith unto her, *Woman*, what have I to do with thee? Mine hour is not yet come" (ii. 3, 4). And again: "When Jesus therefore saw his mother, and the disciple standing by whom he loved, he said unto his mother, *Woman*, behold thy son; then saith he to the disciple, Behold thy mother" (xix. 26, 27). That he once declined to acknowledge her, we read in Luke: "It was told Jesus by certain who said, Thy mother and thy brethren stand without, desiring to see thee: And he answered and said unto them, My mother and my brethren are they who hear the word of God, and do it" (viii. 20, 21; Matt. xii. 46—49; Mark iii. 31—35). In other places Mary is called his mother, but not from his own mouth. The same truth is also confirmed by this circumstance, that he would not acknowledge himself to be the son of David: for we read in the Evangelists, Jesus asked the Pharisees, "saying, What think ye of Christ? whose son is he? They say unto him, The son of David. He saith unth them, How then doth David in spirit call him Lord, saying, the Lord said unto my Lord, Sit thou on my right hand till I make thine enemies thy footstool? If David then call him Lord, how is he his son? And no man was able to answer him a word" (Matt. xxii. 41—45; Mark xii. 35—37; Luke xx. 41—44; Psalm cx. 1). Thus it is evident, that the Lord, in respect to his glorified Human, was neither the son of Mary nor of David. What was the nature of his Glorified Human, he shewed to "Peter, James, and John," when he "was transfigured before them; and his face did shine as the sun and his raimenr was as white as the light;—and a voice came out of the cloud, saying, This is my beloved Son, in whom I am well pleased: hear ye him" (Matt. xvii. 1—8; Mark ix. 2—8; Luke ix. 28

—36). The Lord was also seen by John, "as the sun shining in his strength" (Rev. i. 16).

That the Human of the Lord was glorified, is evident from what is said of his glorification in the Evangelists. Thus in John: "The hour is come that the Son of Man should be glorified." "Father glorify thy name: Then came there a voice from heaven, saying, I have both glorified it, and will glorify it again" (xii. 23, 28). It is said, "I have both glorified it, and will glorify it again," because the Lord's glorification was accomplished by successive steps. Again: "Therefore, when he [Judas] was gone out, Jesus said, Now is the Son of Man glorified, and God is glorified in him,—God shall also glorify him in himself, and shall straightway glorify him" (xiii. 31, 32). Again: Jesus said, "Father, the hour is come; glorify thy Son, that thy Son also may glorify thee" (xvii. 1, 5). And in Luke: "Ought not Christ to have suffered these things, and to enter into his glory?" (xxiv. 16). These words are spoken in reference to his Human. The reason why the Lord said, "God is glorified in him;" and also, "God shall glorify him in himself," and further, "Glorify thy Son, that thy Son may also glorify thee;" was, because the union was reciprocal, being a union of the Divine with the Human, and of the Human with the Divine; which also occasioned him to say, "I am in the Father and the Father in me" (John xiv. 10, 11): and, "All mine are thine, and thine are mine" (John xvii. 10). Thus the union was absolutely full or perfect. It is indeed true of all union, that it is not full and perfect unless it be reciprocal; such, therefore, must be the union of the Lord with man, and of man with the Lord, as he teaches in John: "At that day ye shall know that I am in my Father, and you in me, and I in you" (xiv. 20): And in another place: "Abide in me, and I in you;—he that abideth in me, and I in him, the same bringeth forth much fruit" (xv. 4, 5).

Since the Human of the Lord was glorified, that is, was made Divine, therefore he arose after death on the third day with his whole body; which never happens to any man, for he only rises as to his spirit, and not as to his body. That mankind might be assured, and that no doubt might be entertained, that the Lord arose with his whole body, he not only declared it by the angels who were in the sepulchre, but he also shewed himself in his human body to his disciples: and when they imagined that they saw a spirit, he said to them, "Behold my hands and my feet, that it is I myself: handle me and see; for a spirit hath not flesh and bones, as ye see me have. And when he had thus spoken, he shewed them his hands and his feet" (Luke xxiv. 39, 40; John xx. 20). And further, he said to Thomas, "Reach hither thy finger, and behold my hands; and reach hither thy hand, and thrust it into my side; and be not faithless but believing.

And Thomas answered and said unto him, My Lord and my God" (John xx. 27, 28). And still further, to evince that he was not a spirit but a man, he said to the disciples, "Have ye here any meat? And they gave him a piece of a broiled fish, and of a honey-comb: and he took it and did eat before them" (Luke xxiv. 41—43). As, however, his body was now no longer a material, but a divine substantial body, he came in amongst the disciples whilst "the doors were shut" (John xx. 19, 26). And after he had been seen, "he vanished out of their sight" (Luke xxiv. 31). Being thus wholly Divine, he was taken up, and sat on the right hand of God: for we read in Luke: "And it came to pass while he blessed them [the disciples] he was parted from them, and carried up into heaven" (xxiv. 51). And in Mark: "After he had spoken unto them, he was received up into heaven, and sat on the right hand of God" (xvi. 19). To sit on the right hand of God, means, to possess Divine Omnipotence.

Now, since the Lord ascended into heaven, and sat on the right hand of God, or entered on the exercise of Divine Omnipotence, with his Divine and Human united in one, it follows, that his Human Substance or Essence, is as his Divine. To suppose otherwise, is to imagine that his Divine ascended up into heaven, and sat on the right hand of God, but that his Human did not; a supposition which is contrary to Scripture, and also to the received Christian doctrine, which teaches, That God and Man in Christ are as soul and body; and to separate these is repugnant to sound reason. This union of the Father with the Son, or of the Divine with the Human, is also meant in the following passages: "I came forth from the Father, and am come into the world: again, I leave the world, and go to the Father" (John xvi. 28). "I go away unto him that sent me" (John vii. 33; xvi. 5, 16; xvii. 11, 13; xx. 17). "What and if ye shall see the Son of Man ascend up where he was before?" (John vi. 62). "No man hath ascended up to heaven, but he that came down from heaven" (John iii. 13). Every man that is saved, does indeed ascend into heaven, yet not of himself, but from the Lord; only the Lord ascended of himself.

36. VII. THAT THUS GOD BECAME MAN, AS IN FIRST PRINCIPLES SO ALSO IN ULTIMATES. That God is a man, and that every angel and spirit is a man from God, is shewn in the treatise on *Heaven and Hell;* and more fully in the two treatises entitled *Angelic Wisdom.* God, however, was from the beginning a man in first principles, but not in ultimates; but after he assumed the human in the world, he also became a man in ultimates. This follows from what has just been proved, namely, that the Lord united his Human to his Divine, and thus made his Human Divine also. Hence it is, that the Lord is said to be the Beginning and the End, the First and the Last, and

the Alpha and the Omega; as in the Revelation: "I am Alpha and Omega, the Beginning and the End, saith the Lord, who is, and who was, and who is to come, the Almighty" (i. 8, 11). So when John saw the Son of Man in the midst of the seven candlesticks, he fell at his feet as dead; but he laid his right hand upon him, saying, "I am the First and the Last" (i. 17; ii. 8; xxi. 6). Again: "Behold I come quickly,—to give to every man according as his work shall be. I am Alpha and Omega, the Beginning and the End, the First and the Last" (xxii. 12, 13). And in Isaiah: "Thus saith Jehovah, the King of Israel, and his Redeemer, Jehovah of Hosts: I am the First and I am the Last" (xliv. 6; xlviii. 12).

---

## THE LORD IS THE VERY GOD, FROM WHOM THE WORD IS, AND OF WHOM IT TREATS.

37. In the first section of this work we undertook to shew that the whole Sacred Scripture treats of the Lord, and that the Lord is the Word. This shall now be further demonstrated from those passages of the Word where the Lord is called Jehovah, the God of Israel and of Jacob, the Holy One of Israel, Lord, and God; as also King, the Anointed of Jehovah, and David. It may first be expedient to remark, that it has been granted me to read over all the Prophets, and the Psalms of David, examining every single verse, with a perception of the subject treated of; when I found that the contents relate to nothing else than the church established, and to be established, by the Lord; his coming, his combats, glorification, redemption, and salvation; and of heaven, as existing from him; with, at the same time, their opposites. Now, since all these are the works of the Lord, it was evident to me, that the whole of the Sacred Scripture relates to him, and hence that the Lord is the Word. This, however, cannot be seen, but by those who are inwardly enlightened by the Lord, and who have also a knowledge of the spiritual sense of the Word. All the angels of heaven enjoy this knowledge; and therefore when the Word is read by man, this is the only sense in which they comprehend it: for spirits and angels are present with man continually, and they, being spiritual, understand spiritually what man understands naturally. That the whole Sacred Scripture treats of the Lord, may be seen, but only as through a glass, darkly, from these passages cited from the Word in the first section above,* as also from those which shall now be produced from the Word, to shew how continually he is there called Lord

* N. 1—6

and God; from which, however, this may appear clearly, that it was he who spake by the Prophets, and whom they mean when they say, *Jehovah spake*, *Jehovah said*, and *the saying of Jehovah.*

THAT THE LORD EXISTED BEFORE HIS COMING INTO THE WORLD, appears from these passages: John the Baptist said of the Lord, "He it is who, coming after me, is preferred *before* me, whose shoes' latchet I am not worthy to unloose.—This is he of whom I said, After me cometh a man who is preferred before me, for he *was before* me" (John i. 27, 30). In the Revelation: "And the four-and-twenty elders fell upon their faces, and worshipped God, saying, We give thee thanks, O Lord God Almighty, who art, and *wast*, and art to come" (xi. 16, 17). Also in Micah: "Thou, Bethlehem Ephratah, though thou be little among the thousands of Judah, yet out of thee shall He come forth unto me that is to be ruler in Israel, whose goings forth *have been from old*, *from everlasting*" (v. 2). The Lord himself likewise declares in the Evangelists, that he was before Abraham; that he was in glory with the Father before the foundation of the world; that he came forth from the Father: and John affirms that the Word was from the beginning with God, and that the Word was God, and that it was this which was made flesh.

We will now proceed to shew that the Lord is called Jehovah, the God of Israel and of Jacob, the Holy One of Israel, God, and Lord; also King, the Anointed of Jehovah, and David.

38. I. THAT THE LORD IS CALLED JEHOVAH, appears from these passages: "Thus saith JEHOVAH that created thee, O Jacob, and he that formed thee, O Israel: Fear not; for *I have redeemed thee.*—I am JEHOVAH thy God, the Holy one of Israel, *thy Saviour*" (Isaiah xliii. 1, 3). "I am JEHOVAH your Holy One, the Creator of Israel, your King" (verse 15). "And all flesh shall know, that I JEHOVAH am thy *Saviour and thy Redeemer*, the Mighty One of Jacob" (Isaiah xlix. 26). "Thou shalt know that I JEHOVAH am thy *Saviour and thy Redeemer*, the Mighty One of Jacob" (Isaiah lx. 16). "JEHOVAH that *formed* me from the womb" (Isaiah xlix. 4). "JEHOVAH is my strength and my *Redeemer*" (Psalm xix. 14). "Thus saith JEHOVAH, that made thee and formed thee from the womb.—Thus saith JEHOVAH, the King of Israel, and his *Redeemer*, JEHOVAH OF HOSTS" (Isaiah xlix. 2, 6). "As for our *Redeemer*, JEHOVAH OF HOSTS *is his name*, the Holy One of Israel" (xlvii. 4). "With everlasting kindness will I have mercy on thee, saith JEHOVAH thy *Redeemer*" (Isaiah liv. 8). "*Their Redeemer is strong*, JEHOVAH OF HOSTS *is his name*" (Jerem. l. 34). "JEHOVAH is my rock, and my fortress, and the horn of my salvation,—my *Saviour*" (2 Sam. xxii. 2, 3). "Thus saith

JEHOVAH your *Redeemer*, the Holy One of Israel" (Isaiah xliii. 14; xlviii. 17). "Thus saith JEHOVAH the *Redeemer* of Israel, and his Holy One:—kings shall see and arise" (Isaiah xlix. 7). "I am JEHOVAH, and besides me there is no *Saviour*" (Isaiah xliii. 11). "Who hath declared this from ancient time? Have not I JEHOVAH? and there is no God else beside me:—look unto me, and *be ye saved*, all the ends of the earth" (Isaiah xlv. 21, 22). "I am JEHOVAH thy God,—there is no *Saviour* besides me" (Hosea xiii. 4). "Thou hast *redeemed* me, O JEHOVAH, God of truth" (Psalm xxxi. 5). "Let Israel hope in JEHOVAH; for with JEHOVAH there is mercy, and with him is plenteous *redemption;* he shall *redeem* Israel from all his iniquities" (Psalm cxxx. 7, 8). "JEHOVAH OF HOSTS is his name, and thy *Redeemer*, the Holy One of Israel, the God of the whole earth shall he be called" (Isaiah liv. 5). In these passages, JEHOVAH is called the Redeemer and Saviour; but as the Lord is the only Redeemer and Saviour, it follows that it is he who is there meant by Jehovah.

That the Lord is Jehovah, or that Jehovah is the Lord, also appears from the following passages: "There shall come forth a rod out of the stem of Jesse, and a branch shall grow out of his roots, and the *spirit* of JEHOVAH shall rest upon him" (Isaiah xi. 1, 2). "And it shall be said in that day, Lo, this is our God, we have waited for him, and he will save us; this is JEHOVAH: we have waited for him, we will be glad, and rejoice in his salvation" (Isaiah xxv. 9). "The voice of him that crieth in the wilderness, Prepare ye the way of JEHOVAH, make straight in the desert a highway for our God. And the *glory* of JEHOVAH shall be revealed, and all flesh shall see it together. Behold, THE LORD JEHOVAH will come with a strong hand, and his arm shall rule for him" (Isaiah xl. 3, 5, 10). "I, Jehovah,—will give thee for a covenant of the people, for a light of the Gentiles—I am Jehovah, that is my name, and *my glory will I not give to another*" (Isaiah xlii. 6, 8). "Behold, the days come, saith Jehovah, that I will raise unto David a righteous branch, and a king shall reign and prosper, and shall execute judgment and justice in the earth;—and this is his name whereby he shall be called,—JEHOVAH *our righteousness*" (Jerem. xxiii. 5, 6). "But thou Bethlehem Ephratah,—out of thee shall He come forth unto me, that is to be ruler in Israel. He shall stand and feed in *the strength of* JEHOVAH" (Micah v. 2, 4). "Unto us a child is born, unto us a son is given, and the government shall be upon his shoulder: and his name shall be called,—the Mighty God, the *Everlasting Father:*—upon the throne of David, to order it, and to establish it with judgment and with justice, from henceforth even for ever" (Isaiah ix. 6, 7). "JEHOVAH shall go forth and fight against those nations. *And his feet shall stand in that day upon the*

*Mount of Olives, which is before Jerusalem*" (Zech. xiv. 3, 4). "Lift up your heads, O ye gates, and be ye lift up, ye everlasting doors, and the King of Glory shall come in. Who is the King of Glory? JEHOVAH strong and mighty, JEHOVAH mighty in battle" (Psalm xxiv. 7—10). "In that *day* shall JEHOVAH OF HOSTS be for a crown of glory, and for a diadem of beauty, unto the residue of his people" (Isaiah xxviii. 5). "I will send you Elijah the prophet, before the coming of the great and dreadful *day* of JEHOVAH" (Malachi iv. 5). Not to mention other passages, where mention is made of *the day of* JEHOVAH, and it is said to be great or near; as Ezek. xxx. 3; Joel ii. 11; Amos v. 18, 20; Zeph. i. 14, 15, 18.

39. II. THAT THE LORD IS CALLED THE GOD OF ISRAEL, AND THE GOD OF JACOB, appears from the following passages: "Moses took the blood, and sprinkled it on the people, and said, Behold the blood of the covenant which Jehovah hath made with you: and they saw THE GOD OF ISRAEL; and there was under his feet as it were a paved work of sapphire stone, and as it were the body of heaven" (Exod. xxiv. 8, 10.) "The multitude wondered when they saw the dumb to speak, the maimed to be whole, the lame to walk, and the blind to see; and they glorified THE GOD OF ISRAEL" (Matt. xv. 31). "Blessed be the LORD GOD OF ISRAEL, for he hath visited and redeemed his people, and hath raised up a horn of salvation for us in the house of his servant David" (Luke i. 68, 69). "I will give thee the treasures of darkness and hidden riches of secret places, that thou mayest know that I Jehovah, who call thee by thy name, am THE GOD OF ISRAEL" (Isaiah xlv. 3). "Hear ye this, O house of Jacob,—which swear by the name of Jehovah, and make mention of THE GOD OF ISRAEL:—for they call themselves of the holy city, and stay themselves upon THE GOD OF ISRAEL; Jehovah of Hosts is his name" (Isaiah xlviii. 1, 2). "When he [Jacob] seeth his children—in the midst of him, they shall sanctify my name, and they shall sanctify the Holy One of Jacob, and shall fear THE GOD OF ISRAEL" (Isaiah xxix. 23). "In the last days—many people shall go and say, Come ye, and let us go up to the mountain of Jehovah, to the house of THE GOD OF JACOB; and he will teach us his ways, and we will walk in his paths" (Isaiah ii. 2, 3). "And all flesh shall know that I Jehovah am thy Saviour and *thy Redeemer*, THE MIGHTY ONE OF JACOB" (Isaiah xlix. 26). "I Jehovah am thy *Saviour* and thy *Redeemer*, the MIGHTY ONE OF JACOB" (Isaiah lx. 16). "Tremble, thou earth, at the presence of Jehovah, at the presence of THE GOD OF JACOB" (Psalm cxiv. 7). David "sware unto Jehovah, and vowed unto THE MIGHTY ONE OF JACOB; Surely I will not come into the tabernacle of my house,—until I find out a place for Jehovah, a habitation for the MIGHTY GOD OF JACOB. Lo, we heard of it in Eph

ratah [Bethlehem]" (Psalm cxxxii. 2, 3, 5, 6). "Blessed be Jehovah God, THE GOD OF ISRAEL;—the whole earth shall be filled with his glory" (Psalm lxxii. 18, 19). Not to mention those passages where the Lord is called the God of Israel, the Redeemer and Saviour; as Luke i. 47; Isaiah xlv. 15; Psalm lxxviii. 35; besides many other places, where he is only called the God of Israel; as Isaiah xvii. 6; xxi. 10, 17; xxiv. 15; xxix. 23; Jerem. vii. 3; ix. 15; xi. 3; xiii. 12; xvi. 9; xix. 3, 15; xxiii. 2; xxiv. 5; xxv. 15, 27; xxix. 4, 8, 21, 25; xxx. 2; xxxi. 23; xxxii. 14, 15, 36; xxxiii. 4; xxxiv. 2, 13; xxxv. 13, 17, 18, 19; xxxvii. 7; xxxviii. 17; xxxix. 16; xlii. 9, 15, 18; xliv. 2, 7, 11, 25; xlviii. 1; l. 18; li. 33; Ezek. viii. 4; ix. 3; x. 19, 20; xi. 22; xliii. 2; xliv. 2; Zeph. ii. 9; Psalm xli. 13; lix. 5; lxviii. 8.

40. III. THAT THE LORD IS CALLED THE HOLY ONE OF ISRAEL, appears from these passages: The angel said unto Mary, "That HOLY THING which shall be born of thee shall be called the Son of God" (Luke i. 35). "I saw in the visions of my head upon my bed, and behold, a watcher, and a HOLY ONE came down from heaven" (Dan. iv. 13). "God came from Teman, and the HOLY ONE from Mount Paran" (Habak. iii. 3). "I am Jehovah your HOLY ONE, the Creator of Israel, your king" (Isaiah xliii. 15). "Thus saith Jehovah the Redeemer of Israel, and his HOLY ONE" (Isaiah xlix. 7). "I am Jehovah thy God, THE HOLY ONE of Israel, thy Saviour" (Isaiah xliii. 3). "As for our Redeemer, Jehovah of Hosts is his name, the HOLY ONE OF ISRAEL" (Isaiah xlvii. 4). "Thus saith Jehovah your Redeemer, THE HOLY ONE OF ISRAEL" (Isaiah xliii. 14; xlviii. 17). "Jehovah of Hosts is his name, and thy Redeemer THE HOLY ONE OF ISRAEL" (Isaiah liv. 5). "They tempted God, and limited the HOLY ONE OF ISRAEL" (Psalm lxxviii. 41). "They have forsaken Jehovah, they have provoked THE HOLY ONE OF ISRAEL" (Isaiah i. 4). They say, "Cause THE HOLY ONE OF ISRAEL to cease from before us: wherefore thus saith THE HOLY ONE OF ISRAEL" (Isaiah xxx. 11, 12). They say, "Let him make speed and hasten his work, that we may see it, and let the counsel of THE HOLY ONE OF ISRAEL draw nigh and come" (Isaiah v. 19). "In that day the remnant of Israel, and such as are escaped of the house of Jacob,—shall stay upon Jehovah, THE HOLY ONE OF ISRAEL, in truth" (Isaiah x. 20). "Cry out, and shout, thou inhabitant of Zion, for great is THE HOLY ONE OF ISRAEL in the midst of thee" (Isaiah xii. 6). "Thus saith Jehovah the God of Israel: At that day shall a man look to his Maker, and his eyes shall have respect unto THE HOLY ONE OF ISRAEL" (Isaiah xvii. 6, 7). "The meek shall increase their joy in Jehovah, and the poor among men shall rejoice in THE HOLY ONE OF ISRAEL" (Isaiah xxix. 19; xli. 16). "Nations that knew not thee shall run

unto thee, because of Jehovah thy God, and for THE HOLY ONE OF ISRAEL" (Isaiah lv. 5). "The isles shall wait for me, and the ships of Tarshish first, to bring thy sons from far,—unto the name of Jehovah thy God, and to THE HOLY ONE OF ISRAEL" (Isaiah lx. 9). "Babylon—hath been proud against Jehovah, against THE HOLY ONE OF ISRAEL" (Jerem. l. 29). Not to mention many other passages. By the Holy One of Israel, is signified the Lord with respect to the Divine Human; as is evident from the declaration of the angel Gabriel to Mary: "*That Holy Thing* which shall be born of thee, shall be called the Son of God" (Luke i. 35). That Jehovah and the Holy One of Israel, although they are distinctly named, are but One, is also evident from the places above cited, in which it is said, that Jehovah is himself the Holy One of Israel.

41. IV. THAT THE LORD IS CALLED LORD, AND GOD, appears from so many passages, that, if quoted, they would fill many pages; let these few suffice: In John, when Thomas had been desired by the Lord to behold his hands and feel his side, he said, "*My* LORD, *and my* GOD" (xx. 28). In the Psalms: "They remembered that God was their rock, and the HIGH GOD *their Redeemer*" (lxxviii. 35). In Isaiah: "Jehovah of hosts is his name, and *thy Redeemer* is the Holy One of Israel, *the God of the whole earth shall he be called*" (liv. 5). It also appears from the circumstance of their worshipping him, and falling down on their faces before him; as in Matthew ix. 18; xiv. 33; xv. 25; xxviii. 9; Mark i. 40; v. 22; vii. 25; x. 17; Luke xvii. 15, 16. So in David: "We heard of it in Ephratah—we will go into his tabernacles, *we will worship at his footstool*" (Psalm cxxxii. 6, 7). The same worship is paid him in heaven; as is declared in the Revelation: "I was in the spirit, and behold, a throne was set in heaven, and One sat on the throne—that was to look upon like a jasper and a sardine stone; and there was a rainbow round about the throne, in sight like unto an emerald:—And the four-and-twenty elders *fall down* before him that sat on the throne, *and worship him that liveth forever and ever, and cast their crowns before the throne*" (iv. 2. 3, 10). And again: "I saw in the right hand of him that sat on the throne, a book written within and on the back side, sealed with seven seals:—and no one was able to open the book. And one of the elders said, Behold the lion of the tribe of Judah, the root of David, hath prevailed to open the book and to loose the seven seals thereof. And I beheld—in the midst of the throne—a Lamb,—and he came and took the book.—*And [the four-and-twenty elders] fell down before the Lamb,—and worshipped him that liveth forever and ever*" (v. 1, 5—8, 14).

42. V. THAT THE LORD IS CALLED A KING, AND THE ANOINTED. He is so called because he was the Messiah or Christ, and the word Messiah, or Christ, signifies king and

the Anointed; hence it is that the name of king is applied to the Lord, as also that of David, who was king over Judah and Israel. That the name of king is applied to the Lord, and that he is also called the Anointed of Jehovah, is evident from many passages of the Word; thus it is said in the Revelation: "The Lamb shall overcome them, for he is *Lord of lords, and* KING OF KINGS" (xvii. 14). And in another place: "And he that sat upon the white horse had on his vesture a name written, KING OF KINGS *and Lord of lords*" (xix. 11, 16). It is on account of the Lord's being called a king that heaven and the church are said to be *his kingdom*, and that the annunciation of his coming into the world is called the *gospel* (*or good news*) *of the kingdom. That heaven and the church are called his kingdom*, may be seen in Matthew xii. 28; xvi. 28; Mark i. 14, 15; ix. 1; xv. 43; Luke i. 33: iv. 43; viii. 1, 10; ix. 2, 11, 60; x. 11; xix. 11; xxi. 31; xxii. 18; xxiii. 51. So in Daniel: "God shall set up a *kingdom*, which shall never be destroyed.—It shall break in pieces and consume all these kingdoms, and it shall stand for ever" (ii. 44). Again: "I saw in the night visions, and behold, one like the Son of Man came,—and there was given him *dominion*, and glory, and *a kingdom*, that all people nations, and languages, should serve him; his *dominion* is an everlasting *dominion*,—and his *kingdom* that which shall not be destroyed" (vii. 13, 14, 27). *That his coming is called the gospel of the kingdom*, may be seen in Matthew iv. 23; ix. 35; xxiv. 14.

43. VI. THAT THE LORD IS CALLED DAVID, appears from the following passages: "They shall serve Jehovah their God, and DAVID their king, whom I will raise up to them" (Jerem. xxx. 9). "Afterward the children of Israel shall return, and seek Jehovah their God, and DAVID their king, and shall fear Jehovah and his goodness in the latter days" (Hosea iii. 5). "And I will set up one shepherd over them, and he shall feed them, even my servant DAVID; he shall feed them and he shall be their shepherd: And I Jehovah will be their God, and my servant DAVID a prince among them" (Ezek. xxxiv. 23, 24). "They shall be my people, and I will be their God: and DAVID my servant shall be king over them; and they all shall have one shepherd;—and they shall dwell in the land,—even they, and their children, and their children's children, for ever, and my servant DAVID shall be their prince for ever; I will make a covenant of peace with them, it shall be an everlasting covenant with them" (Ezek. xxxvii. 23—26). "I will make an everlasting covenant with you, even the sure mercies of DAVID. Behold, I have given him for a witness to the people, a leader and commander to the people" (Isaiah lv. 3, 4). "In that day I will raise up the tabernacle of DAVID that is fallen, and close up the breaches thereof, and I will raise up his ruins, and I

will build it as in the days of old" (Amos ix. 11). "The house of DAVID shall be as God, as the angel of Jehovah before them" (Zech. xii. 8). "In that day there shall be a fountain open to the house of DAVID" (Zech. xiii. 1).

44. He who knows that by David is meant the Lord, is enabled to comprehend how David in his Psalms so often wrote concerning the Lord, whilst he seems to speak only of himself; as in Psalm lxxxix., where is the following passage: "I have made a covenant with my chosen, I have sworn unto David my servant; thy seed will I establish for ever, and build up thy throne to all generations; and the heavens shall praise thy wonders, O Jehovah; thy faithfulness also in the congregation of the saints. Thou spakest in vision to thy Holy One, and saidst, I have laid help upon one that is mighty, I have exalted one chosen out of the people: I have found David my servant; with my holy oil have I anointed him: with whom my hand shall be established: mine arm also shall strengthen him: my faithfulness and my mercy shall be with him, and in my name shall his horn be exalted: I will set his hand also in the sea, and his right hand in the rivers. He shall cry unto me, Thou art my Father, my God, and the Rock of my Salvation: Also I will make him my First-born, higher than the kings of the earth:—my covenant shall stand fast with him: his seed also will I make to endure for ever, and his throne as the days of heaven. Once have I sworn by my holiness, that I will not lie unto David; his seed shall endure for ever, and his throne as the sun before me: It shall be established for ever as the moon, and as a faithful witness in heaven" (verses 3—5, 19—21, 24—29, 35—37). So, also in other Psalms; as Psalm xlv. 2—17; cxxii. 4, 5; cxxxii. 8—18.

---

## GOD IS ONE, AND THE LORD IS THAT GOD.

45. From the numerous passages adduced from the Word in the preceding article, it may appear, that the Lord is called Jehovah, the God of Israel and of Jacob, the Holy one of Israel, the Lord, and God; as also King, the Anointed, and David; whence it may be seen, though still but as through a glass, darkly, that the Lord is the very God, from whom the Word is, and of whom it treats. Now it is generally known throughout the world, that God is One; a truth which no man, possessed of sound reason, denies; what further, then, remains to be done, is, to confirm this truth from the Word; and to shew, in addition, that the Lord is that God.

I. THAT GOD IS ONE, is confirmed by these passages of the

Word: Jesus said, "The first of all the commandments is, Hear, O Israel, *The Lord our God is* ONE LORD; and thou shalt love the Lord thy God with all thy heart, and with all thy soul, and with all thy mind" (Mark xii. 29, 30). "Hear, O Israel, *Jehovah our God is* ONE JEHOVAH. And thou shalt love Jehovah thy God with all thy heart, and with all thy soul" (Deut. vi. 4, 5). One came unto Jesus and said, "Good master, what good thing shall I do that I may have eternal life? And he said unto him, Why callest thou me good? *There is none good but the* ONE GOD" (Matt. xix. 16, 17). "That all the kingdoms of the earth may know, that *thou art Jehovah, even* THOU ONLY" (Isaiah xxxvii. 20). "*I am Jehovah and there is* NONE ELSE; *there is* NO GOD BESIDE ME;—that they may know from the rising of the sun, and from the west, that there is NONE BESIDE ME. *I am Jehovah, and there is* NONE ELSE" (Isaiah xlv. 5, 6). "O Jehovah of Hosts, God of Israel, that dwellest between the cherubim, *Thou art the God, even* THOU ALONE, of all the kingdoms of the earth" (Isaiah xxxvii. 16). "Is there a God BESIDE ME? yea, there is NO GOD; I KNOW NOT ANY" (Isaiah xliv. 8). "Who is God SAVE JEHOVAH, or who is a Rock, SAVE OUR GOD?" (Psalm xviii. 31).

II. THAT THE LORD IS THAT GOD, is confirmed from the following passages of the Word: "Surely God is in thee, *and there is* NONE ELSE, there is *no* GOD; verily, thou art a God that hidest thyself, O God of Israel, the *Saviour*" (Isaiah xlv. 14, 15). "Who hath declared this from ancient time?—Have not I Jehovah? and *there is* NO GOD ELSE BESIDE ME, a just God and a SAVIOUR, *there is* NONE BESIDE ME. Look unto ME, *and be ye* SAVED, all the ends of the earth; for *I am God, and there is* NONE ELSE" (Isaiah xlv. 21, 22). "I am Jehovah, *and* BESIDE ME *there is* NO SAVIOUR" (Isaiah xliii. 11). "I am Jehovah thy God,—and *thou shalt know* NO GOD BUT ME, for *there is* NO SAVIOUR BESIDE ME" (Hosea xiii. 4). "Thus saith Jehovah the King of Israel, and his REDEEMER, Jehovah of Hosts, I am the First, and I am the Last, and BESIDE ME *there is* NO GOD" (Isaiah xliv. 6). "Jehovah of Hosts is his name, and thy REDEEMER the Holy One of Israel; *the God of the whole earth shall be called*" (Isaiah liv. 5). "Jehovah shall be king over all the earth, and in that day there shall be ONE JEHOVAH, and his name ONE" (Zech. xiv. 9).

Now as the Lord is the only Saviour and Redeemer; and yet it is said, that Jehovah is the Saviour and Redeemer, and that there is none beside him; it follows, that the One God is no other than the Lord.

---

## THE HOLY SPIRIT IS THE DIVINE PROCEEDING FROM THE LORD, AND THIS IS THE LORD HIMSELF.

46. JESUS says in Matthew, "All power is given unto me in heaven and on earth; go ye therefore and teach all nations, baptizing them in the name of the Father, and of the Son, and of the Holy Spirit; teaching them to observe all things whatsoever I have commanded you: and lo, I am with you always, even unto the consummation of the age" (xxviii. 18, 20). It has been already shewn, that the Divine which is called the Father, and the Divine which is called the Son, are a One in the Lord; it shall therefore now be shewn that the Holy Spirit is the same with the Lord. The reason why the Lord enjoined the disciples to baptize in the name of the Father, of the Son, and of the Holy Spirit, was because there is in the Lord a trine or threefold nature, consisting of the Divine which is called the Father, the Divine Human which is called the Son, and the Divine Proceeding which is called the Holy Spirit. The Divine which is the Father and the Divine, which is the Son, is the all-originating Divine [est Divinum ex quo], and the Divine Proceeding, which is the Holy Spirit, is the Divine Medium of operation [Divinum per quod]. That the Divine proceeding from the Lord is no other than the Divine which is himself, will be seen in the tracts on the Divine Providence, Omnipotence, Omnipresence, and Omniscience; for it is a subject that requires deep investigation. That there is a trine or threefold nature in the Lord, may be illustrated by comparison with an angel, who has a soul and a body, and also a proceeding [sphere] which proceeds from him, which is still himself, although external to himself. It has been granted me to know many particulars concerning this proceeding [sphere], but this is not the place to introduce them. Every man who in his life looks to God, is first of all, after death, instructed by the angels, that the Holy Spirit is not a person separate from the Lord, and that the terms *to go forth*, and *to proceed*, mean no other [in reference to the Lord], than to enlighten and teach by his presence, which is always according to the reception of him. Hence many, after death, relinquish the idea of the Holy Spirit which they had conceived in the world, and receive this idea, that it is the presence of the Lord with man by angels and spirits, by, and according to which, man is enlightened and instructed. It is moreover, customary in the Word, to name, as it were, two Divines, and sometimes three, which, notwithstanding, are but one; as Jehovah and God, Jehovah and the Holy One of Israel, Jehovah and the Mighty One of Jacob, also God and the Lamb; yet as these are but one, it is also said in other places, that Jehovah is God alone, Jehovah only

is Holy, that he is the Holy One of Israel, and that there is none beside him. Further, the word Lamb is sometimes used to express God, and the word God to express the Lamb: the latter case occurs in the Revelation, the former in the Prophets. But that it is the Lord alone who is understood by the terms Father, Son, and Holy Spirit, in Matt. xxviii. 19, appears from the verses which precede and follow. In the preceding verse the Lord says, "All power is given unto ME in heaven and in earth;" and in the subsequent verse, "Lo, *I* am with you always, even unto the consummation of the age;" Thus he speaks of himself alone; and the reason why he mentioned the Father, Son, and Holy Spirit, was, to instruct the disciples that the Trinity was in him.

To prove more clearly that the Holy Spirit is not a Divine distinct from the Lord, it may be expedient to shew the meanings attached in the Word to the term *Spirit.* It means, I. The life of man in general. II. As the life of man varies according to his state, by Spirit is also signified the particular affection of his life. III. Also the life of the regenerate which is called spiritual life. IV. But where Spirit is mentioned in reference to the Lord, it signifies his Divine Life, consequently the Lord himself. V. And specifically the life of his Wisdom, which is called Divine Truth. In the last place it shall be shewn, that Jehovah himself, that is, the Lord, spoke the Word by the prophets.

47. I. BY THE TERM "SPIRIT" IS MEANT THE LIFE OF MAN, as is evident from common discourse, in which it is usual to say, when a man dies, that he has yielded up the spirit: where the term spirit is used to signify the life of respiration. Indeed, "spirit" is a Latin word which is derived from another that signifies to breathe; and in the Hebrew language, spirit, breath, and wind are expressed by the same word. There are with man two fountains of life; one is the motion of the heart, the other is the respiration of the lungs: and the life originating in the respiration of the lungs, is what is properly meant by the term "spirit," and also by the term "soul." That this acts in unity with the thought of man from his understanding, whilst the life originating in the motion of the heart acts in unity with the love of his will, will be shewn in its proper place. That the life of man is meant by the term "spirit" in the Word, appears from the following passages: "Thou takest away their *breath* [*spirit*], they die, and return to their dust" (Psalm civ. 29). "He remembered that they were but flesh, *a wind* [*spirit*] that passeth away, and cometh not again" (Psalm lxxviii. 39). "His *breath* [*spirit*] goeth forth, he returneth to his earth" (Psalm cxlvi. 4). Hezekiah lamented that *the life of his spirit* should depart (Isaiah xxxviii. 16). "*The Spirit of Jacob* revived" (Gen. xlv. 27). "A molten image is falsehood, and there

is no *breath* [*spirit*] in them" (Jerem. li. 16). The Lord Jehovih said unto the dry bones, "I will cause *breath* [*spirit*] to enter into you, and ye shall shall live. Come from the four winds, O *breath* [*spirit*], and *breathe* upon these slain that they may live. And the *breath* [*spirit*] came into them, and they lived" (Ezek. xxxviii. 5, 6, 9, 10). Jesus took the maiden by the hand, "and her *spirit* came again, and she arose straightway" (Luke viii. 54, 55).

48. II. SINCE THE LIFE OF MAN VARIES ACCORDING TO HIS STATE, THEREFORE BY THE TERM "SPIRIT" IS ALSO SIGNIFIED THE PECULIAR AFFECTION OF HIS LIFE: as 1. *A life of wisdom.* Bezaleel was filled with the *spirit of wisdom*, of understanding, and of knowledge (Exod. xxxi. 3). "Thou shalt speak unto all that are wise hearted, whom I have filled *with the spirit of wisdom*" (Exod. xxviii. 3). "Joshua was full *of the spirit of wisdom*" (Deut. xxxiv. 9). It is said of Daniel, that "*an excellent spirit, and knowledge, and understanding*," were in him (Dan. v. 12). "They also that erred *in spirit* shall come to *understanding*" (Isaiah xxix. 24.) 2. *The excitement of life.* "Jehovah hath *raised* up *the spirit* of the kings of the Medes" (Jerem. li. 11). "And Jehovah *stirred up the spirit* of Zerubbabel,—and *the spirit* of all the remnant of the people" (Haggai i. 14). "Behold, I will send *a blast* [*a spirit*] *upon the King of Assyria*, and he shall hear a rumour, and return to his own land" (Isaiah xxxvii. 7). Jehovah *hardened the spirit* of Sihon the king (Deut. ii. 30). "And that *which cometh into your mind* [*spirit*] shall not be at all" (Ezek. xx. 32). 3. *Liberty of life.* It is said of the four living creatures, which were cherubs, seen by the prophet, that "whithersoever *the spirit* was to go, they went" (Ezek. i. 20). 4. *Life in fear, pain, and anger.* "Every heart shall melt, and all hands shall be feeble, *and every spirit shall faint*" (Ezek. xxi. 7). "Therefore is my *spirit overwhelmed* within me, my heart within me is desolate" (Psalm cxliii 4). "My *spirit faileth*" (Psalm cxliii. 7). "I, Daniel, was *grieved in my spirit*" (Dan. vii. 15). "The *spirit of Pharaoh was troubled*" (Gen. xli. 8). Nebuchadnezzar said, "*My spirit was troubled* to know the dream" (Dan. ii. 3). "I went in bitterness in the *heat of my spirit*" (Ezek. iii. 14). 5. *A life of various evil affections.* "Blessed is the man—*in whose spirit there is no guile*" (Psalm xxxii. 2). "Jehovah had mingled *a perverse spirit* in the midst thereof" (Isaiah xix. 14). "Woe unto the *foolish* prophets that follow their own *spirit*" (Ezek. xiii. 3). "The prophet is a fool, the *spiritual man is mad*" (Hosea ix. 7). "Take heed to *your spirit*, that you deal not *treacherously*" (Malachi ii. 16). "*The spirit of whoredoms* hath caused them to err" (Hosea iv. 12). "*The spirit of whoredoms* is in the midst of them" (Hosea v. 4). "If *the spirit of jealousy* come upon him" (Numb. v. 14). If a man that walketh "in *spirit and falsehood do lie*"

(Micah ii. 11). "A generation—*whose spirit was not steadfast with God*" (Psalm lxxviii. 8). "Jehovah hath poured out upon you *the spirit of deep sleep*" (Isaiah xxix. 10). "Ye shall conceive chaff, ye shall bring forth stubble; *your breath [spirit] as fire* shall devour you" (Isaiah xxxiii. 11). 6. *Infernal life.* "I will cause *the unclean spirit* to pass out of the land" (Zech. xiii. 2). "When the *unclean spirit* is gone out of a man, he walketh through dry places,—then goeth he and taketh—seven *other spirits more wicked* than himself, and they enter in and dwell there" (Matt. xii. 43, 45). "Babylon—is become the hold *of every foul spirit*" (Apoc. xviii. 2). 7. *The term "spirit" further signifies the infernal spirits themselves, by whom mankind are troubled.* See Matt. viii. 16; x. 1; xii. 43—45; Mark i. 23—28; ix. 17—29; Luke iv. 33—36; vi. 17, 18; vii. 21; viii. 2, 29; ix. 39, 42, 55; xi. 24, 25, 26; xiii. 11; Rev. xvi. 13, 14.

49. III. By the term "Spirit" is also signified the Life of the Regenerate, which is called Spiritual Life. "Jesus said,—Except a man be born of water, *and of the spirit*, he cannot enter into the kingdom of God" (John iii. 5). "A new heart also will I give you, and a *new spirit* will I put within you.—And I will put *my spirit* within you, and cause you to walk in my statutes" (Ezek. xxxvi. 26, 27). "I will give them one heart, and put a *new spirit* within you" (Ezek. xi. 19). "Create in me a clean heart, O God, and renew *a right spirit* within me. Restore unto me the joy of thy salvation, and uphold me with thy *free spirit*" (Psalm li. 10, 12). "Make you a new heart, and a *new spirit*; for why will ye die, O house of Israel?" (Ezek. xviii. 31). "Thou sendest forth thy *spirit*, they are created, and thou renewest the face of the earth" (Psalm civ. 30). "The hour cometh, and now is, when the true worshippers shall worship the Father in *spirit* and in truth" (John iv. 23). "Thus saith Jehovah God—he that spread forth the earth,—he that giveth breath into the people upon it, and *spirit* to them that walk therein" (Isaiah xlii. 5). "Jehovah —which formeth *the spirit of man* within him" (Zech. xii. 1). "With my soul have I desired thee in the night, yea, *with my spirit* within me will I seek thee early" (Isaiah xxvi. 9). In that day shall Jehovah be—for a *spirit of judgment* to him that sitteth in judgment" (Isaiah xxviii. 5, 6). "*My spirit* hath rejoiced in God my Saviour" (Luke i. 47). "These that go toward the north country have quieted *my spirit* in the north country" (Zech. vi. 8). "Into thy hands I commit *my spirit*; thou hast redeemed me" (Psalms xxxi. 5). "Did not he make ona? yet had he the residue of *the spirit*" (Malachi ii. 15). "And after three days and a half, *the spirit of life* from God entered into them" (Apoc. xi. 11). "He that formeth the mountains, and createth *the wind [spirit]*"—is Jehovah (Amos

iv. 13). "O God, *the God of the spirits* of all flesh" (Numb. xvi. 22); [see also] xxvii. 18. "And I will pour upon the house of David, and upon the inhabitants of Jerusalem, *the spirit from on high*" (Zech. xii. 10). "Until the *spirit* be poured upon us *from on high*" (Isaiah xxxii. 15). "I will pour water upon him that is thirsty, and floods upon the dry ground; *I will pour my spirit* upon thy seed" (Isaiah xliv. 3). "I will pour out *my spirit* upon all flesh,—also upon the servants and upon the handmaids, in those days, *will I pour out my spirit*" (Joel ii. 28, 29). By pouring out *the spirit* is signified to regenerate: the same is meant by giving a new heart and a new spirit.

*By the spirit is also signified spiritual life communicated to those who are in humiliation.* "I dwell—with him that is of a contrite and *humble spirit*, to revive the *spirit of the humble*, and to revive the hearts of the contrite ones" (Isaiah lvii. 15). "The sacrifices of God are a *broken spirit;* a broken and a contrite heart, O God, thou wilt not despise" (Psalm li. 17). "To give—the oil of joy for mourning, the garment of praise for the *spirit* of heaviness" (Isaiah lxi. 3). "The Lord hath called thee as a woman forsaken, and *grieved in spirit*" (Isaiah liv. 6). "Blessed are *the poor in spirit*, for theirs is the kingdom of heaven" (Matt. v. 3).

50. IV. Where the term "Spirit" is mentioned in reference to the Lord, it signifies his Divine Life, consequently the Lord Himself. The truth of the first part of this proposition appears from the following passages: "He whom God hath sent speaketh the words of God, for God giveth not *the spirit* by measure unto him. The Father loveth the Son, and hath given all things into his hand" (John iii. 34, 35). "There shall come forth a rod out of the stem of Jesse,—and *the spirit of Jehovah* shall rest upon him, *the spirit of wisdom and understanding, the spirit of council and might*" (Isaiah xi. 1, 2). "I have put *my spirit* upon him, he shall bring forth judgment to the Gentiles" (Isaiah xlii. 1). "When the enemy shall come in like a flood, *the spirit of Jehovah* shall lift up a standard against him; and the Redeemer shall come to Zion" (Isaiah lix. 19, 20). "*The spirit of the Lord Jehovah* is upon me:—Jehovah hath anointed me to speak good tidings unto the meek" (Isaiah lxi. 1; Luke iv. 18). "Jesus perceived *in his spirit* that they so reasoned within themselves" (Mark ii. 8). "Jesus rejoiced *in spirit*, and said" (Luke x. 21). "Jesus was troubled *in spirit*" (John xiii. 21). "Jesus sighed deeply *in his spirit*" (Mark viii. 12).

*The term "Spirit" is used to denote Jehovah Himself, or the Lord*, as is evident from these passages: "God is a *spirit*" (John iv. 24). "Who hath directed *the spirit of Jehovah*, or, being his counsellor, hath taught him?" (Isaiah xl. 13). "They rebelled and vexed his *holy spirit:*" and he said, "Where is he that put his *holy spirit* within him, that led them by the right hand of Moses" (Isaiah lxiii. 10, 11, 12). "Whither shall I go *from thy spirit*, or whither shall I flee from thy presence?" (Psalm cxxxix. 7). "Not by might,—but by *my spirit*, saith Jehovah of hosts" (Zech. iv. 6). "They provoked *his spirit;*—therefore he abhorred his own inheritance" (Psalm cvi. 33, 40). "*My spirit* shall not always strive with man, for that he also is flesh" (Gen. vi. 3). "I will not contend for ever,—for *the spirit* should fail before me" (Isaiah lvii. 16). "The blasphemy against the *Holy Spirit* shall not be forgiven; and whosoever speaketh a word against the Son of Man, it shall be forgiven him" (Matt. xii. 31, 32; Mark iii. 28, 29, 30; Luke xii. 10). Blasphemy against the Holy Spirit is blasphemy against the Divine of the Lord;—against the Son of Man is to contradict the Word by giving it a wrong interpretation: for the Son of Man is the Lord as to the Word, as was shewn above.

51. V. By the term "Spirit," when mentioned in reference to the Lord is signified specifically the Life of His Wisdom, which is the Divine Truth. This appears from the following passages: "Nevertheless I tell you *the truth;* it is expedient for you that I go away, for if I go not away, *the Comforter* will not come unto you; but if I depart, I will send him unto you" (John xvi. 7). "When he, *the Spirit of truth*, is come, he will guide you into *all truth;* for he shall not speak of himself, but whatsoever he shall hear that shall he speak" (John xvi. 13). "He shall glorify me, for he shall receive *of mine*, and shall shew it unto you. All things that the Father hath are mine; therefore said I that he shall take *of mine*, and shall shew it unto you" (John xvi. 14, 15). "I will pray the Father, and he shall give you another *Comforter—the Spirit of truth*, whom the world cannot receive, because it seeth him not, neither knoweth him, but ye know him, for he dwelleth with you, and shall be in you. I will not leave you comfortless; I will come to you,"—and ye shall see me (John xiv. 16—19) "When the *Comforter* is come, whom I will send unto you from the Father, even *the Spirit of truth*,—he shall testify of me" (John xv. 26). "Jesus cried, saying, If any man thirst let him come unto me, and drink. He that believeth on me, as the Scripture hath said, out of his belly shall flow rivers of living water.—This spake he *of the Spirit*, which they that believe on him should receive. For the *Holy Spirit* was not yet, because Jesus was not yet glorified" (John vii. 37—39). Jesus breathed on his disciples, "and saith unto them, Receive ye the *Holy Spirit*" (John xx. 22). That by the Comforter, the Spirit of Truth, and the Holy Spirit, the Lord meant himself, appears from his own words when he said, that the world did not as yet know him; for they did not as yet know the Lord;

so when he said, that he would send the Holy Spirit, he added, "*I* will not leave you comfortless, *I* will come unto you," and ye shall see me (John xiv. 16—19, 26, 28). And again: "Lo, *I* am with you always, even to the consummation of the age" (Matt. xxviii. 20). And when Thomas said, We know not whither thou goest, Jesus said, "*I* am the way and *the truth*" (John xiv. 5, 6). And because the Spirit of Truth, or the Holy Spirit, is the same with the Lord, who is the Truth itself, it is therefore also said, "The *Holy Spirit* was not yet, because Jesus was not yet glorified" (John vii. 39): for after his glorification, or full union with the Father, which was effected by the passion of the cross, he was then the Divine Wisdom and the Divine Truth itself, consequently the Holy Spirit. The reason why the Lord breathed on the disciples and said, "Receive the *Holy Spirit*," was, because all the respiration of heaven is from the Lord: for angels, as well as men, have both respiration and the pulsation of the heart; and their respiration is according to their reception of divine wisdom from the Lord, and their pulsation of the heart according to their reception of divine love from him. But more of this in its proper place.

That the Holy Spirit is the Divine Truth from the Lord, further appears from the following passages: "When they bring you unto the synagogues,—take ye no thought—what ye shall say, for *the Holy Spirit* shall teach you in the same hour what ye ought to say" (Luke xii. 11, 12; Mark xiii. 11). "Thus saith Jehovah, *My Spirit* that is upon thee, and my words which I have put in thy mouth, shall not depart out of thy mouth" (Isaiah lix. 21). "There shall come forth a rod out of the stem of Jesse;—and he shall smite the earth with the rod of his mouth, *and with the breath* [*spirit*] *of his lips* shall he slay the wicked; and righteousness shall be the girdle of his reins" (Isaiah xi. 1, 4, 5). "For my mouth, it hath commanded; and *his spirit*, it hath gathered them" (Isaiah xxxiv. 16). "God is a spirit, and they who worship him must worship him *in spirit and in truth*" (John iv. 24). "It is the *spirit* that quickeneth, the flesh profiteth nothing; the words that I speak unto you, *they are spirit and they are life*" (John vi. 63). John said, "I indeed baptize you with water unto repentance; but he that cometh after me—shall baptize you with *the Holy Spirit* and with fire" (Matt. iii. 11; Mark i. 8; Luke iii. 16). To baptize with the Holy Spirit and with fire, is to regenerate by the Divine Truth, which is of faith, and by the Divine Good, which is of love. "And Jesus when he was baptized, went up straightway out of the water; and the heavens were opened unto him, and he saw *the Spirit of God* descending like a dove" (Matt. iii. 16; Mark i. 10; Luke iii. 22; John i. 32, 33). A dove is a representative of purification and regeneration by divine truth.

As by the Holy Spirit, when treating of the Lord, is meant his Divine Life, consequently himself, and in particular the life of his wisdom, which is called the Divine Truth; therefore by the spirit of the prophets, which is also called the Holy Spirit, is signified the Divine Truth from the Lord; as in the following passages: "*The Spirit* saith unto the churches" (Rev. ii. 7, 11, 29; iii. 1, 6, 13, 32). "There were seven lamps of fire burning before the throne, which are *the seven spirits of God*" (Rev. iv. 5). "In the midst of the elders stood a Lamb,—having seven eyes, which are the *seven spirits of God* sent forth into all the earth" (Rev. v. 6). Lamps of fire, and the eyes of the Lord, signify divine truths, and the number seven signifies what is holy. "Yea, saith *the Spirit*, that they may rest from their labours" (Rev. xiv. 13.) "*The Spirit* and the Bride say, Come" (Rev. xxii .17). "They made their hearts as an adamant stone, lest they should hear the law, and the words which Jehovah of hosts hath sent *in his spirit* by the former prophets" (Zech. vii. 12). "*The spirit* of Elijah doth rest on Elisha" (2 Kings ii. 15). "He [John] shall go before him in *the spirit* and power of Elias" (Luke i. 17). "Elizabeth was filled with the *Holy Spirit*" (Luke i. 41). "Zacharias was filled with the *Holy Spirit*, and prophesied" (Luke i. 67). "David said, by *the Holy Spirit*, The Lord said to my Lord, Sit thou on my right hand" (Mark xii. 36). "The testimony of Jesus is *the spirit of prophecy*" (Rev. xix. 10). Hence then we see why the offices of the Holy Spirit are said to be to *enlighten, to teach and inspire*, since by the Holy Spirit is specifically signified the Lord in respect to his Divine Wisdom, and thus as to Divine Truth.

52. VI. JEHOVAH HIMSELF, THAT IS, THE LORD, SPAKE THE WORD BY THE PROPHETS. We read of the prophets that they were *in vision*, and that *Jehovah spake to them*. When they were in vision they were not in the body, but in the spirit, in which state they saw such things as are in heaven; but when Jehovah spake with them, they were in the body, and heard him speaking. These two states of the prophets should be accurately distinguished. In their state of vision, the eyes of their spirits were open, and those of their bodies shut; at which time also they appeared to themselves to be carried from place to place, the body still remaining where it was. In this state, at times, were Ezekiel, Zechariah, and Daniel; as also John, when he wrote the Revelation; and it is then said, that they were in *vision*, or in *the spirit*. Ezekiel says, "The spirit lifted me up,—and brought me in a *vision* by the Spirit of God into Chaldea to them of the captivity.—So *the vision* that I had seen went up from me" (xi. 1, 24). He says too, that the spirit took him up, and he heard behind him a voice of great rushing [or earthquake] with other things (iii. 12, 14). Also, "The spirit lifted me up between the earth and heaven, and

brought me *in the visions of God* to Jerusalem," where he saw their abominations (viii. 3). He was likewise in the vision of God, or in the spirit, when he saw the four living creatures, which were cherubs (i. and x.); also a new earth and a new temple, and an angel measuring it, as is related from chap xl. to xlviii. That he was then *in the visions of God*, he says himself (xl. 2); and that *the spirit* took him up (xliii. 5). The like happened to Zechariah, who was accompanied by an angel, when he saw a man riding among the myrtle trees (Zech. i. 8). When he saw four horns, and afterwards a man who had a measuring line in his hand (i. 18; ii. 1). When he saw Joshua the high priest (iii. 1, &c.). When he saw a candlestick, and two olive trees (iv. 2, 3). When he saw a flying roll and ephah (v. 1, 6). And when he saw four chariots coming out from between two mountains, with horses (vi. 1). In the same state was Daniel, when he saw four beasts ascend out of the sea (Dan. vii. 3); and when he saw the battle between the ram and the he-goat (viii. 1, &c.). That he saw these things in visions, is stated in chap. vii. 1, 2, 7, 13; viii. 2; x. 1, 7, 8. It was also in vision that the angel Gabriel was seen by him, and spake with him (ix. 21, 22). The like happened to John, when he wrote the Revelation, who says, that he was *in the spirit* on the Lord's day (Rev. i. 10). That he was carried away *in the spirit* into the wilderness (xvii. 3); also *in the spirit* to a high mountain (xxi. 10). That he saw horses *in the vision* (ix. 17). In other places he declares, that *he saw* those things which he describes; of course he must have been at the time in the spirit, or in vision: as in chap. i. 12; iv. 1; v. 1; vi. 1; and in each of the subsequent chapters.

53. But in respect to the Word itself, it is never said, by the prophets, that they spake it from the Holy Spirit, but that they spake it from Jehovah, Jehovah of hosts, and the Lord Jehovih. Thus we continually find them saying, "*The word of Jehovah came to me;*" "*Jehovah spake to me:*" also, very often, "*Thus saith Jehovah;*" and "*The saying of Jehovah.*" Now as we have already shewn that the Lord is Jehovah, it follows that the whole Word was spoken by him. To remove all doubt on this subject, I will only point out those passages in Jeremiah alone, where it is said, "The word of Jehovah came unto me;" "Jehovah said unto me;" "Thus saith Jehovah;" and "The saying of Jehovah;" which are the following: chap. i. 4, 7, 11—14, 19; ii. 1—5, 9, 19, 22, 29, 31; iii. 1, 6, 10, 12, 14, 16; iv. 1, 3, 9, 17, 27; v. 11, 14, 18, 22, 29; vi. 6, 9, 12, 15, 16, 21, 22; vii. 1, 3, 11, 13, 19—21; viii. 1, 3, 12, 13; ix. 3, 6, 7, 9, 12, 13, 15, 17, 22, 23, 25; x. 2, 18; xi. 1, 6, 9, 11, 18, 21, 22; xii. 14, 17; xiii. 1, 6, 9, 11—15, 25; xiv. 1, 10, 14, 15, xv. 1—3, 6, 11, 19, 20; xvi. 1, 3, 5, 9, 14, 16; xvii. 5, 19—21, 24; xviii. 1, 5, 6, 11, 13; xix. 1, 3, 6, 12, 15; xx. 4; xxi. 1, 4,

7, 8, 11, 12; xxii. 2, 3, 6, 11, 16, 18, 24, 29, 30; xxiii. 2, 5, 7, 11, 12, 15, 16, 24, 29, 31—33, 38; xxiv. 3, 5, 8; xxv. 1, 3, 7—9, 15, 27—29, 32; xxvi. 1, 2, 18; xxvii. 1, 2, 4, 8, 11, 16, 19, 21, 22; xxviii. 2, 12, 14, 16; xxix. 4, 8, 9, 16, 19—21, 25, 30—32; xxx. 1—5, 8, 10—12, 17, 18; xxxi. 1, 2, 7, 10, 15—17, 23, 27, 28, 31—38; xxxii. 1, 6, 14, 15, 25, 26, 28, 30, 36 42, 44; xxxiii. 1, 2, 4, 10—13, 17, 19, 20, 23, 25; xxxiv. 1, 2, 4, 8, 12, 13, 17, 22; xxxv. 1, 13, 17—19; xxxvi. 1, 6, 27, 29, 30; xxxvii. 6, 7, 9; xxxviii. 2, 3, 17; xxxix. 15—18; xl. 1; xlii. 7, 9, 15, 18, 19; xliii. 8, 10; xliv. 1, 2, 7, 11, 24—26, 30; xlv. 1, 2, 5; xlvi. 1, 23, 25, 28; xlvii. 1; xlviii. 1, 8, 12, 30, 35, 38, 40, 43, 44, 47; xlix. 2, 5—7, 12, 13, 16, 18, 26, 28, 30, 32, 35, 37—39; l. 1, 4, 10, 18, 20, 21, 30, 31, 33, 35, 40; li. 25, 33, 36, 39, 52, 58. These instances occur in Jeremiah only. All the other prophets speak in the same manner, and none ever say that the Holy Spirit spoke to them, or that Jehovah spoke to them by the Holy Spirit.

54. These conclusions then follow from the whole: That *Jehovah,* who is *the Lord from eternity,* is he who spake by the prophets, and where *the Holy Spirit* is mentioned, it means and is himself: consequently, THAT GOD IS ONE IN ESSENCE AND IN PERSON, AND THAT GOD IS THE LORD.

---

## THE DOCTRINE OF THE ATHANASIAN CREED AGREES WITH THE TRUTH, PROVIDED THE TRINITY OF PERSONS OF WHICH IT SPEAKS BE UNDERSTOOD TO MEAN A TRINITY OF PERSON, AND THAT THIS TRINITY IS IN THE LORD.

55. THE acknowledgement, by Christians, of three divine persons, and thus as it were of three gods, has arisen from there being in the Lord a Trine, one of which is called the Father, another the Son, and the third the Holy Spirit; and this Trine is mentioned in the Word under distinct names, just as, in common discourse, we speak by distinct names of the soul and body, and what proceeds from them, notwithstanding they are a One. Such also is the nature of the Word in its literal sense, that it distinguishes things which form a One, as if they were not so: hence Jehovah, who is the Lord from eternity, is in one place named in the Word *Jehovah;* in another, *Jehovah of Hosts;* in another *God;* in another, the *Lord;* and at the same time he is called *the Creator, Saviour, Redeemer,* and *Former,* or *Maker;* also *Shaddai:* so, too, his Human, which he assumed in the world, is named *Jesus Christ, the Messiah, the Son of God, the Son of Man;* and in the Word of the Old Testament, *God, the Holy One of Israel, the Anointed of Jeho-*

*vah*, *King*, *Prince*, *Counsellor*, *an Angel*, and *David*. Now since the Word, in its literal sense, is of such a nature as to apply several names where but One Being is meant, therefore, Christians, who in the first ages were simple men, who understood everything according to the literal import of the words, came to distinguish the Divinity into three persons; and this, on account of their simplicity, was permitted; yet with this restriction, that they should believe THE SON to be Infinite, Uncreate, Almighty, God, and Lord, and altogether equal to the Father; and further, that they were not two or three, but one, in Essence, Majesty, and Glory, consequently in Divinity. Those who thus believe in simplicity according to the doctrine which is taught them, and do not confirm themselves in the notion of three gods, but consider the three as one, are, after their decease, instructed from the Lord by angels, that he himself is that One, and that Trine. This faith is received by all who enter into heaven: for no one can be admitted into heaven who has three gods in his thoughts, howsoever with his lips he may say that they are one: for the life of all heaven, and the wisdom of all the angels, is founded on the acknowledgment and consequent confession of one God, and on the faith that this one God is also a Man, and that the Lord, who is at once both God and Man, is he. Hence it appears, that the reception by Christians at first of the doctrine concerning three persons, was of divine permission, provided they accompanied it with the belief that the Lord was God, Infinite, Almighty, and Jehovah; for had they not received this belief also, the church must have perished: since the church exists as such only from the Lord, and from him, and from no other, is the eternal life of all. That a church exists as such only from the Lord, may appear from this single fact, that the whole Word, from beginning to end, treats of him alone, as was shewn above; and also from the declaration that he must be believed in, and that he that believeth not in him shall not see life; nay, that the wrath of God abideth on him (John iii. 36). Now, since every one sees intuitively, that if God is one, HE MUST BE ONE BOTH IN PERSON AND IN ESSENCE, (for no one does or can think otherwise, whilst he thinks that God is one,) I will here cite the whole of the Athanasian Creed, and then demonstrate that all its contents are true, provided, instead of a trinity of persons, we understand a trinity of person.

56. THE CREED is as follows: "Whosoever will be saved, before all things, it is necessary that he hold the Catholic (some copies have *Christian*) Faith; which faith, except every one do keep whole and undefiled, without doubt he shall perish everlastingly. And the Catholic (some copies have *Christian*) Faith is this: That we worship One God in Trinity, and the Trinity in Unity, neither confounding the persons, nor dividing

the substance (some copies have *essence*). For there is one person of the Father, another of the Son, and another of the Holy Spirit; but the Godhead of the Father, of the Son, and of the Holy Spirit, is all one, the glory equal, the majesty co-eternal. Such as the Father is, such is the Son, and such is the Holy Spirit. The Father uncreate, the Son uncreate, and the Holy Spirit uncreate. The Father incomprehensible,* the Son incomprehensible, and the Holy Spirit incomprehensible. The Father eternal, the Son eternal, and the Holy Spirit eternal: and yet there are not three eternals, but One Eternal: as also there are not three incomprehensibles,† nor three uncreates, but one uncreate, and one incomprehensible. So likewise the Father is almighty, the Son almighty, and the Holy Spirit almighty; and yet they are not three Almighties, but One Almighty. So the Father is God, the Son is God, and the Holy Spirit is God: and yet they are not three gods, but One God. So—the Father is Lord, the Son Lord, and the Holy Spirit Lord: and yet they are not three lords, but One Lord. For like as we are compelled, by the Christian verity, to acknowledge every person by himself to be God and Lord, so we are forbidden, by the Catholic Religion, to say, there are three gods or three lords (some copies have, "Still we cannot, according to the Christian faith, mention three gods or three lords"). The Father is made of none, neither created, nor begotten:‡ the Son is of the Father alone, not made, nor created, but begotten:‡ the Holy Spirit is of the Father and of the Son, neither made, nor created, nor begotten,‡ ut proceeding. So there is one Father, not three Fathers; one Son, not three Sons; one Holy Spirit, not three Holy Spirits. And in this Trinity none is before or after another; none is greater or less than another; but the whole three persons are co-eternal together, and co-equal. So that in all things, as is aforesaid, the Unity in Trinity, and the Trinity in Unity, is to be worshipped (some copies have "three persons in one Godhead, and one God in three persons, is to be worshipped"). He therefore that will be saved, must thus think of the Trinity.

"Furthermore, it is necessary to everlasting salvation, that he also believe rightly the incarnation of our Lord Jesus Christ (some copies have, "that he firmly believes that our Lord is very Man"). For the right faith is, that we believe and confess, that our Lord Jesus Christ, the Son of God, is God and Man; God of the substance (some copies have *essence*, others *nature*) of the Father, begotten before the worlds; and Man of the substance (some copies have *essence*, others *nature*) of his mo-

* The Latin here is *infinite.*

† Or *infinites.*

‡ In these places the Latin is *born.*

ther, born in the world; perfect God, and perfect Man, of a reasonable soul, and human flesh* subsisting; equal to the Father as touching his Godhead, and inferior to the Father as touching his manhood. Who although he be God and Man, yet he is not two, but one Christ; one, not by conversion of the Godhead into flesh,* but by taking of the manhood into God (some copies have, "he is one, yet not that the Godhead was transmuted into manhood, but the Godhead took up the Manhood to itself"); one altogether, not by confusion (in some copies *commixtion*) of substance, but by unity of person (some copies have, "He is altogether One, not that the two are natures commixed, but he is one person"). For as the reasonable soul and flesh* is one man, so God and man is one Christ. Who suffered for our salvation, descended into hell, rose again the third day from the dead, he ascended into heaven, and sitteth on the right hand of the Father, God Almighty, from whence he shall come to judge the quick and the dead; at whose coming all men shall rise again with their bodies, and shall give account for their own works: and they that have done good shall go into life everlasting, and they that have done evil into everlasting fire."

57. That all the contents of this Creed are true, if instead of a trinity of persons we understand a trinity of person, will be seen if we transcribe it again, with this trinity substituted for the former, as is done below. A trinity of person is this: THAT THE DIVINE OF THE LORD IS THE FATHER, THE DIVINE HUMAN THE SON, AND THE DIVINE PROCEEDING THE HOLY SPIRIT. When this trinity is understood, a man may then conceive one God in his thoughts, and also profess one God with his lips; otherwise he must needs conceive three gods in his thoughts, as must be evident to every one, and as was evident to Athanasius himself, which is the reason that he inserted in his creed these words: "*As we are compelled by the Christian verity to acknowledge every person by himself to be God and Lord; so are we forbidden by the Catholic religion to say there are three gods or three lords:*" which amounts to this, that, "although it is allowable, by the Christian verity, to *acknowledge*, or *think of*, three gods and lords, yet it is not allowable, by the Catholic religion, to say that there is more than one." And yet it is acknowledgment and thought that conjoin man with the Lord and heaven, and not mere speech. Besides no one can comprehend how the Godhead, which is allowed to be one, and is incapable of division, can be divided among three persons, every one of whom is God: whilst to make the three one in essence or substance, does not take away the idea of three gods, but only conveys that of unanimity beween them

* The Latin has *body*.

58. To prove, however, that all the contents of that creed, even to the very words, are agreeable to the truth, provided a trinity of *person* be understood instead of a trinity of *persons* it is here transcribed again with this alteration. "Whosoever will be saved, it is necessary that he hold the Christian Faith; and the Christian Faith is, that we worship one God in Trinity, and Trinity in Unity, not confounding the Trinity of person, nor separating the essence. The trinity of one person is what is called the Father, the Son, and the Holy Spirit. The Godhead of the Father, of the Son, and of the Holy Spirit, is all one, the glory and the majesty equal. Such as the Father is, such is the Son, and such is the Holy Spirit. The Father is uncreate, the Son uncreate, the Holy Spirit uncreate: the Father is infinite, the Son infinite, and the Holy Spirit infinite; and yet there are not three infinites, nor three uncreates, but one Uncreate, and one Infinite. So, likewise, the Father is almighty, the Son almighty, and the Holy Spirit almighty; and yet there are not three almighties, but one Almighty. So, the Father is God, the Son is God, and the Holy Spirit is God; and yet there are not three Gods, but one God. So, likewise, the Father is Lord, the Son is Lord, and the Holy Spirit is Lord; and yet there are not three Lords, but one Lord. For as by the Christian verity we acknowledge a trinity in one person, who is God and Lord: so by the Christian faith we can say that there is one God and one Lord. The Father is made of none, neither created, nor born; the Son is of the Father alone, not made, nor created, but born; the Holy Spirit is of the Father and of the Son, not made nor created, nor born, but proceeding. So there is one Father, not three Fathers; one Son, not three Sons; one Holy Spirit, not three Holy Spirits. And in this Trinity none is greatest or least, but they are altogether equal. So that in all things, as is beforesaid, the Unity in Trinity, and Trinity in Unity, is to be worshipped."

59. So far as to the doctrine of the trinity and unity of God: next is delivered the doctrine concerning the assumption of the Human by the Lord in the world, which is called the incarnation. What is said on this subject is also in each and every respect true, if we distinguish between what is understood of the Human from the mother, in which the Lord was when in a state of humiliation or exinanition,—as when he suffered temptations and the passion of the cross,—and what of the Human from the Father, in which he was when in the state of glorification or union. For the Lord assumed in the world a Human conceived of Jehovah, who is the Lord from eternity, and born of the Virgin Mary; hence he hath both a Divine and a Human,—a Divine from his Divine from eternity, and a Human from the mother Mary in time: this Human he moreover put off, and put on a Divine Human. This is the Human

which is called the Divine Human, and which is meant in the Word by the Son of God. When, therefore, what has been stated in the doctrine of incarnation is understood of the maternal Human, in which he was when in the state of humiliation; and what follows of the Divine Human in which he was when in the state of glorification; the whole will be found to coincide with the truth. *The following passages apply to the maternal Human, in which he was when in a state of humiliation:* "That Jesus Christ was God and Man, God of the substance of the Father, and Man of the substance of the mother, born in the world; perfect God and perfect man, of a [rational] reasonable soul and human flesh subsisting; equal to the Father as touching the Godhead, but inferior to the Father as touching the manhood." *Also,* "That this manhood was not converted into the Godhead, nor commixed therewith; it being put off, and the Divine Human assumed in its place. *The following passages apply to the Divine Human, in which he was when in the state of glorification, and* **is** *now to eternity:*" "Although our Lord Jesus Christ, the Son of God, be God and Man, yet he is not two, but one Christ; yea, he is altogether one, for he is one person; for as the reasonable soul and body are one man, so God and Man are one Christ."

60. That God and Man, in the Lord, are, as stated in the above doctrine, not two, but one person, yea, altogether one, as the soul and body, appears clearly from many declarations of the Lord himself;—as, that the Father and he are one;—that all things of the Father are his, and all his the Father's;—that he is in the Father, and the Father in him;—that all things are given unto his hand;—that he has all power;—that he is the God of heaven and earth; that whosoever believeth in him hath eternal life: and also, from its being said of him;—that he ascended into heaven, both as to his Divine and Human, and that, with respect to both, he sits on the right hand of God, which means that he is Almighty: not to repeat many passages of the Word, which are copiously quoted in the former part of this work, concerning his Divine Human. All which testify that GOD IS ONE AS WELL IN PERSON AS IN ESSENCE; THAT IN HIM IS A TRINITY; AND THAT GOD IS THE LORD.

61. The reason why these truths relative to the Lord are now for the first time made publicly known, is, because it is foretold in the Revelation, chap. xxi. and xxii., that a New Church, in which this doctrine will hold the chief place, should be established by the Lord at the end of the former. This church is what is meant by the New Jerusalem there mentioned; and none can enter into it, but such as acknowledge the Lord alone as the God of heaven and earth. This I am enabled further to declare, that the Lord alone is acknowledged in the

universal heaven, and that whosoever is not in this acknowledgment cannot enter there. For heaven is heaven from the Lord; and that acknowledgement, from love and faith, is what causes its inhabitants to be in the Lord, and the Lord in them; as the Lord himself teaches, "At that day ye shall know that I am in my Father, and *you* in me, and *I* in *you*" (John xiv. 20). And again: "Abide in ME, and *I* in *you:* I am the vine, ye are the branches: he that abideth in ME and *I* in *him*, the same bringeth forth much fruit; for without ME ye can do nothing: if a man abide not in ME, he is cast forth" (xv. 4—6; xvii. 22, 23). The reason that this has not been previously seen from the Word is, because, if it had been previously seen, still it would not have been received, because the last judgment had not been as yet accomplished; and prior to that, the power of hell prevailed over the power of heaven: and, as man is in the midst between heaven and hell, had this doctrine been seen before, the devil, that is, hell, would have plucked it from the heart, and would, moreover, have profaned it. This state of predominance on the part of hell was altogether destroyed by the last judgment, which is now accomplished. Since this,—thus *now*—every one who desires it, may become enlightened and wise. On this subject more may be seen in the work on *Heaven and Hell*, n. 589—596, and n. 597—603; also in the tract on the *Last Judgment*, n. 65—72, and n. 73, 74.

---

## BY THE NEW JERUSALEM, MENTIONED IN THE REVELATION, IS MEANT A NEW CHURCH.

62. IN the Revelation, after a representation of the state of the Christian Church, such as it would be at its end, which is now arrived; and after those professing members of the church who are meant by the false prophet, the dragon, the harlot, and the beasts, are described as being cast into hell;—thus, after the predictions relating to the accomplishment of the last judgment;—it is said, "I saw a new heaven and a new earth; for the first heaven and the first earth were passed away.—And I John saw the *Holy City*, *New Jerusalem*, coming down from God out of heaven.—And I heard a great voice out of heaven, saying, Behold, the tabernacle of God is with men, and he will dwell with them, and they shall be his people, and God himself shall be with them—their God.—And he that sat upon the throne said, Behold, I make all things new. And he said unto me, Write, for these words are true and faithful" (Rev xxi. 1—3, 5). By the new heaven and the new earth which John saw, after the first heaven and the first earth had passed away, is not mean

a new starry and atmospherical heaven, such as appears before the bodily eyes, neither a new earth such as that on which men dwell; but *new* is to be understood of the church, both in the spiritual world and in the natural world. As a new [formation] of the church, both in the spiritual and natural worlds, was effected by the Lord when upon earth, a similar prediction,—that a new heaven and a new earth should then exist,—is found in the prophets of the Old Testament, as in Isaiah lxv. 17; lxvi. 22; and elsewhere; which it is plain, therefore, cannot relate to the visible heaven, or the earth inhabited by men. By the spiritual world we mean the world which is the abode of angels and spirits; and by the natural world, that which is the abode of men. That a new formation of the church has lately been effected in the spiritual world, and that it will be followed by a new formation of the church in the natural world, is in some measure shewn in the tract on *The Last Judgment*, and more fully in *The Continuation*.

63. By the holy city, New Jerusalem, is meant this new church as to its doctrine; wherefore it was seen descending out of heaven from God; for the doctrine of genuine truth can come from no other origin than from the Lord through heaven. And as the church in respect to doctrine is meant by the city, New Jerusalem, it is therefore said to be "prepared as a bride adorned for her husband" (verse 2); and afterwards, that "there came unto me one of the seven angels—and talked with me, saying, Come hither, I will shew thee the bride, the Lamb's wife. And he carried me away in the spirit to a great and high mountain, and shewed me that great city, the Holy Jerusalem, descending out of heaven from God" (verse 9, 10). That by a bride and wife is meant the church, when the Lord is understood to be the bridegroom and husband, is well known. The church is a bride, when she is desirous to receive the Lord, and a wife, when she actually does receive him. That the Lord is here understood to be the husband, is evident from its being said, THE BRIDE, THE LAMB'S WIFE.

64. The reason why by Jerusalem, in the Word, is meant the church in respect to doctrine, is, because at Jerusalem in the land of Canaan, and in no other place, were the temple and the altar, the offering of sacrifices, and the whole celebration of divine worship; there also the three yearly festivals were kept at which every male in the whole land was required to be present. It is on this account that by Jerusalem is signified the church as to worship, and consequently also as to doctrine; for worship is prescribed in doctrine, and performed according to it. An additional reason is, because the Lord came to Jerusalem, and taught in his temple, and afterwards there glorified his Human. Moreover, by a city in general, when mentioned in the Word, doctrine is signified in the spiritual sense: hence by

the holy city is signified the doctrine of divine truth from the Lord.* That by Jerusalem is meant the church as to doctrine, is also evident from other passages in the Word, such as the following, in Isaiah: "For Zion's sake I will not hold my peace, and for *Jerusalem's* sake I will not rest, until the righteousness thereof go forth as brightness, and the salvation thereof as a lamp that burneth. And the Gentiles shall see thy righteousness and all kings thy glory. And thou shalt be called by a new name, which the mouth of Jehovah shall name. Thou shalt also be a crown of glory in the hand of Jehovah, and a royal diadem in the hand of thy God:—for Jehovah delighteth in thee, and thy land shall be married.—Behold, thy salvation cometh,—his reward is with him.—And they shall call them the holy people, the redeemed of Jehovah. And thou shalt be called, Sought out, a city not forsaken" (lxii. 1—4, 11, 12). The whole of this chapter treats of the coming of the Lord, and of the new church that was to be established by him: this new church is what is here signified by Jerusalem, which, it is said, shall be called by a new name, which the mouth of Jehovah shall name, and shall be a crown of glory in the hand of Jehovah, and a royal diadem in the hand of God; in which Jehovah shall delight, and which shall be called a city sought out and not forsaken. This description is not at all applicable to the city of Jerusalem inhabited by the Jews, when the Lord came into the world, for this was entirely of a contrary character, and ought rather to have been called Sodom, as it is also called in the Rev. xi. See Isa. iii. 9; Jer. xxiii. 14; Ezek. xvi. 46, 48. Again, in Isaiah: "Behold, I create new heavens and a new earth, and the former shall not be remembered.—Be ye glad and rejoice for ever in that which I create: for behold I create *Jerusalem* a rejoicing, and her people a joy: and I will rejoice in *Jerusalem*, and joy in my people.—The wolf and the lamb shall feed together: they shall not hurt nor destroy in all my holy mountain" (lxv. 17—19, 25). This chapter also treats of the coming of the Lord, and of the church that was to be established by him; which was not established with those who dwelt in the natural Jerusalem, but with such as were without it: it is this church which is signified by the Jerusalem that should be a rejoicing to the Lord, and whose people should be to him a joy; where, also, the wolf and the lamb should feed together, and where they should do no hurt. Here also it is said, as in the Revelation, that the Lord would create a new heaven and a new earth; which expressions have,

* That by a city, when spoken of in the Word, is signified the doctrine of the church and of religion, may be seen in the *Arcana Cœlestia*, at n. 402, 2451, 2943, 3216, 4492, 4493. That by the gate of a city is signified, in the same sense, a doctrine by which there is an entrance into the church, n. 2943, 4447, 4478. And that therefore the elders sat in the gates of the city, and judged, *ibid.* That to go out at the gate is to recede from doctrine, n. 4492, 4493. The cities and palaces are represented in heaven, when the angels converse on matters of doctrine, n. 3216.

in both places, a similar meaning: it is also said, that he would create Jerusalem. Again: "Awake, awake! put on thy strength, O Zion; put on thy beautiful garments, O *Jerusalem*, the holy city: for henceforth there shall no more come into thee the uncircumcised, and the unclean. Shake thyself from the dust; arise, and sit down, O Jerusalem.—My people shall know my name in that day,—that I am he that doth speak. Behold it is I.—Jehovah hath comforted his people, he hath redeemed Jerusalem" (lii. 1, 2, 6, 9). This chapter also treats of the coming of the Lord, and of the church to be established by him; wherefore, by that Jerusalem into which the uncircumcised and unclean should no more enter, and which the Lord should redeem, is signified the church; and by Jerusalem the holy city, the church as to doctrine from the Lord. So in Zephaniah: "Sing, O daughter of Zion;—rejoice with all the heart, O daughter of *Jerusalem:* — the king of Israel—is in the midst of thee. Thou shalt not see evil any more.—Jehovah thy God—will rejoice over thee with joy: he will rest in his love, he will joy over thee with singing.—I will make you a name and a praise among all people of the earth" (iii. 14, 15, 17, 20). Here likewise the subject is the Lord, and the church to be founded by him; over which the King of Israel, who is the Lord, will rejoice with joy, and exult with singing; in whose love he will rest, and which he will make a name and a praise among all the people of the earth. So in Isaiah: "Thus saith Jehovah thy Reedeemer and he that formed thee,—to *Jerusalem*, Thou shalt be inhabited; and to the cities of Judah, Ye shall be built" (xliv. 24, 26). And in Daniel: "Know therefore and understand, that from the going forth of the commandment to restore and to build *Jerusalem*, unto the Messiah the Prince, shall be seven weeks" (ix. 25). That by Jerusalem is here also meant the church, is evident, because this was restored and established by the Lord, but not so Jerusalem, the metropolis of the Jews. By Jerusalem is signified the church from the Lord also in the following passages: in Zechariah: "Thus saith Jehovah, I am returned unto Zion, and will dwell in the midst of *Jerusalem:* and *Jerusalem* shall be called the City of truth; and the mountain of Jehovah of hosts, the Holy Mountain" (viii. 3, and 20—23). In Joel: "So shall ye know that I am Jehovah your God, dwelling in Zion, my holy mountain. Then shall *Jerusalem* be holy.—And it shall come to pass in that day, that the mountains shall drop down new wine, and the hills shall flow with milk;—and *Jerusalem* [shall dwell] from generation to generation" (iii. 17, 18, 20). In Isaiah: "In that day shall the branch of Jehovah be beautiful and glorious.—And it shall come to pass, that he that is left in Zion, and he that remaineth in *Jerusalem*, shall be called holy: even every one that is written among the living in Jerusalem"

(iv. 2, 3). In Micah: "In the last days it shall come to pass, that the mountain of the house of Jehovah shall be established in the top of the mountains: for the law shall go forth of Zion, and the Word of Jehovah from *Jerusalem.*—Unto thee shall it come, even the first dominion, the kingdom shall come to the daughter of *Jerusalem*" (iv. 1, 2, 8). In Jeremiah: "At that time they shall call *Jerusalem* the throne of Jehovah, and all nations shall be gathered—to the name of Jehovah to *Jerusalem:* neither shall they walk any more after the imagination of their evil heart" (iii. 17). In Isaiah: "Look upon Zion the city of our solemnities. Thine eyes shall see *Jerusalem* a quiet habitation, a tabernacle that shall not be taken down; not one of the stakes thereof shall ever be removed, neither shall any of the cords thereof be broken" (xxxiii. 20). Not to mention many other places; as in Isaiah xxiv. 23; xxxvii. 32; lxvi. 10—14; in Zech. xii. 3, 6, 8, 9, 10; xiv. 8, 11, 12, 21; in Malachi iii. 1, 4; in David, Psalm cxxii.1—7; Psalm cxxxvii. 5, 6. That by Jerusalem, in these places, is meant the church which was to be, and which became established, by the Lord, and not the Jerusalem inhabited by the Jews in the Land of Canaan, may also appear from those passages in the Word, where it is said of the latter, that it would be wholly ruined, and that it would be destroyed; as Jeremiah v. 1; vi. 6, 7; vii. 17, 20, &c.; viii. 5—7, &c.; ix. 11, 13, &c.; xiii. 9, 10, 14; xiv. 16; Lam. i. 8, 9, 15, 17; Ezek. iv. 1 to the end; v. 9 to the end; xii. 18, 19; xv. 6—8; xvi. 1 to the end; xxiii. 1—39; and 37, 39; Luke xix. 41—44; xxi. 20, 21, 22; xxiii. 28—30: and in many other places.

65. When it is said in the Revelation, "*I saw a new heaven and a new earth;*" and afterwards, "*Behold, I make all things new;*" nothing else is meant than that in the church now to be established by the Lord, *there will be new doctrine*, which did not exist in the former church. The reason why this doctrine was not discerned before, is, because if it had been seen, it would not have been received; for the last judgment was not as yet accomplished, prior to which the power of hell prevailed over the power of heaven, as was observed above; wherefore, if the doctrine had been before delivered, even from the mouth of the Lord, it would not have remained with man: nor indeed will it now remain with any but those, who in worship approach the Lord alone, and acknowledge him as the God of heaven and earth. [See above, n. 61.] This same doctrine was indeed before delivered in the Word; but as the church, not long after its first establishment was turned into Babylon, and since then, among others, into Philistia, that doctrine could not be seen from the Word; for the church always looks at the Word from its own religious principles and doctrines.

The new things which are discovered in this little work, are in general these. I. God is One in Person and in Essence; and the Lord is that God. II. The whole Sacred Scripture treats of him alone. III. He came into the world to subdue the hells, and to glorify his Human; and he accomplished both by admitting temptations to assail him, and fully by the last of them, which was the passion of the cross; by this he became a Saviour and Redeemer; and again by this, merit and righteousness belong to him alone. IV. When it is said that he fulfilled the whole of the law, the meaning is that he fulfilled the whole of the Word. V. He did not take away the sins of mankind by the passion of the cross, but he bore them, in his character of prophet; that is, he suffered a representation of the church to be made in himself, in respect to the manner in which it had maltreated the Word. VI. The imputation of his merit is a phrase without meaning, unless it be understood to denote the remission of sins after repentance. These are contained in this little work; in the treatises *on the Sacred Scripture*, *the Doctrine of Life*, *the Doctrine of Faith*, and *on the Divine Love and Divine Wisdom* still more new truths will be shewn.

**END OF THE DOCTRINE CONCERNING THE LORD.**

# NINE QUESTIONS,

CHIEFLY RELATING TO

## THE LORD, THE TRINITY, AND THE HOLY SPIRIT,

PROPOSED BY THE

## REV. T. HARTLEY, A.M.,

*Late Rector of Winwick in Northampton,*

TO

## EMANUEL SWEDENBORG:

WITH HIS ANSWERS.

---

*Question* 1. In what sense did the Lord call himself the Son of Man, if he only took flesh from his mother, and not a rational soul? Had the human sonship respect only to the human flesh?

*Answer.* The Lord called himself the Son of Man because he was the Word, or Divine Truth, even as to his Human; for the title "Son of Man," in the spiritual sense, signifies the truth of the church derived from the Word. The same was signified by the term "prophet," because the prophets taught truths derived from the Word: wherefore the Lord, who in a super-eminent degree was THE PROPHET, and also THE WORD, and thence Divine Truth, called himself, as to his Human, the Son of Man. Hence it is that, throughout the prophets, and also in David, where the subject is the devastation of truth in the church, it is said that the son of man doth not abide there: and hence also it is, that the prophets themselves were likewise called sons of man, as Ezek. (ii. 1, 3, 6, 8; iii. 1, 3, 4, 10, 17, 25: and very frequently in the succeeding chapters); so also was Daniel. This is shewn by the quotation of many passages in the *Doctrine of the New Jerusalem concerning the Lord.*

*Question* II. Had the Lord his rational soul from Jehovah the Father, to which was united the Divine Esse, whence he became very God and very Man?

*Answer.* The Lord from eternity, or Jehovah, was Divine Love and Divine Wisdom; and he then had a Divine Celestial and a Divine Spiritual Principle, but not a Divine Natural before he assumed the Human; and as the rational principle is only predicated of the celestial-and-spiritual-natural, therefore

Jehovah the Lord, by the assumption of the Human, did also put on the Divine Rational. Before the assumption of the Human, he had a Divine Rational; but it then existed by influx into the angelic heaven; and when he manifested himself in the world, he had it by an angel whom he filled with his Divine; for the Essence purely Divine,—which, as just stated, was the purely Divine Celestial and Divine Spiritual Essence,—transcends both the angelic and the human rational. But the nature of the Divine Rational which existed by influx may be concluded from the answer to the 6th question beneath. Luther and Melancthon teach, that in Christ Man is God and God is Man; which is also agreeable to the Sacred Scripture:* but Calvin denied this, and merely affirmed that Christ is God and Man.

*Question* III. Was there not always a Trinity in the Divine Nature, to be understood in this manner, viz. Divine Love, Divine Wisdom, and the Quickening Spirit, or Holy Proceeding?

*Answer.* The Divine Trinity in one Person is to be understood as soul, body, and proceeding operation, which together constitute one essence, for the one is from the other, consequently the one belongs to the other. There is a similar trinity in every individual man, which together constitutes one person, namely, the soul, body, and proceeding operation. But in man this trinity is finite, for man is only an organ of life; whereas in the Lord the Trinity is Infinite, and thus Divine, for the Lord is life itself even with respect to his Human; as he himself teaches in John (chap. v. 26; xiv. 6; and elsewhere).

*Question* IV. Does not the Son, by whom Jehovah is said to have created the worlds (Heb. i. 2), signify the same thing as the Divine Wisdom in Jerem. x. 12; li. 15; so that the essential Wisdom, or *Logos* of God, in first principles, is now become the truth, or *Logos* of God, in ultimates?

*Answer.* That the Lord, that is, the Word or Divine Truth, by which all things were made that were made, and by which the world was created (John i. 3, 10), was the Divine Wisdom, which with the Divine Love constitutes the Divine Essence, and thus one and the same God, is a natural consequence; for Divine Wisdom is also Divine Truth, since all things appertaining to wisdom are truths, and wisdom produces nothing but truths, it containing in itself all truths, according to Jeremiah x. 12, and li. 15. The same is also understood by that passage in David, Psalm xxxiii. 6. The spirit or breath of the Lord's mouth also is wisdom, and the word there mentioned is

* See the *True Christian Religion*, n. 137.

the Divine Love and Divine Wisdom together; for it is said, "*And the Word was God.*" (John i. 1).

*Question* V. Is not the Holy Spirit in the New Testament the same as the Spirit of God in the Old Testament, with this only difference, that before the Lord's incarnation it proceeded from the Divine Esse or Jehovah immediately, or mediately by angels; and after the incarnation, through the Son or the Divine Human?

Is not the Holy Spirit the same as the sphere of God?

*Answer.* The Spirit of God and the Holy Spirit are two distinct things. The Spirit of God neither did nor could operate on man, otherwise than imperceptibly; whereas the Holy Spirit, which proceeds solely from the Lord, operates on man perceptibly, and enables him to comprehend spiritual truths after a natural manner; for to the Divine Celestial and the Divine Spiritual Principles the Lord hath united the Divine Natural also, by which he operates from them. Besides, the term "Holy," in the Word, is solely predicated of the Divine Truth, consequently of the Lord, who is the Divine Truth, not only in the celestial and spiritual sense, but also in the natural sense: wherefore it is said in the Apocalypse, that the Lord alone is holy (xv. 3, 4).* It is also said in John: "the Holy Spirit was not yet, because that Jesus was not yet glorified" (vii. 39).

The Holy Spirit is the same as the Divine Sphere, if by this be meant the Divine Love and the Divine Wisdom, which two proceed from Jehovah the Lord out of the sun of the angelic heaven, like heat and light from the sun of the natural world, and compose its sphere: for the heat proceeding out of the sun of the angelic heaven is in its essence love, and the light thence in its essence wisdom; to which two the heat and light proceeding out of the sun of the natural world correspond.

*Question* VI. Was the Divine Human of Jehovah, before the incarnation, a person subsisting by itself, as the *existere*, form, or body of God, or was it an angelic form, occasionally assumed for the purpose of manifestation?

Does it not follow, that the Divine Human before the incarnation was different from the Divine Human which now is since the incarnation, seeing the Divine Trinity is in the person of the Lord?

*Answer.* Before the incarnation there was not any Divine Human, except a representative one by means of some angel, whom Jehovah the Lord filled with his spirit, as has been said above; and as that was a representative one, so all things of

* See moreover the *Apocalypse Revealed,* n. 137.

the church at that time were representatives, and like shadows; but after the incarnation representatives ceased, like the shadows of evening or night at the rising of the sun. But the representative human, in which Jehovah was then manifested in the world, before his actual advent, was not of such efficacy as that it could spiritually enlighten men; wherefore illumination was then effected only by types and figures.

*Question* VII. May not the Trinity be properly said to be one and the same Lord under three characters, distinctions of office, or relations towards man, namely, as Creator, Redeemer, and Sanctifier,—as Father, Son, and Holy Spirit,—as Divine Esse, Divine Human, and Holy Proceeding; not as three Persons, which would of necessity be making three Gods?

*Answer.* The most Holy Trinity in one Person is to be apprehended as the Divine Esse, the Divine Human, and the Divine Proceeding, and thus as soul, body, and operation thence proceeding, altogether as described in the Memorable Relation inserted in the work, entitled, *The True Christian Religion.** As productions from these, follow in their order, creation, redemption, and regeneration; for creation is the attribute of the Divine Esse, redemption is the attribute of the Divine Human from the Divine Esse, and regeneration is the attribute of the Holy Spirit, which is the primary power or operation of the Divine Human from the Divine Esse: agreeably to what is said in *The True Christian Religion.*†

*Question* VIII. It is said in 1 Cor. xv. 45, "The first man Adam was made a living soul;" and in the genealogy in Luke iii., he is placed first after God, thus, "*Who was the son of God.*" Does not the regarding Adam as a church contradict this?

*Answer.* In the genealogy in Luke, it is said, that Adam was "of God" that is, created by God, and not the son of God.

*Question* IX. If there was no individual man called Noah, how comes it to be said in Ezek. xiv. 14, "Though these three men, Noah, Daniel, and Job," &c.?

[I lay no great stress upon these two questions, (says Mr. Hartley,) but I had a mind to propose them.]

*Answer.* The reason why Noah is mentioned in Ezek. xiv. is, because he was mentioned in Genesis, and hence the same is signified in the prophet as in Moses; namely, that the man with his three sons were significative of the succeeding church; on which subject see what is said in the *Arcana Cœlestia.*

* n. 18 † n. 153—155.

THE

# DOCTRINE

OF

# THE NEW JERUSALEM

RESPECTING THE

# SACRED SCRIPTURE.

# THE DOCTRINE

OF

# THE NEW JERUSALEM

RESPECTING THE

# SACRED SCRIPTURE.

---

BY EMANUEL SWEDENBORG,

*Servant of the Lord Jesus Christ.*

---

BEING A TRANSLATION OF HIS WORK ENTITLED

"DOCTRINA NOVÆ HIEROSOLYMÆ DE SCRIPTURA SACRA.

Amstelodami, 1763.

NEW YORK:

AMERICAN SWEDENBORG PRINTING AND PUBLISHING SOCIETY

1873.

# THE DOCTRINE

OF

# THE NEW JERUSALEM

RESPECTING THE

# SACRED SCRIPTURE.

---

### I. THAT THE SACRED SCRIPTURE, OR THE WORD, IS DIVINE TRUTH ITSELF.

1. It is universally confessed, that the Word is from God, is divinely inspired, and of consequence holy; but still it has remained a secret to this day in what part of the Word its divinity resides, inasmuch as in the letter it appears like a common writing, composed in a strange style, neither so sublime nor so elegant as that which distinguishes the best secular compositions. Hence it is, that whosoever worships nature instead of God, or in preference to God, and in consequence of such worship makes himself and his own *proprium* the centre and fountain of his thoughts, instead of deriving them out of heaven from the Lord, may easily fall into error concerning the Word, and into contempt for it, and say within himself whilst he reads it, "What is the meaning of this passage? What is the meaning of that? Is it possible this should be divine? Is it possible that God, whose wisdom is infinite, should speak in this manner? Where is its sanctity, or whence can it be derived, but from superstition and credulity?"

2. But he who reasons thus, does not reflect that Jehovah the Lord, who is God of heaven and earth, spake the Word by Moses and the prophets, and that consequently, it must be Divine Truth, inasmuch as what Jehovah the Lord Himself speaks can be nothing else; nor does such a one consider that the Lord, who is the same with Jehovah, spake the Word written by the Evangelists, many parts from his own mouth, and the rest from the spirit of his mouth, which is the Holy Spirit. Hence it is, as He Himself declares, that in His words there is life, and that He is the light which enlightens, and that He is the truth. That Jehovah himself spake the Word by the pro-

phets, has been shewn in THE DOCTRINE OF THE NEW JERUSALEM RESPECTING THE LORD, n. 52, 53. That the words which the Lord Himself spake in the writings of the Evangelists are life, is declared in John: "The words that I speak unto you, they are *spirit*, and they are *life*" (John vi. 63); Jesus said to the woman at Jacob's well, "If thou knewest the gift of God, and who it is that saith to thee, Give me to drink, thou wouldest have asked of Him, and he would have given thee living water. Whosoever drinketh of the water that I shall give him shall never thirst; but the water that I shall give him shall be in him a well of water springing up into everlasting life" (John iv. 10, 14). By Jacob's well is here signified the Word, as also in Deut. xxxiii. 28; for which reason the Lord, who is the Word, sat there, and conversed with the woman; and by water is signified the truth of the word. "Jesus said, If any man thirst, let him come unto me, and drink. He that believeth on me, as the Scripture hath said, out of his belly shall flow rivers of living water" (John vii. 37, 38): Peter said unto Jesus, "Thou hast the words of eternal life" (John vi. 68): Jesus said, "Heaven and earth shall pass away; but my words shall not pass away" (Mark. xiii. 31). The reason why the words of the Lord are truth and life is, because He is the truth and the life, as He teaches in John: "I am the Way, the Truth, and the Life" (xiv. 6); and in another place: "In the beginning was the Word, and the Word was with God, and the Word was God. In him was life; and the life was the light of men" (John i. 1, 4). By the word is meant the Lord with respect to Divine Truth, in which alone there is life and light. Hence it is, that the Word, which is from the Lord, and which is the Lord, is called "A FOUNTAIN OF LIVING WATERS" (Jerem. ii. 13; xvii. 13; xxxi. 9); "A WELL OF SALVATION" (Isaiah xii. 3); "A FOUNTAIN" (Zech. xiii. 1); and "A RIVER OF WATER OF LIFE" (Apoc. xxii. 1); and it is said, that "the Lamb which is in the midst of the throne shall feed them, and shall lead them unto living fountains of waters" (Apoc. vii. 17). Not to mention other passages, where the Word is also called THE SANCTUARY, and THE TABERNACLE, wherein the Lord dwells with man.

3. The natural man, however, cannot still be persuaded to believe, that the Word is Divine Truth itself, in which is Divine Wisdom and Divine Life, inasmuch as he judges of it by its style, in which no such things appear. Nevertheless, the style in which the Word is written, is a truly Divine style, with which no other style, however sublime and excellent it may seem, is at all comparable, for it is as darkness compared to light. The style of the Word is of such a nature as to contain what is holy in every verse, in every word, and in some cases in every letter; and hence the Word conjoins man with the Lord,

and opens heaven. There are two things which proceed from the Lord, Divine Love and Divine Wisdom, or what is the same, Divine Good and Divine Truth; for Divine Good is of Divine Love itself, and Divine Truth is of Divine Wisdom itself: and the Word, in its essence, is both of these; and inasmuch as it conjoins man with the Lord, and opens heaven, as just observed, therefore the Word fills the man who reads it under the Lord's influence, and not under the influence of his proprium or self, with the good of love and the truth of wisdom, his will with the good of love, and his understanding with the truths of wisdom. Hence man has life by and through the Word.

4. Lest therefore mankind should remain any longer in doubt concerning the divinity of the Word, it has pleased the Lord to reveal to me its internal sense, which in its essence is spiritual, and which is, to the external sense, which is natural, what the soul is to the body. This internal sense is the spirit which gives life to the letter; wherefore this sense will evince the divinity and sanctity of the Word, and may convince even the natural man, if he is in a disposition to be convinced.

---

## II. THAT IN THE WORD THERE IS A SPIRITUAL SENSE, HERETOFORE UNKNOWN.

THIS subject we will consider in the following order. 1. *What the spiritual sense is.* 2. *That this sense is in all and every part of the Word.* 3. *That it is owing to this sense that the Word is divinely inspired, and holy in every syllable.* 4. *That this sense has heretofore been unknown.* 5. *That hereafter it will be made known to none but those who are principled in genuine truths from the Lord.*

5. 1. *What the spiritual sense is.*

The spiritual sense of the Word is not that which breaks forth as light out of the literal sense, whilst a person is studying and explaining the Word, with intent to establish some particular tenet of the church: this sense may be called the literal sense of the Word: but the spiritual sense does not appear in the literal sense, being within it, as the soul is in the body, or as the thought of the understanding is in the eye, or as the affection of love is in the countenance, which act together as cause and effect. It is this sense, principally, which renders the Word spiritual, and by which it is adapted not only to the use of men, but also of angels; whence also, by means of that sense, the Word communicates with the heavens.

6. From the Lord proceed these principles; the celestial, the spiritual, and the natural, one after another. Whatsoever proceeds from His Divine Love is called celestial, and is Divine

Good; whatsoever proceeds from His Divine Wisdom is called spiritual, and is Divine Truth: the natural partakes of both, and is their complex in ultimates. The angels of the celestial kingdom, who compose the third or highest heaven, are in that Divine Principle which proceeds from the Lord that is called celestial, for they are in the good of love from the Lord; the angels of the Lord's spiritual kingdom, who compose the second or middle heaven, are in that Divine Principle which proceeds from the Lord that is called spiritual, for they are in the truths of wisdom from the Lord:* but men, who compose the Lord's church on earth, are in the Divine-natural, which also proceeds from the Lord. Hence it follows, that the Divine Principle proceeding from the Lord, in its progress to its ultimates, descends through three degrees, and is termed celestial, spiritual, and natural. The Divine Principle which proceeds from the Lord and descends to men, descends through those three degrees and when it has descended, it contains those three degrees in itself. Such is the nature of every Divine Principle proceeding from the Lord; wherefore, when it is in its last degree, it is in its fulness. Such is the nature and quality of the Word; in its last sense it is natural, in its interior sense it is spiritual, and in its inmost sense it is celestial; and in each sense it is divine. That the Word is of such a nature and quality, does not appear in the sense of the letter, which is natural, by reason that man has heretofore been altogether unacquainted with the state of the heavens, and consequently with the nature of the spiritual principle, and the celestial, and of course with the distinction between them and the natural principle.

7. The distinction between these degrees cannot be known, except by the knowledge of correspondence; for these three degrees are altogether distinct from each other, like end, cause, and effect, or like what is prior, posterior, and postreme, but yet make one by correspondences; for the natural degree or principle corresponds with the spiritual, and also with the celestial. The nature and meaning of correspondence may be seen more fully explained in the treatise concerning HEAVEN AND HELL, being there digested under these two articles, 1st. *Concerning the correspondence of all things in heaven with all things in man*, n. 87—102; 2ndly. *Concerning the correspondence of all things in heaven with all things on earth*, n. 102—115; and it will be further seen below by examples adduced from the Word.

8. Inasmuch as the Word in its interior is spiritual and celestial, therefore it is written by mere correspondences, and what is written by mere correspondences, in its ultimate sense

* That there are two kingdoms of which the heavens consist, one of which is called the celestial kingdom, and the other the spiritual kingdom, may be seen in the Treatise concerning HEAVEN AND HELL, n. 20—28.

is written in such a style as that of the prophets and evangelists, which notwithstanding its apparent commonness, contains in it all divine and angelic wisdom.

9. 2. *That the Spiritual Sense is in all and every part of the Word.*

This cannot be better seen than by examples; as for instance: John says in the Apocalypse, "I saw heaven opened, and behold a white horse, and He that sat upon him was called Faithful and True, and in righteousness He doth judge and make war. His eyes were as a flame of fire, and on His head were many crowns, and He had a name written that no man knew but He Himself; and he was clothed with a vesture dipped in blood, and His name is called THE WORD OF GOD. And the armies which were in heaven followed Him upon white horses, clothed in fine linen, white and clean. And He hath on His vesture and on His thigh a name written, KING OF KINGS AND LORD OF LORDS. And I saw an angel standing in the sun, and He cried with a loud voice, saying to all the fowls that fly in the midst of heaven, Come and gather yourselves together unto the supper of the great God, that ye may eat the flesh of kings, and the flesh of captains, and the flesh of mighty men, and the flesh of horses, and of them that sit on them, and the flesh of all men, both free and bond, both small and great" (xix. 11—18). What these words signify cannot possibly be known, but from the spiritual sense of the Word; and the spiritual sense of the Word cannot possibly be known, but from the science of correspondences; for all the above words are correspondences, and there is not one without a meaning. The science of correspondences teaches what is signified by a white horse, what by Him that sat upon him, what by his eyes which were as a flame of fire, what by the crowns which He wore on His head, what by His vesture dipped in blood, what by white linen with which the armies that followed Him in heaven were clothed, what by the angel standing in the sun, what by the great supper to which they should come and gather themselves, what by the flesh of kings, and captains, and others, which they should eat. The particular signification of all these expressions in their spiritual sense may be seen explained in the small treatise on the WHITE HORSE; wherefore it is needless to repeat the explanation. In that work it is shewn that, in the passage here quoted, the Lord is described as to the Word; and that by His eyes, which were like a flame of fire, and by the crowns which He wore on His head, and by the name which no one knew but Himself, are meant the spiritual sense of the Word, and that no one knows what the Word is, in its spiritual sense, except the Lord, and those to whom He reveals it; also, that by His vesture dipped in blood is meant the natural sense of the Word, which is its literal sense, to which violence has been offered.

That it is the Word which is thus described, is very evident from its being said, *His name is called* THE WORD OF GOD; and that it is the Lord who is meant, is likewise evident, for it is said that the name of Him who sat on the white horse was KING OF KINGS AND LORD OF LORDS. That the spiritual sense of the Word is to be opened at the end of the church, is signified, not only by what is said of the white horse and of Him that sat upon it, but also by the great supper to which all were invited by the angel standing in the sun, to come and to eat the flesh of kings and captains, of mighty men, of horses, and them that sat on them, and of men both free and bond. All these expressions would be idle unmeaning words, and without life and spirit, unless there was a spiritual sense within them, as the soul is in the body.

10. In the Apocalypse, chap. xxi., the New Jerusalem is thus described: "Her light was like unto a stone most precious, even like a jasper-stone, clear as crystal; and she had a wall great and high, and had twelve gates, and at the gates twelve angels, and names written thereon, which are the names of the twelve tribes of the children of Israel. And the wall was a hundred and forty-four cubits, according to the measure of a man, that is, of the angel; and the building of the wall was of jasper; and the foundations of all manner of precious stones, of jasper, sapphire, chalcedony, emerald, sardonyx, sardius, chrysolite, beryl, topaz, chrysoprasus, jacinth, and amethyst. And the gates were twelve pearls. And the city was pure gold, as it were transparent glass; and it was four square; the length, and the breadth, and the height of it equal, twelve thousand furlongs;" with many other circumstances. That all these things are to be understood spiritually, appears from hence; that by the New Jerusalem is meant a new church, which is to be established by the Lord, as is shewn in THE DOCTRINE OF THE LORD, n. 62—65; and since by Jerusalem is there signified the church, it follows of consequence that all things spoken of it as of a city, respecting its wall, the foundations of the wall, and their measures, contain a spiritual sense, inasmuch as all things relating to the church are spiritual. What the expressions in the above description particularly signify, is shewn in the work ON THE NEW JERUSALEM, n. 1; wherefore it is needless here to repeat the explanation. It is enough to understand from thence, that there is a spiritual sense in every part of the description, like a soul in its body, and that without such a sense the expressions could have no reference to the church; as where it is said that the city was of pure gold, its gates of pearls, the wall of jasper, the foundation of the wall of precious stones, that the wall was a hundred and forty-four cubits, which is the measure of a man, that is, an angel, and that the city was in length, breadth, and height, twelve thousand furlongs, with

many other particulars: but whosoever, by the science of correspondences, is acquainted with the spiritual sense of the Word, will understand those expressions, and will see, for instance, that the wall and its foundations signify the doctrinal tenets of the New Church, derived from the literal sense of the Word. and that the numbers twelve, one hundred and forty-four, twelve thousand, signify similar things, namely, all the truths and goods of the church in one complex.

11. Again, in the Apocalypse, chap. vii., it is written, that there were sealed, of all the tribes of the children of Israel, one hundred and forty-four thousand, twelve thousand of each particular tribe; of the tribe of Judah, of the tribe of Reuben, of Gad, of Ashur, of Naphtali, of Manasses, of Simeon, of Levi, of Issachar, of Zebulon, of Joseph, and of Benjamin. The spiritual sense of these words teaches, that all are saved in whom the Lord has established His church, for, in a spiritual sense, by being marked in the forehead, or sealed, is signified to be acknowledged by the Lord, and to be saved. By the twelve tribes of Israel are signified all of that church; by twelve, twelve thousand, and one hundred and forty-four thousand, are signified all; by Israel is signified the church, and by each particular tribe some particular specific principle of character of the church. If this spiritual meaning of these words be not known, it may be imagined that salvation is confined to a certain number, and to those of the Israelitish and Jewish nation.

12. Again, in the Apocalypse, chap. vi., it is written, that when the Lamb opened one of the seals of the book, there went forth a white horse, and that he who sat thereon had a bow, and that a crown was given unto him; and that when he opened the second seal there went forth a red horse, and that to him who sat thereon was given a great sword; and that when he opened the third seal, there went forth a black horse, and that he that sat thereon, held in his hand a pair of balances: and that when he opened the fourth seal, there went forth a pale horse, and that the name of him who sat thereon was Death. What these words signify can only be unfolded by the spiritual sense; and it is fully unfolded when it is known what is signified by opening the seals, by horses, and by the other things therein mentioned. Thereby are described the successive states of the church from its beginning to its end, as to the understanding of the Word: by the Lamb's opening the seals of the book, is signified the manifestation of those states of the church by the Lord; by a horse is signified the understanding of the Word; by a white horse the understanding of truth from the Word in the first state of the church; by the bow of him that sat upon that horse, the doctrine of charity and faith combating against false principles; by a crown, eternal life the reward of victory; by a red horse is signified the un

derstanding of the Word destroyed, as to the principle of good, in the second state of the church; by a great sword, falsity combating against truth: by a black horse is signified the understanding of the Word destroyed, as to the principle of truth, in the third state of the church; by a pair of balances, the estimation of truth so small as scarce to be of any amount: by a pale horse is signified the understanding of the Word annihilated, by the evils of life and the falsities thence derived, in the fourth and last state of the church: and by death, eternal damnation. That such is the signification of the contents of the above passage in the spiritual sense, does not appear in the sense of the letter, or the natural sense; wherefore unless the spiritual sense had been now for once opened, the Word, as to this and other passages in the Apocalypse, must have been closed up, so that at length no one would know how, and in what, any thing holy lay therein concealed. The case is the same, in respect to the signification of the four horses and the four chariots that came forth from between two mountains of brass; see Zechariah vi. 1—8.

13. Again, in the Apocalypse, chap. ix., it is written, "The fifth angel sounded, and I saw a star fall from heaven unto the earth, and to him was given the key of the bottomless pit: and he opened the bottomless pit, and there arose a smoke out of the pit as the smoke of a great furnace; and the sun and the air were darkened by reason of the smoke of the pit; and there came out of the smoke locusts upon the earth, and unto them was given power as the scorpions of the earth have power; the shapes of the locusts were like unto horses prepared for battle; and on their heads were as it were crowns like gold; and their faces were as the faces of men, and they had hair as the hair of women, and their teeth were as the teeth of lions; and they had breast-plates as it were breast-plates of iron; and the sound of their wings was as the sound of chariots of many horses running to battle: and they had tails like unto scorpions, and there were stings in their tails; and their power was to hurt men five months: and they had a king over them, which is the angel of the bottomless pit, whose name in the Hebrew tongue is Abaddon, but in the Greek tongue hath his name Apollyon." These words, in like manner, must needs be unintelligible to every one who is not acquainted by revelation with the spiritual sense; for there is nothing said in this passage without a meaning, but the whole thereof and every particular expression therein is significative. The subject here treated of is concerning the state of the church, when all the knowledges of truth from the Word are destroyed, in consequence whereof man, becoming sensual, persuades himself that falsities are truths. By a star fallen from heaven, are signified the knowledges of truth destroyed: by the sun and air being darkened is signified

the light of truth made darkness: by locusts which came forth from the smoke of the pit, are signified falsities in the extremes, such as appertain to those who are become sensual, and who see and judge all things according to fallacies: by a scorpion is signified their persuasive principle or faculty: by the locusts appearing as horses prepared for battle, is signified their ratiocinations as from the understanding of truth: by the locusts having crowns like unto gold upon their heads, and having faces as the faces of men, is signified that they appeared to themselves as conquerors and as wise: by their having hair as the hair of women, is signified that they appeared to themselves as if they were in the affection of truth: by their having teeth as lions' teeth, is signified that sensual things, which are the ultimates of the natural man, appeared to them as if they had power over all things: by their having breast-plates as breast-plates of iron, are signified argumentations grounded in fallacies, by which they fight and prevail: by the sound of their wings being as the sound of chariots of horses running to battle, are signified ratiocinations as if grounded in the truths of doctrine from the Word, for which they were to combat: by their having tails as scorpions, are signified persuasions: by their having stings in their tails, are signified the cunning arts of deceiving thereby: by their having power to hurt men five months is signified that they induce a kind of stupor on those who are principled in the understanding of truth and in the perception of good: by their having a king over them, the angel of the bottomless pit, whose name is Abaddon or Apollyon, is signified that their falsities were from hell, the abode of those who are merely natural, and principled in self-intelligence. This is the spiritual sense of these words, whereof nothing appears in the sense of the letter: and the like spiritual sense is contained in every part of the book of the Apocalypse. It is to be observed, that, in the spiritual sense, the whole has a regular connexion and coherence, to effect and perfect which, each particular expression in the literal or natural sense is conducive, insomuch that if a single word were taken away, the connexion would be broken and the coherence perish; therefore to prevent this, it is added at the end of this prophetical book, that not a word shall be taken away (Apoc. xxii. 19). The case is similar in regard to the books of the prophets of the Old Testament; from which, lest any thing should be taken away, it was effected by the Divine Providence of the Lord, that each particular therein, even to the letters, should be counted or numbered; which was done by the Masorites.

14. Where the Lord speaks to His disciples about the consummation of the age, which is the last time of the church, at the end of His predictions concerning its successive changes of state, He says, "Immediately after the tribulation of those

days, shall the sun be darkened, and the moon shall not give her light, and the stars shall fall from heaven, and the powers of the heaven shall be taken. And then shall appear the sign of the Son of Man in heaven; and then shall all the tribes of the earth mourn, and they shall see the Son of Man coming in the clouds of heaven with power and great glory. And He shall send His angels with a great sound of a trumpet, and they shall gather together His elect from the four winds, from one end of heaven to the other" (Matt. xxiv. 29, 30, 31). By these words, in their spiritual sense, is not meant that the sun and the moon should be darkened, that the stars should fall from heaven, and that the sign of the Lord should appear in the heavens, and that He should be seen in the clouds, attended by His angels with trumpets; but by all these expressions are meant spiritual things relating to the church, of the final state or period of which, they are spoken. For, in the spiritual sense, by the sun which shall be darkened, is meant the Lord as to love; by the moon which shall not give her light, is meant the Lord as to faith; by the stars which shall fall from heaven, are meant the knowledges of truth and good which would perish; by the sign of the Son of Man in heaven, is meant the appearance of Divine Truth; by the tribes of the earth which shall mourn, is meant the failure of all truth which should be the object of faith, and of all good which should be the object of love; by the coming of the Son of Man in the clouds of heaven with power and glory, is meant the presence of the Lord in the Word, and revelation; by the clouds of heaven is signified the literal sense of the Word, and by glory, the spiritual sense; by the angels with a great sound of a trumpet, is meant heaven, whence Divine Truth comes; by gathering together the elect from the four winds from one end of heaven to the other, is meant a new church as to love and faith. That in this passage we are not to understand the darkening of the sun and moon, and the falling of the stars upon the earth, is evident from the writings of the prophets, where mention is made of the same circumstances in reference to the state of the church at the time when the Lord should come into the world; as in Isaiah: "Behold, the day of Jehovah cometh, cruel both with wrath and fierce anger; for the stars of heaven, and the constellations thereof, shall not give their light; the sun shall be darkened in his going forth, and the moon shall not cause her light to shine; and I will punish the world for their evil" (xiii. 9, 10, 11). And in Joel: "The day of Jehovah cometh,—a day of darkness—and of thick darkness. The sun and the moon shall be darkened, and the stars shall withdraw their shining" (ii. 1, 2; iii. 15). And in Ezekiel: "I will cover the heaven, and make the stars thereof dark; I will cover the sun with a cloud, and the moon shall not give her light; all the bright lights of heaven will I make dark over thee, and set darkness upon thy land" (xxxii. 7, 8). By the day of Jehovah is meant the Lord's advent, which was at a time when there was no longer any goodness and truth remaining in the church, nor any knowledge of the Lord.

15. In order to shew more clearly that the prophetical parts of the Word of the Old Testament are, in many places unintelligible without a spiritual sense, I shall here adduce a few passages; as this in Isaiah: "Jehovah of hosts shall stir up a scourge for him, according to the slaughter of Midian at the rock of Oreb; and as his rod was upon the sea, so shall he lift it up after the manner of Egypt. And it shall come to pass in that day, that his burden shall be taken away from off thy shoulder, and his yoke from off thy neck. He is come to Aiath, he shall pass to Migron, at Michmash he hath laid up his carriages. They are gone over the passage; they have taken up their lodging at Gebah; Ramah is afraid, Gibeah of Saul is fled. Lift up thy voice, O daughter of Gallim, cause it to be heard unto, O Laish, O poor Anathoth; Madmenah is removed; the inhabitants of Gebim gather themselves together; as yet shall he remain at Nob that day; he shall shake his hand against the mount of the daughter of Zion; the hill of Jerusalem; he shall cut down the thickets of the forest with iron, and Lebanon shall fall by a mighty one" (x. 26—34). In this passage there occur only mere names, from which no meaning can be drawn but by the help of the spiritual sense; in which sense, all names throughout the Word signify things appertaining to heaven and the church. By virtue of this sense is discovered the signification of the contents of the above passage, as denoting that the whole church was brought into devastation by means of scientifics perverting all truth, and confirming all falsity. Again, in the same prophet: "In that day the envy also of Ephraim shall depart, and the adversaries of Judah shall be cut off; Ephraim shall not envy Judah, and Judah shall not vex Ephraim; but they shall fly upon the shoulders of the Philistines toward the west, they shall spoil them of the east together; they shall lay their hand upon Edom and Moab. Jehovah shall utterly destroy the tongue of the Egyptian sea, and with his mighty wind shall He shake His hand over the river, and shall smite it in the seven streams, and make men go over dry-shod; and there shall be a highway for the remnant of His people which shall be left from Assyria" (xi. 13—16). In this passage, also, it is impossible to see any thing divine, unless it be known what is signified by each particular name, notwithstanding the subject here treated of is concerning the coming of the Lord, and what shall come to pass at that time, as plainly appears from verses 1—10: without the help therefore of the spiritual sense, how is it possible for any one to discern the genuine signification of these words in their

order, as denoting that they who through ignorance are principled in falses, and do not suffer themselves to be seduced by evils, will come to the Lord, and that the Word will then be understood by the church, and that falsities will then be no longer hurtful to them. The case is the same in those passages where no names occur, as in Ezekiel: "Thus saith the Lord Jehovah; Thou son of man, speak unto every feathered fowl, and to every beast of the field, Assemble yourselves, and come; gather yourselves from every side to my sacrifice which I do sacrifice for you, even a great sacrifice upon the mountains of Israel, that ye may eat flesh and drink blood. Ye shall eat the flesh of the mighty, and drink the blood of the princes of the earth;—ye shall eat fat till ye be full, and drink blood till ye be drunken, of my sacrifice which I have sacrificed for you. Ye shall be filled at my table with horses and chariots, with mighty men, and with all men of war. And I will set my glory amongst the heathen" (xxxix. 17—21). If it be not known by the spiritual sense what is signified by sacrifice, what by flesh and blood, what by horses and chariots, mighty men, and men of war, it must needs appear as if those things were to be eaten and drunken; but the spiritual sense teaches, that by eating flesh and drinking blood of the sacrifice which the Lord Jehovah shall sacrifice on the mountains of Israel, is signified to appropriate Divine Good and Divine Truth from the Word; for this passage treats of the calling together of all to the Lord's kingdom, and in particular of the establishment of the church amongst the Gentiles by the Lord. Who cannot see that by flesh is not here meant flesh, nor by blood, blood?—as where it is said that they should drink blood till they were drunken, and that they should be filled with horses, chariots, mighty men, and all men of war? The case is similar in a thousand other passages in the prophets.

16. Without the spiritual sense it is impossible for any one to know why the prophet Jeremiah was commanded to buy himself a girdle, and put it on his loins, and not to draw it through the waters, but to go to Euphrates, and hide it there in a hole in the rock (Jer. xiii. 1—7); or why Isaiah the prophet was commanded to loose the sackcloth from off his loins, and to put off his shoe from off his foot, and to go naked and barefoot three years (Isaiah xx. 2, 3.); or why Ezekiel the prophet was commanded to make a razor pass upon his head, and upon his beard, and afterwards to divide them, and to burn a third part in the midst of the city, and to smite a third part with the sword, and to scatter a third part in the wind, and to bind a little of them in his skirts, and at last to cast them into the midst of the fire (Ezek. v. 1—4); or why the same prophet was commanded to lie upon his left side three hundred and ninety days, and upon his right side forty days, and to make

himself a cake of wheat, and barley, and millet, and fitches, with cow's dung, and eat it; and in the meantime to raise a rampart and a mound against Jerusalem, and besiege it (Ezek. iv. 1—15); or why Hosea was twice commanded to take to himself a harlot to wife (Hosea i. 2—9; iii. 2, 3): with several other things of a like nature. Moreover, who can know, without the spiritual sense, what is signified by all things appertaining to the tabernacle; as by the ark, the mercy-seat, the cherubim, the candlestick, the altar of incense, the shew-bread on the table, and the vails and curtains? Or who would know, without the spiritual sense, what is signified by Aaron's holy garments; as by his coat, his cloak, the ephod, the urim and thummim, the mitre, and several things besides? Or, without the spiritual sense, who would know what is signified by all those particulars which were enjoined concerning burnt-offerings, sacrifices, meat-offerings, and drink-offerings; and also concerning sabbaths and feasts? The truth is, that nothing was enjoined, be it ever so minute, but what was significative of something appertaining to the Lord, to heaven, and to the church. From these few instances then it may be plainly seen, that there is a spiritual sense in all and every part of the Word.

17. That the Lord, during his abode in the world, spoke by correspondences, and thus both spiritually and naturally at the same time, may appear from His parables, in which every single expression contains in it a spiritual sense. As, for example, in the parable of the ten virgins, He says, "Then shall the kingdom of heaven be likened unto ten virgins, who took their lamps, and went forth to meet the bridegroom. And five of them were wise, and five were foolish: they that were foolish, took their lamps, and took no oil with them, but the wise took oil in their vessels with their lamps. Whilst the bridegroom tarried, they all slumbered and slept: and at midnight there was a cry made, Behold, the bridegroom cometh, go ye out to meet him. Then all those virgins arose, and trimmed their lamps; and the foolish said unto the wise, Give us of your oil, for our lamps are gone out: but the wise answered, saying, Not so, lest there be not enough for us and you: but go ye rather to them that sell, and buy for yourselves. And while they went to buy, the bridegroom came, and they that were ready went in with him to the marriage, and the door was shut. Afterwards came also the other virgins, saying, Lord, Lord, open to us; but He answered and said, Verily, I say unto you, I know you not" (Matt. xxv. 1—13). That there is a spiritual sense in every part of this parable, and consequently a divine holiness, can only be seen by those who are apprised of the existence of a spiritual sense, and are acquainted with its nature. In the spiritual sense, by the kingdom of God is meant heaven and the church; by the bridegroom, the Lord; by a

wedding, the marriage of the Lord with heaven and the church by the good of love and faith; by virgins, those who belong to the church; by ten, all; by five, some part; by lamps, the truths of faith; by oil, the good of love; by sleeping and awaking, the life of man in the world, which is natural life, and his life after death, which is spiritual; by buying, to procure for themselves; by going to them that sell and buying oil, to procure for themselves the good of love from others after death; and because this is then impracticable, therefore, although they came with their lamps and the oil they had bought to the marriage door, yet the bridegroom said unto them, "I know you not;" the reason is, because man, after the conclusion of his life in this world, retains the nature and quality which he had acquired by that life. From hence it is evident, that the Lord spoke by mere correspondences, and this in consequence of speaking from the Divinity which was in Him, and belonged to Him. That the bridegroom signifies the Lord, that the kingdom of God signifies heaven and the church, and that a marriage signifies the Lord's marriage with the church by the good of love and of faith; that virgins signify those who are of the church; ten, all; five, some; to sleep, a natural state; to buy, to procure for themselves; a door, entrance into heaven; and not to know, when spoken by the Lord, not to be principled in the love of Him;—all this may appear from many passages in the prophetical parts of the Word, where the same expressions have a similar signification. Because virgins signify those who belong to the church, therefore in the prophetical parts of the Word we find so frequent mention made of the virgin and daughter of Zion, of Jerusalem, of Judah, and of Israel; and because oil signifies the good of love, therefore all the holy things of the Israelitish church were anointed with oil. It is also similar in respect to the other parables, and all the words spoken by the Lord; and it was from this ground that the Lord declares that his "words are spirit and are life" (John vi. 63). The case is the same with all the Lord's miracles, which were divine, as signifying various states amongst those with whom the church was to be established by the Lord. Thus when the blind received sight, it signified, that they who were in ignorance of the truth should receive understanding; when the deaf received hearing, it signified, that they who had heard nothing before concerning the Lord, and concerning the Word, should hearken and obey: when the dead were raised, it signified, that they who otherwise would have spiritually perished should become alive: and so in other cases. This is meant by the Lord's reply to the disciples of John, who sent to ask whether He was He who should come: "Go and shew John again those things which ye do hear and see: the blind receive their sight, and the lame walk, the lepers are cleansed, and the deaf hear, the dead are raised up, and the poor have the Gospel preached to them" (Matt. xi. 3, 4, 5). Moreover, all the miracles related in the Word contain in them such things as relate to the Lord, to heaven, and the church; on which account they are divine miracles, and are distinguished from miracles not divine. These few observations may serve to illustrate the nature and meaning of the spiritual sense of the Word, and to shew that it exists in the whole of it, and in every part.

18. III. *That it is owing to the spiritual sense that the Word is divinely inspired, and holy in every syllable.* It is asserted in the church, that the Word is holy, inasmuch as Jehovah God spoke it; but because its holiness does not appear in its literal sense, they who once begin to doubt about its holiness on that account, in the future course of their reading confirm their doubts by many passages they meet with, suggesting these questions: "Can this be holy? Can this be divine?" In order therefore to prevent the influence of such doubts on men's minds, lest they should destroy the Lord's conjunction with the church that is in possession of the Word, it has pleased the Lord, at this time, to reveal its spiritual sense, for the purpose of discovering to mankind in what part of it its divine sanctity lies concealed. But to illustrate this, let us apply to examples. In the Word we find frequent mention made, sometimes of Egypt, sometimes of Assyria, sometimes of Edom, of Moab, of the children of Ammon, of Tyre and Sidon, and of Gog: they, now, who do not know that by those names things relating to heaven and the church are signified, may easily be led into the erroneous notion, that the Word treats much of people and nations, and but little of heaven and the church, thus much about earthly things, and but little about heavenly things; whereas, were such persons acquainted with what is signified by those people and nations, or by their names, this might be a means to lead them out of error into truth. In like manner, when it is observed, that in the Word frequent mention is made of gardens, groves, and woods; and also of the trees that grow therein, as the olive, the vine, the cedar, the poplar, and the oak; and also of lambs, sheep, goats, calves, oxen; and likewise of mountains, hills, valleys, fountains, rivers, waters, and the like: he who knows nothing of the spiritual sense of the Word must of necessity be led to suppose, that nothing further is meant by these things than what is expressed in the letter; for he little thinks that by a garden, a grove, and a wood, are meant wisdom, intelligence, and science; that by the olive, the vine, and the cedar, the poplar, and the oak, are meant the good and truth of the church, under the different qualities of celestial, spiritual, rational, natural, and sensual; that by a lamb, a sheep, a goat, a calf, and an ox, are meant innocence, charity, and natural affection; that by mountains, hills, and

valleys, are meant the higher, the lower, and the lowest things relating to the church. The case is in like manner altered, when the reader is aware, that by Egypt is signified what is scientific, by Assyria what is rational, by Edom what is natural, by Moab the adulteration of good, by the children of Ammon the adulteration of truth, by Tyre and Sidon the knowledges of goodness and truth, and by Gog external worship without internal. When the mind is opened to this knowledge, it may then be able to conceive that the Word treats solely of heavenly things, and that the earthly things mentioned in it are only the subjects wherein those heavenly ones are contained. But it may be expedient to illustrate this also by an example taken from the Word. It is written in David: "The voice of Jehovah is upon the waters: the God of glory thundereth; Jehovah is upon many waters; the voice of Jehovah breaketh the cedars: yea, Jehovah breaketh the cedars of Lebanon. He maketh them also to skip like a calf, Lebanon and Sirion, like a young unicorn: the voice of Jehovah divideth the flames of fire; the voice of Jehovah shaketh the wilderness, Jehovah shaketh the wilderness of Kadesh; the voice of Jehovah maketh the hinds to calve, and discovereth the forests; but in his temple doth every one speak of his glory" (Psalm xxix. 3—9). In this passage, if the reader is not aware that all the particulars thereof are holy and divine as to each single expression, he may say within himself, if he be a merely natural man, "What can this mean, that Jehovah sits upon the waters, that by His voice He breaks the cedars, that He causes them to skip like a calf, and Lebanon like a young unicorn; and that He causes the hinds to calve;" not to mention other particulars: for He knows not that the power of Divine Truth, or the Word, is described by these things in the spiritual sense; for in that sense, by the voice of Jehovah, which is there called thunder, is meant the Divine Truth or Word in its power; by the many waters on which Jehovah sits, are meant the truths thereof; by cedars and by Lebanon, which He breaks and bruises, are meant the falsities of the rational man; by a calf and a young unicorn, are meant the falsities of the natural and sensual man; by a flame of fire, the affection of falsity; by the wilderness, and the wilderness of Kadesh, the church where there is no truth and goodness; by hinds, which the voice of Jehovah causes to calve, are meant the Gentiles who are principled in natural good; and by the forests which He discovers, are meant the sciences and knowledges which the Word opens to them: wherefore it follows, that in His temple every one declares glory; by which is meant, that in all the particulars of the Word there are contained divine truths; for a temple signifies the Lord, and consequently the Word, and also heaven and the church, and glory signifies Divine Truth. Hence it appears, that there is not a single expression in this passage, but what describes the divine power of the Word put forth against falsities of every kind amongst natural men, and the divine power exerted in reforming the Gentiles.

19. There is in the Word a sense still more internal, which is called CELESTIAL, concerning which somewhat was said above, n. 6; but this sense cannot easily be unfolded, not being so much the object of intellectual thought, as of will-affection. The true ground and reason why there is in the Word a sense still more interior, which is called celestial, is, because from the Lord proceed Divine Good and Divine Truth, Divine Good from His Divine Love, and Divine Truth from His Divine Wisdom; each is in the Word, for the Word is the Divine proceeding. It is on this account that the Word imparts life to those that read it under holy influence: but more will be said on this subject in another place, where it will be shewn that a marriage of the Lord with the church, and consequently a marriage of goodness and truth, is contained in every particular of the Word.

20. IV. *That the spiritual sense of the Word has heretofore remained unknown.* That all things in nature, both in general and in particular, correspond to things spiritual, and, in like manner, all and singular the things in the human body, is shewn in the treatise concerning HEAVEN AND HELL, n. 87—105. But what is meant by correspondence, has to this day remained unknown, notwithstanding it was a subject most familiar to the men of the most ancient times, who esteemed it the chief of sciences, and cultivated it so universally, that all their books and tracts were written by correspondences. The book of Job, which was a book of the ancient church, is full of correspondences. The hieroglyphics of the Egyptians, and the fabulous stories of antiquity, were founded on the same science. All the ancient churches were churches representative of spiritual things; and their ceremonies, and also their statutes, which were rules for the institution of their worship, consisted of mere correspondences; in like manner, every thing in the Israelitish church, their burnt-offerings and sacrifices, with all the particulars belonging to each, were correspondences: so also was the tabernacle, with all things contained in it; and likewise their festivals, as the feast of unleavened bread, the feast of tabernacles, the feast of the first fruits; also the priesthood of Aaron and the Levites, and their garments of holiness; and beside the things above-mentioned, all their statutes and judgments, relating to worship and life, were correspondences. Now, forasmuch as divine things fix their existence in outward nature in correspondences, therefore the Word was written by mere correspondences; and for the same reason the Lord, in consequence of speaking from Divinity, spoke by correspondences:

for whatever proceeds from Divinity, when it comes into outward nature, manifests itself in such outward things as correspond with what is divine; which outward things become then the depositories of divine things, otherwise called celestial and spiritual, which lie concealed within them.

21. I have been informed, that the men of the Most Ancient Church, which was before the flood, were of so heavenly a genius, that they conversed with angels, and that they had the power of holding such converse by means of correspondences; hence the state of their wisdom became such, that, on viewing any of the objects of this world, they not only thought of them naturally, but also spiritually, thus in conjunction with the angels of heaven. I have been further informed, that Enoch, who is spoken of in Genesis, chap. v. 21—24, together with his associates, collected correspondences from the lips of the celestial men, and transmitted the science of them to posterity; in consequence of which, the science of correspondences was not only known in many kingdoms of Asia, but also much cultivated, particularly in the land of Canaan, Egypt, Assyria, Chaldea, Syria, and Arabia, and in Tyre, Sidon, and Nineveh; and that from thence it was conveyed into Greece, where it was changed into fable, as may appear from the works of the oldest writers of that country.

22. But as the representative rites of the church, which were correspondences, began in process of time to be corrupted by idolatrous and likewise magical applications of them, therefore the science of correspondences was, by the divine providence of the Lord, gradually lost, and amongst the Israelitish and Jewish people entirely obliterated. The divine worship of that people consisted indeed of mere correspondences, and consequently was representative of heavenly things; but still they had no knowledge of a single thing represented; for they were altogether natural men, and therefore had neither inclination nor ability to gain any knowledge of spiritual and celestial subjects: for the same reason they were necessarily ignorant of correspondences, these being representations of things spiritual and celestial in things natural.

23. The reason why the idolatries of the Gentiles of old took their rise from the science of correspondences, was, because all things that appear on the face of the earth have correspondence; consequently, not only trees and vegetables, but also beasts and birds of every kind; with fishes and all other things. The ancients, who were versed in the science of correspondences, made themselves images which corresponded with heavenly things; and were greatly delighted with them by reason of their signification, and because they could discern in them what related to heaven and the church: they therefore placed those images not only in their temples, but also in their houses;

not with any intention to worship them, but to serve as means of recollecting the heavenly things signified by them. Hence in Egypt, and in other places, they made images of calves, oxen, and serpents, and also of children, old men, and virgins; because calves and oxen signified the affections and powers of the natural man; serpents, the prudence of the sensual man; children, innocence and charity; old men, wisdom; and virgins, the affections of truth; and so in other instances. Succeeding ages, when the science of correspondences was obliterated, began to adore as holy, and at length to worship as deities, the images and resemblances set up by their forefathers, because they found them in and about their temples. The case was the same with other nations; as with the Philistines in Ashdod, whose god Dagon (concerning whom, see 1 Sam. v. 1 to the end) was, in its upper part, like a man, and in its lower part like a fish; the reason of which was, because a man signifies intelligence, and a fish science, which make a one. For the same reason, the ancients performed their worship in gardens and in groves, according to the different kinds of trees growing in them, and also on mountains and hills; for gardens and groves signified wisdom and intelligence, and every particular tree something that had relation thereto; as the olive, the good of love; the vine, truth derived from that good; the cedar, good and truth rational; a mountain signified the highest heaven; a hill, the heaven beneath. That the science of correspondences remained amongst many eastern nations, even till the coming of the Lord, may appear also from the wise men of the east who visited the Lord at His nativity; wherefore a star went before them, and they brought with them gifts, gold, frankincense, and myrrh (Matt. ii. 1, 2, 9, 10, 11); for the star which went before them signified knowledge from heaven; gold signified celestial good; frankincense, spiritual good; and myrrh, natural good; which are the three constituents of all worship. But still there was no knowledge whatever of the science of correspondences amongst the Israelitish and Jewish people, although all parts of their worship, and all the statutes and judgments given them by Moses, and all things contained in the Word, were mere correspondences: the reason was, because they were idolaters at heart, and consequently of such a nature and genius, that they were not even willing to know that any part of their worship had a celestial and spiritual signification, for they believed that all the parts of it were holy of themselves; wherefore had the celestial and spiritual significations been revealed to them, they would not only have rejected, but also have profaned them; for this reason heaven was so shut to them, that they scarcely knew whether there was such a thing as eternal life. That such was the case with them, appears evident from the circumstance, that they did not acknowledge

117

the Lord, although the whole Scripture throughout prophesied concerning Him, and foretold His coming; and they rejected Him solely on this account, because He instructed them about a heavenly kingdom, and not about an earthly one; for they wanted a Messiah who should exalt them above all nations in the world, and not a Messiah who should provide only for their eternal salvation. They affirm, however, that in the Word are contained many arcana, which are called mystical; but they have no inclination to learn that those arcana relate to the Lord. Tell them that they relate to gold, and they immediately desire to know them.

24. The reason why the science of correspondences, which is the key to the spiritual sense of the Word, was not discovered to later ages, was, because the Christians of the primitive church were men of such great simplicity, that it was impossible to discover it to them; for had it been discovered, they would have found no use in it, nor would they have understood it. After those first ages of Christianity, there arose thick clouds of darkness, and overspread the whole Christian world, in consequence of the establishment of the papal dominion; and they who are subject thereto, and have confirmed themselves in its false doctrines, have neither capacity nor inclination to apprehend anything of a spiritual nature, consequently, what is the nature of the correspondence of things natural with things spiritual in the Word: for by this they would be convinced, that by Peter is not meant Peter, but the Lord as a rock, signified by Peter: and they would also be convinced, that the Word, even to its inmost contents, is divine, and that the papal decrees respectively are of no account. But after the reformation, as men began to divide faith from charity, and to worship God under three persons, consequently, three gods, whom they conceive to be one, therefore at that time heavenly truths were concealed from them: for if they had been discovered they would have been falsified, and would have been abused to the confirmation of faith alone without being at all applied to charity and love: thus also men would have closed heaven against themselves.

25. The reason why the spiritual sense of the Word is at this day made known by the Lord, is, because the doctrine of genuine truth is now revealed; and this doctrine, and no other, agrees with the spiritual sense of the Word. This sense is likewise signified by the Lord's appearing in the clouds with glory and power (see Matthew xxiv. 30, 31: which treats of the consummation of the age, by which is meant the last time of the church). The opening of the Word as to its spiritual sense was also promised in the Apocalypse, and that sense is there meant by the white horse, and by the great supper to which all are invited (chap. xix. 11—18). That the spiritual sense for

a long time will not be acknowledged, and that this will be solely owing to the influence of those who are principled in fal sities of doctrine, particularly concerning the Lord, and therefore do not admit truths, is meant in the Apocalypse by the beast, and by the kings of the earth, who would make war with him that sat on the white horse (chap. xix. 19): by the beast are meant the Roman Catholics (as chap. xvii. 3); and by the kings of the earth are meant the Reformed, who are principled in falsities of doctrine.

26. V. *That hereafter the spiritual sense of the Word will be made known unto none, but those who are principled in genuine truths from the Lord.* The reason is, because no one can see the spiritual sense, except it be given him by the Lord alone, and except he be principled in divine truths from the Lord. For the spiritual sense of the Word treats solely of the Lord and of his kingdom, and that is the sense which his angels in heaven are in the perception of, for it is his divine truth there. This it is possible for man to violate, supposing him versed in the science of correspondences, and desirous thereby to explore the spiritual sense of the Word, under the influence of his own self-derived intelligence alone; for by some correspondences with which he is acquainted, he may pervert the spiritual sense, and force it even to confirm what is false; and this would be to offer violence to divine truth, and consequently to heaven also; wherefore, if any one wishes to open that sense by virtue of his own power, and not of the Lord's, heaven is closed against him; in which case he either loses sight of all truth, or falls into spiritual insanity. To this may be added another reason, namely, that the Lord teaches every one by means of the Word, and grounds his teaching on the knowledges which man is in possession of, never infusing new ones immediately; wherefore unless a man be principled in divine truths, or if he be only in possession of a few truths, and in falsities at the same time, he may falsify truths by falsities, as is done by every heretic, as is well known, with regard to the literal sense of the Word. To prevent, therefore, any person from entering into the spiritual sense, and perverting the genuine truth which belongs to that sense, there are guards set by the Lord, which are signified in the Word by the cherubs. This was made known to me by the following representation: "It was given to me to see great purses which had the appearance of bags, in which money was stored up in great abundance: and as they were open, it seemed as if any one might take out, yea, steal away, the money therein deposited; but near those two purses sat two angels as guards. The place where they were laid appeared like a manger in a stable. In a neighbouring apartment were seen modest virgins with a chaste wife; and near that apartment stood two infants, and information was given that they were to be treated in their

sports, not in a childish way, but according to wisdom. Afterwards there appeared a harlot; and, lastly, a horse lying dead On seeing these things I was instructed, that thereby was represented the literal sense of the Word, in which is contained the spiritual sense. Those large purses full of money signified the knowledges of truth in great abundance. Their being open, and yet guarded by angels, signified that any one might take thence the knowledges of truth, but that there was need of caution lest he should falsify the spiritual sense, in which are naked truths. The manger in the stable, in which the purses lay, signified spiritual instruction for the understanding; this is the signification of a manger, because a horse that feeds there signifies understanding. The modest virgins who were seen in a neighbouring apartment, signified the affections of truth; and the chaste wife signified the conjunction of goodness and truth. The infants signified the innocence of wisdom therein; they were angels from the third heaven, who all appear as infants. The harlot with the dead horse, signified the falsification of the Word by many at this day, whereby all understanding of the Word is destroyed: a harlot signifies falsification, and a dead horse signifies the non-understanding of truth."

---

### III. THAT THE LITERAL SENSE OF THE WORD IS THE BASIS, THE CONTINENT, AND THE FIRMAMENT, OF ITS SPIRITUAL AND CELESTIAL SENSES.

27. In every divine work there is a first, a middle, and a last, and the first passes through the middle to the last, and thereby exists and subsists; hence the last is the basis. The first also is in the middle, and by means of the middle in the last; and thus the last is the continent. And because the last is the continent and the basis, it is also the firmament.

28. The learned reader will be able to comprehend the propriety of calling those three, end, cause, and effect, and also *esse*, *fieri*, and *existere*;* and that the end answers to *esse*, the cause to *fieri*, and the effect to *existere*; consequently, that in every complete thing there is a trinity, which is called first, middle and last; likewise end, cause, and effect; and also, *esse*, *fieri*, and *existere*. He who comprehends this reasoning will be able to comprehend also, that every divine work is complete and perfect in the last; and likewise that in the last is contained the whole, because the prior things are contained together in it.

29. From this ground it is, that by the number three, in the Word, according to its spiritual sense, is signified what is

* These terms literally signify, *to be*, *to become*, and *to exist*.

complete and perfect; and also, the all or whole together. Because this is the signification of that number, therefore it is so frequently applied in the Word, when that signification is intended to be expressed; as in the following places: Isaiah was to go naked and barefoot *three years* (Isaiah xx. 3); Jehovah called Samuel *three times*, and Samuel ran *three times* to Eli, and Eli understood him the *third time* (1 Sam. iii. 1—8); David said to Jonathan, that he would hide himself in the field *three days;* and Jonathan afterwards shot *three arrows* beside the stone; and David, lastly, bowed himself *three times* before Jonathan (1 Sam. xx. 5, 12—42); Elijah stetched himself *three times* on the widow's son (1 Kings xvii. 21); Elijah commanded to pour water on the burnt-offering *three times* (1 Kings xviii. 34); "Jesus said, The kingdom of heaven is like unto leaven, which a woman took and hid in *three measures* of meal, till the whole was leavened" (Matt. xiii. 33); Jesus said to Peter, that he should deny Him *thrice* (Matt. xxvi. 34); Jesus said *three times* unto Peter, Lovest thou me? (John xxi. 15, 16, 17). Jonah was in the whale's belly *three days and three nights* (Jonah i. 17); "Jesus said, Destroy this temple, and in *three days* I will raise it up" (John ii. 19); Jesus prayed *three times* in the garden of Gethsemane (Matt. xxvi. 39—44); Jesus rose again on the *third day* (Matt. xxviii. 1); beside many other passages, where the number three is mentioned; and it is mentioned where a work finished and perfect is the subject treated of, because such a work is signified by that number.

30. These observations are premised with a view to the conclusions which follow, in order that they may be intellectually comprehended; particularly at present, that it may be fully understood, that the natural sense of the Word, which is its literal sense, is the basis, continent, and firmament, of its spiritual and celestial senses.

31. That in the Word there are three senses, was shewn above, n. 6, 19; also, that the celestial sense is its first sense, the spiritual sense its middle sense, and the natural sense its last sense.: hence the rational man may conclude, that the first, which is celestial, passes by its middle, which is spiritual, to its last, which is natural; and that thus its last is the basis: also, that its first, which is celestial, is in its middle, which is spiritual, and by this in its last, which is natural; and hence its last which is natural, and is the literal sense of the Word, is the continent; and whereas it is the continent and basis, that it is also the firmament.

32. But how these things are, would require many pages to explain fully, as they are arcana of heaven, and subjects of angelic contemplation; nevertheless, they will be elucidated as far as possible, in the treatises ON ANGELIC WISDOM CONCERNING THE DIVINE LOVE AND WISDOM, and CONCERNING THE

DIVINE PROVIDENCE. It is sufficient for the present, if, from what has been said above, we are enabled to draw this conclusion: that in the Word, which is a divine work expressly given for the salvation of mankind, the ultimate sense, which is natural, and is called the literal sense, is the basis, continent, and firmament of the two interior senses.

33. Hence it follows, that the Word, without its literal sense, would be like a palace without a foundation; that is, like a palace in the air and not on the ground, which could only be the shadow of a palace, and must vanish away; also, that the Word, without its literal sense, would be like a temple in which there are many holy things, and in the midst thereof the holy of holies, without a roof and walls to form the continents thereof; in which case its holy things would be plundered by thieves, or be violated by the beasts of the earth and the birds of heaven, and thus be dissipated. In the same manner, it would be like the tabernacle, in the inmost place whereof was the ark of the covenant, and in the middle part the golden candlestick, the golden altar for incense, and also the table for shew-bread, which were its holy things, without its ultimates, which were the curtains and vails. Yea, the Word without its literal sense would be like the human body without its coverings, which are called skins, and without its supporters, which are called bones, of which, supposing it to be deprived, its inner parts must of necessity be dispersed and perish. It would also be like the heart and the lungs in the thorax, deprived of their covering, which is called the *pleura*, and their supporters, which are called the ribs; or like the brain without its coverings, which are called the *dura mater* and *pia mater*, and without its common covering, continent, and firmament, which is called the skull. Such would be the state of the Word without its literal sense; wherefore it is said in Isaiah, that "the Lord will create upon all the glory a covering" (iv. 5).

34. Similar to this would be the state of the heavens, where the angels dwell, without the world, where men dwell; mankind being the basis, continent, and firmament thereof, and the Word being with men and in them. For all the heavens are distinguished into two kingdoms, which are called the celestial kingdom and the spiritual kingdom; and these two kingdoms are founded on the natural kingdom, the subjects of which are men. That the angelic heavens are distinguished into two kingdoms, the celestial and the spiritual, may be seen in the treatise on HEAVEN AND HELL, n. 20—28.

35. That the prophets of the Old Testament represented the Lord as to the Word, and thereby signified the doctrine of the church derived from the Word, and that hence they were called sons of man, was shewn in the DOCTRINE RESPECTING THE LORD, n. 28; whence it follows, that by the the various things

which they suffered and endured, they represented the violence offered by the Jews to the literal sense of the Word; as where Isaiah was commanded to put off the sackcloth from his loins, and his shoes from his feet, and to go naked and barefoot three years (Isaiah xx. 2, 3); in like manner where Ezekiel was commanded to take a barber's razor, and cause it to pass upon his head and upon his beard, and to burn a third part in the midst of the city, and to smite a third part with the sword, and to disperse a third part to the wind, and to bind a little thereof in his skirts, and at length to cast it in the midst of the fire and burn it (Ezek. v. 1—4). The ground and reason of this signification and representation, is, because by the head is signified wisdom derived from the Word, hence by the hair and by the beard is signified the ultimate of truth. In consequence of this signification it was a mark of great mourning, and also a great disgrace, for any one to make himself bald, and likewise to appear bald. For this cause, and no other, the prophet was directed to shave the hair of his head and his beard, that thereby he might represent the state of the Jewish church as to the Word: this, too, and no other, was the reason, why the forty and two children, who called Elisha bald head, were torn in pieces by two bears (2 Kings ii. 23, 24, 25); for the prophet, as was before observed, represented the Word, and baldness signifies the Word without its ultimate sense. That the Nazarites represented the Lord as to the Word in its ultimates, will be seen below, n. 49; and therefore it was an ordinance with them that they should cause their hair to grow, and should shave no part of it: the term Nazarite, also, in the Hebrew tongue, signifies the head of hair. It was also an ordinance for the high priest, that he should not shave his head (Levit. xxi. 10); and in like manner for the father of a family (Levit. xxi. 5). Hence it was that baldness was esteemed a great disgrace; as may appear from the following passages: "On all their heads shall be *baldness*, and every beard shall be cut off" (Isaiah xv. 2; Jerem. xlviii. 37). "Shame shall be upon all faces, and *baldness* upon all their heads" (Ezek. vii. 18). "Every head was made *bald*, and every shoulder was peeled" (Ezek. xxix. 18). "I will bring up sackcloth upon all loins, and *baldness* upon every head" (Amos viii. 10). "Make thee *bald*, and poll thee for thy delicate children, enlarge thy *baldness* as the eagle; for they are gone into captivity from thee" (Micah i. 16); where, by putting on and enlarging baldness, is signified to falsify the truths of the Word in its ultimates; for when these are falsified, as was done by the Jews, the whole Word is destroyed; for the ultimates of the Word are its props and supports, yea, every single expression is a prop and support of its celestial and spiritual truths. As hair of the head signifies truth in its ultimates, therefore, in the spiritual world.

all who despise the Word, and falsify its literal sense, appear bald; but they who honor and love it, appear adorned with decent and becoming hair. On this subject see also below, n. 49.

36. The Word in its ultimate or natural sense, which is the sense of the letter, is signified also by the wall of the holy Jerusalem; the building whereof was jasper; and by the foundations of the wall, which were precious stones; and also by the gates, which were pearls (Rev. xxi. 18—21); for by Jerusalem is signified the church as to doctrine; but more may be seen on this subject in the following article. From what has been here observed it may appear, that the literal sense of the Word, which is its natural sense, is the basis, continent, and firmament, of its interior senses which are spiritual and celestial.

---

## IV. THAT IN THE LITERAL SENSE OF THE WORD, DIVINE TRUTH IS IN ITS FULNESS, IN ITS SANCTITY, AND IN ITS POWER.

37. The reason why the Word, in its literal sense, is in its fulness, in its sanctity, and in its power, is, because the two prior or interior senses, which are called the spiritual and celestial senses, are simultaneously contained in the natural sense, which is the sense of the letter, as was said above, n. 29; but in what manner they are so simultaneously contained shall be now shewn.

38. Both in heaven and in the world, there are two kinds of order, successive order, and simultaneous order. In successive order one thing succeeds and follows another, from what is highest to what is lowest; but in simultaneous order one thing adjoins to another, from what is innermost to what is outermost. Successive order is like a column with degrees from highest to lowest; but simultaneous order is like a work whose centre and circumferences have a regular coherence, all the way to the surface. We shall now shew in what manner successive order becomes, in its ultimates, simultaneous order, which is thus: the highest parts of successive order become the inmost of simultaneous order, and the lowest parts of successive order become the outermost of simultaneous order, just as would be the case with a column of degrees, were it to sink down and become a coherent body in a plane. Thus what is simultaneous is formed from what is successive; and this is the case in all and every thing in the natural world, and in all and every thing in the spiritual world; for there is every where a first, a middle,

and a last; and the first, by means of the middle, tends and proceeds to the last. To apply now this reasoning to the Word: the celestial, spiritual, and natural principles proceed from the Lord in successive order, and in their last, or ultimate, they are in simultaneous order: thus, then, the celestial and spiritual senses of the Word are simultaneously contained in its natural sense. When this truth is comprehended, it will be easy to see how the natural sense of the Word, which is its literal sense, is the continent, basis, and firmament, of its spiritual and celestial senses: and also, in what manner divine good and divine truth, in the literal sense of the Word, are in their fulness, in their sanctity, and in their power.

39. From hence it must appear evident, that the Word is pre-eminently the Word in its literal sense; for in this sense, spirit, and life are inwardly contained; and this is what the Lord meant when he said, "The words which I speak unto you, they are spirit and they are life" (John vi. 63); for the Lord spoke his words before the world, and in the natural sense. The celestial and spiritual senses are not the Word without the natural sense, which is the sense of the letter; for in such case they would be like spirit and life without a body; or, as was said above, n. 33, like a palace which has no foundation.

40. The truths of the literal sense of the Word are, in some cases, not naked truths, but only appearances of truth, and are like similitudes and comparisons taken from the objects of nature, and thus accommodated and brought down to the apprehension of simple minds and of children. But whereas they are at the same time correspondences, they are the receptacles and abodes of genuine truth; and they are like containing vessels,—like a crystalline cup containing excellent wine, or a silver dish containing rich meats; or they are like garments clothing the body,—like swaddling clothes on an infant, or an elegant dress on a beautiful virgin: they are also like the scientifics of the natural man, which comprehend in them the perceptions and affections of truth of the spiritual man. The naked truths themselves, which are included, contained, attired, and comprehended, are in the spiritual sense of the Word, and the naked principles of good are in its celestial sense. But let us illustrate this by instances from the Word. Jesus said, "Wo unto you, Scribes and Pharisees, hypocrites! for ye make clean the outside of the cup and of the platter, but within they are full of extortion and excess; thou blind Pharisee! cleanse first that which is within the cup and platter, that the outside of them may be clean also" (Matt. xxiii. 25, 26). In this passage the Lord spoke by ultimates, or things of the lowest order, which at the same time are continents: he uses the words "cup and platter," because by the cup is meant wine, and by wine is signified the truth of the Word; and by the platter is meant

meat, and by meat is signified the good of the Word; wherefore by making clean the inside of the cup and platter, is signified to purify the interiors of the mind, which relate to the will and the thoughts, thus to the love and faith, by means of the Word; and by the consequent cleansing of the outside is signified, that thus the exteriors are purified, which are the words and works, inasmuch as these derive their essence from the former. Again: Jesus said, "There was a certain rich man, who was clothed in purple and fine linen, and fared sumptuously every day; and there was a certain beggar, named Lazarus, who was laid at his gate, full of sores" (Luke xvi. 19, 20). In this passage also, the Lord spoke by natural things, which were correspondences, and contained in them spiritual things: by the rich man is meant the Jewish nation, who are called rich, because they were in possession of the Word, in which there are spiritual riches; by the purple and fine linen, with which the rich man was clothed, are signified the good and truth of the Word; by purple its good, and by fine linen its truth; by faring sumptuously every day, is signified the delight which the Jewish people took in possessing and reading the Word; by the beggar Lazarus are meant the Gentiles, because they were not in possession of the Word; by Lazarus lying at the rich man's gate, is meant that the Gentiles were despised and rejected by the Jews; by being full of sores, is signified that the Gentiles, by reason of their ignorance of truth, were in many falsities. The reason why the Gentiles are meant by Lazarus, is, because the Gentiles were beloved by the Lord, as was Lazarus whom he raised from the dead (John xi. 3, 5, 26); who is called his friend (John xi. 11); and who sat with him at table (John xii. 2). From these two passages it is evident, that the truths and goods of the literal sense of the Word are like vessels and garments, to contain and cover the naked good and truth, which are concealed in the spiritual and celestial senses.

41. Since the Word, in its literal sense, is of such a nature, it follows of consequence, that they who are principled in divine truths, and in a belief that the Word, in its internal parts, is divine and holy, see divine truths in natural light, whilst they read the Word in a state of illustration from the Lord, and more especially if they believe that the Word is of such a nature by virtue of its spiritual and celestial senses; for the light of heaven, in which the spiritual sense of the Word is, descends by influx into the natural light, in which the literal sense of the Word is, and illuminates the intellectual principle of man, which is called his rational principle, and makes him see and acknowledge divine truths, both where they are manifest, and where they are concealed. This effect of the influx of light from heaven, takes place with some, even when they are not aware of it.

42. As the Word, in its inmost contents, by virtue of its celestial sense, is like a gentle burning flame, and in its middle contents, by virtue of its spiritual sense, is like an illustrating light; it follows hence, that in its ultimate or last contents, by virtue of its natural sense, in which are the two other senses, it is like a ruby, and like a diamond; by virtue of the celestial flame like a ruby, and by virtue of the spiritual light like a diamond. And since this is the nature and quality of the Word in its literal sense, therefore the Word is meant, in that sense, by the precious stones of which the foundations of the New Jerusalem were built; also by the urim and thummim on the ephod of Aaron; and likewise by the precious stones in the garden of Eden, wherein the king of Tyre is said to have been; and further, by the curtains and vails of the tabernacle; in like manner, by the external part of the temple at Jerusalem. And the Word, in all its glory, was represented in the person of the Lord, when he was transfigured.

43. I. *That the truths of the literal sense of the Word are meant by the precious stones of which the foundations of the New Jerusalem were built, as mentioned in the Apocalypse*, chap. xxi. 17—21, follows from this circumstance; that by the New Jerusalem is signified the New Church in respect to doctrine derived from the Word, as is shewn in the DOCTRINE OF THE LORD, n. 62, 63; wherefore, by its wall, and the foundations of the wall, nothing can be meant but the external of the Word, which is its literal sense; for it is this sense from which doctrine is derived, and, by doctrine, the church; and this sense is like a wall with its foundations, that encompasses and secures the city. The New Jerusalem and its foundations are thus described in the Apocalypse: "The angel measured the wall thereof, a hundred forty and four cubits, according to the measure of a man, that is, of an angel. And the wall had twelve foundations, garnished with all manner of precious stones. The first foundation was a jasper; the second, a sapphire; the third, a chalcedony; the fourth, an emerald; the fifth, a sardonyx; the sixth, a sardius; the seventh, a chrysolite; the eighth, a beryl; the ninth, a topaz; the tenth, a chrysoprasus; the eleventh, a jacinth; the twelfth, an amethyst" (xxi. 17—20). By the number one hundred and forty-four, are signified all the truths and goods of the church derived from doctrine grounded in the literal sense of the Word; the same is signified by twelve; by a man is signified intelligence; by an angel is signified the Divine Truth, whence intelligence is derived; by measure is signified their quality; by a wall and its foundations is signified the sense of the letter of the Word; and by precious stones, the truths and goods of the Word in their order, from whence doctrine is derived, and, by doctrine, the church.

44. II. *That the truths and goods of the literal sense of the Word are meant by the urim and thummim.* The urim and thummim were on Aaron's ephod, whose priesthood was representative of the Lord with respect to Divine Good, and the work of salvation. By the garments of the priesthood, or of holiness, was represented Divine Truth from Divine Good; by the ephod was represented Divine Truth in its last or ultimate state, consequently, the Word in its literal sense, for this is Divine Truth in its ultimate, as was shewn above; hence by the twelve precious stones, with the names of the twelve tribes of Israel, which were the urim and thummim, were represented Divine Truths, as derived from Divine Good, in their whole complex. Concerning the ephod, with the urim and thummim, Moses has these words: "They shall make the ephod of gold, of blue, and of purple, of scarlet and fine twined linen, with cunning work; and they shall make the breast-plate of judgment with cunning work, after the work of the ephod, and shall set it in settings of stones, even four rows of stones. The first row shall be a sardius, a topaz, and a carbuncle; and the second row shall be an emerald, a sapphire, and a diamond; and the third row, a ligure, an agate, and an amethyst; and the fourth row, a beryl, an onyx, and a jasper; and the stones shall be according to the names of the children of Israel; the engravings of a signet, every one with his name, they shall be according to the twelve tribes; and Aaron shall bear the judgment of the children of Israel upon his heart, before Jehovah, continually" (Exod. xxviii. 6, 15—21, 30). What is represented by Aaron's garments, his ephod, his robe, his coat, his mitre, and his belt, is explained in the work entitled ARCANA CŒLESTIA; where, in treating on that chapter, it is shewn, that by the ephod is represented Divine Truth in its last or ultimate; by the precious stones therein are signified truths transparent by virtue of good; by twelve precious stones, all ultimate truths rendered transparent by the good of love in its order; by the twelve tribes of Israel, all things relating to the church; by the breast-plate, Divine Truth derived from Divine Good: by the urim and thummim, the brilliancy of Divine Truth derived from Divine Good in its ultimates: for urim signifies a shining fire, and thummim, brilliancy, in the angelic tongue, and, in the Hebrew tongue, integrity. In the same work it is also shewn, that responses were given by variegations of light, accompanied by a tacit perception, or by an audible voice; with many other circumstances. Hence it may appear evident, that by those stones were likewise signified truths derived from good in the ultimate sense of the Word; nor are responses from heaven given by any other means, inasmuch as in that sense the Divine Proceeding is in its fulness. That precious stones and diadems signify Divine Truths in their ultimates, such as

are the truths of the literal sense of the Word, was made manifest to me from the precious stones and diadems which I saw in the spiritual world amongst the angels and spirits there: they served in some cases for ornaments of dress, and in others they were deposited in cabinets, and it was given me to know, that they corresponded to truths in the ultimates, nay, that they even had thence their origin and brilliant appearance. It was by reason of their bearing such a signification, that crowns were seen by John on the head of the dragon (Apoc. xii. 3); and on the horns of the beast (Apoc. xiii. 1); and that precious stones were seen on the harlot who sat on the scarlet beast (Apoc. xvii. 4). Such ornaments were seen by John, because by the dragon, the beast, and the harlot, are signified those in the Christian world who are in possession of the Word.

45. III. *That the truths of the literal sense of the Word are meant by the precious stones in the garden of Eden, wherein the king of Tyre is said to have been.* It is written in Ezekiel: "King of Tyrus, thou sealest up thy sum, full of wisdom and perfect in beauty; thou hast been in Eden, the garden of God: every precious stone was thy covering; the sardius, the topaz, and the diamond; the beryl, the onyx, and the jasper; the sapphire, the emerald, and the carbuncle; and gold" (xxviii. 12, 13). By Tyrus, in the Word, are signified the knowledges of good and truth; by a king is signified the truth of the church; by the garden of Eden are signified wisdom and intelligence derived from the Word; by precious stones are signified truths, such as are in the literal sense of the Word, bright and transparent by virtue of good; and because these are signified by those stones, therefore they are called his covering; for that the literal sense of the Word serves as a covering for the interior senses, may be seen above.

46. IV. *That the literal sense of the Word is signified by the curtains and vails of the tabernacle.* By the tabernacle, heaven and the church were represented, wherefore the pattern of it was shewn to Moses by Jehovah on Mount Sinai. Hence by all things contained in that tabernacle, as the candlestick, the golden altar for incense, and the table whereon was the shewbread, were represented and signified the holy things of heaven and the church; by the holy of holies, where was the ark of the covenant, was represented and thence signified the inmost of heaven and the church; and by the law written on two tables, and inclosed in the ark, the Lord as respects the Word was signified. Now as externals derive their essence from internals, and both the one and the other from what is inmost, which in the tabernacle was the law, therefore the holy things of the Word were represented and signified by all things belonging to the tabernacle: hence it follows, that by the ultimates of the tabernacle, as the curtains and the vails, which

were its coverings and continents, are signified the ultimates of the Word, which are the truths and goods of its literal sense; and because those things were signified, therefore all the curtains and vails were made of fine twined linen, and blue, and scarlet double-dyed, with cherubs (Exod. xxvi. 1, 31, 36). The general and particular representations and significations of the tabernacle, and all that was in it, are explained in the ARCANA CŒLESTIA. It is there shewn, in treating on that chapter of Exodus, that by the curtains and vails were represented the externals of heaven and the church, consequently also the externals of the Word; and, further, that by fine linen is signified truth from a spiritual origin; by blue, truth from a celestial origin; by purple, celestial good; by double-dyed scarlet, spiritual good; and by cherubs, the guards of the interiors of the Word.

47. V. *That the externals of the Word, or the things appertaining to the literal sense, were represented by the externals of the temple at Jerusalem.* The reason of this is, because the temple, as well as the tabernacle, was representative of heaven and the church, and thence, also, of the Word. That by the temple at Jerusalem was signified the Divine Humanity of the Lord, He Himself teaches in these words: "Destroy this temple, and in three days I will raise it up;—but He spake of *the temple of His body*" (John ii. 19, 21): and wherever the Lord is meant, there also the Word is meant, inasmuch as He is the Word. Now, since the interiors of the temple were representative of the interiors of heaven and the church, and so also of the Word, therefore its exteriors were representative and significative of the exteriors of heaven and the church, and consequently of the exteriors of the Word, which are its literal sense. Concerning the exteriors of the temple it is written, that they were built of whole stones not hewn, and of cedar within, and that all its walls within were carved with figures of cherubs, palm-trees, and openings of flowers; and that the floor was overlaid with gold (1 Kings vi. 7, 29, 30); by all which are likewise signified the externals of the Word, which are the holy things of its literal sense.

48. VI. *That the Word in its glory was represented in the person of the Lord at His transfiguration.* Concerning the Lord's transfiguration in the presence of Peter, James, and John, it is written, "That His face did shine as the sun, and that His raiment was as the light; and there appeared Moses and Elias talking with Him; and that a bright cloud overshadowed Him: and that a voice came out of the cloud, saying, This is my beloved Son, hear ye Him" (Matt. xvii. 1—5). I have been informed, that the Lord, on this occasion, represented the Word: by His face, which shone as the sun, was represented His Divine Good; by His raiment which was as the light, His Divine

Truth; by Moses and Elias, the historical and prophetical Word; by Moses, the Word which was written by him, and in general the historical Word, and by Elias, the whole prophetical Word; by the bright cloud which overshadowed the disciples, the Word in its literal sense; wherefore out of this a voice was heard, saying, "This is my beloved Son, hear ye Him:" for all declarations and responses from heaven are constantly delivered by means of ultimates, such as are in the literal sense of the Word; for they are delivered in fulness from the Lord.

49. Thus far we have shewn, that the Word in its natural sense, which is the sense of the letter, is in its sanctity and in its fulness; something now shall be said to shew, that the Word in that sense is in its *power*. What and how great is the power of the Divine Truth in the heavens, and also on earth, may appear from what is said, in the treatise ON HEAVEN AND HELL, concerning the power of the angels of heaven (n. 228—233). The power of the Divine Truth operates especially against falsities and evils, consequently against the hells: whoever engages in combat against these, must support it by truths from the literal sense of the Word. The Lord's power of saving, also, is exerted by means of the truths which are with man; for by truths derived from the literal sense of the Word, man is reformed and regenerated, and is then taken out of hell, and introduced into heaven. This power the Lord took upon Him even as to His Divine Humanity, after He had fulfilled all the contents of the Word even to its ultimates; wherefore he said to the high-priest, speaking of the time when, by the passion of the cross, He should have completed what remained to be fulfilled, "Hereafter ye shall see the Son of Man sitting on the right hand of power, and coming in the clouds of heaven" (Matt. xxvi. 64; Mark xiv. 62). The Son of Man is the Lord as to the Word; the clouds of heaven signify the Word in the sense of the letter; to sit on the right hand of God is omnipotence by the Word; as also Mark xvi. 19. The power of the Word, in its ultimates, was represented by the Nazarites in the Jewish church, and by Samson, of whom it is said, that he was a Nazarite from his mother's womb, and that his strength lay in his hair; by the word Nazarite, and Nazariteship, also, is signified hair. That Samson's strength lay in his hair, is plain from his own words: "There hath not come a razor upon my head, for I have been a Nazarite unto God from my mother's womb; if I be shaven, then my strength will go from me, and I shall become weak, and be like any other man" (Judges xvi. 17). It is impossible for any one to know why the Nazariteship, by which is signified hair, was instituted, and on what ground it was that Samson derived strength from his hair, unless he is first acquainted with the signification of the head in the

Word: by the head is signified intelligence, which angels and men have from the Lord by means of Divine Truth; hence by the hair is signified celestial wisdom in its ultimates, and also Divine Truth in its ultimates. As this is the signification of hair from its correspondence with the heavens, therefore it was ordained as a law for the Nazarites, That they should not shave the hair of their heads, because that is the Nazariteship of God upon their heads (Numb. vi. 1—21). For the same reason it was likewise ordained, that the high priest and his sons should not shave their heads, lest they should die, and wrath should come upon the whole house of Israel (Levit. x. 6). Since the hair, by reason of this signification, grounded in correspondence, was so holy, therefore the *Son of Man*, who is the Lord in respect to the Word, is described even as to His hairs, that they "were white like wool, as white as snow" (Apoc. i. 14); in like manner the *Ancient of days* is described (Dan. vii. 9). On this subject also something may be seen above, n. 35. In fine, the reason why the power of Divine Truth, or the Word, resides in its literal sense, is, because the Word in that sense is in its fulness, and the angels of both the Lord's kingdoms, and men on earth, are in that sense simultaneously.

---

## V. THAT THE DOCTRINE OF THE CHURCH OUGHT TO BE DRAWN FROM THE LITERAL SENSE OF THE WORD, AND TO BE CONFIRMED THEREBY.

50. It was shewn in the foregoing article, that the Word, in its literal sense, is in its fulness, in its holiness, and in its power: and since the Lord is the Word, being the all of the Word, it follows that the Lord, in that sense, is most eminently present, and that from that sense he teaches and enlightens mankind. But the truth of this will fall under the following propositions: I. *That the Word, without doctrine, cannot be understood.* II. *That doctrine ought to be drawn from the literal sense of the Word.* III. *But that divine truth, which doctrine is to teach, appears to none but those who are in illustration from the Lord.*

51. I. *That the Word, without doctrine, cannot be understood.* The reason is, because the Word, in its literal sense, consists of mere correspondences, to the end that spiritual and celestial things may be simultaneously in it, and that every single expression may afford them a continent and support; therefore divine truths in the literal sense are rarely found naked, but clothed; in which state they are called the appearances of truth, and are more accommodated to the apprehension of the simple, who are not used to any elevation of their thoughts

above visible objects. There are also some things which appear like contradictions, when nevertheless there is not a single contradiction in the Word, if it be viewed in its own spiritual light. In some parts, likewise, of the prophetic writings, there is a collection of names of places and persons, from which in the letter no sense can be gathered, as in the passages above adduced, n. 15. Such, then, being the nature of the Word in its literal sense, it must be very evident, that without doctrine it cannot possibly be understood. But this will be best illustrated by examples. It is said, for instance, "that Jehovah repenteth" (Exod. xxxii. 12, 14; Jonah iii. 9; iv. 2); and it is also said, "that Jehovah doth not repent" (Numb. xxiii. 19: 1 Sam. xv. 29); which apparently contradictory passages without doctrine, are not reconcileable. It is said, that Jehovah visiteth "the iniquity of the fathers upon the children, to the third and fourth generation" (Numb. xiv. 18); and it is likewise said, "that the fathers shall not be put to death for the children, neither the children for the fathers, but every man shall be put to death for his own sin" (Deut. xxiv. 16). These passages, without doctrine, seem contradictory, but when illustrated by doctrine, they are in perfect agreement. Jesus saith, "Ask, and it shall be given you; seek, and ye shall find; knock, and it shall be opened unto you." Without doctrine, it might be supposed, from these words, that every one would certainly receive what he requests; but doctrine teaches, that whatsoever a man asks, not from himself, but from the Lord. that is granted him; for thus the Lord explains himself: "If ye abide in me, and my words abide in you, ye shall ask what ye will, and it shall be done unto you" (John xv. 7). The Lord says, "Blessed are the poor, for theirs is the kingdom of God" (Luke vi. 20). Without doctrine it may be imagined, that heaven is designed for the poor, and not for the rich: but doctrine teaches that the poor in spirit are here meant; for the Lord says in another place, "Blessed are the poor in spirit, for theirs is the kingdom of heaven" (Matt. v. 5). Again, the Lord says, "Judge not, that ye be not judged; for with what judgment ye judge, ye shall be judged (Matt. vii. 1, 2; Luke vi. 37). Without doctrine a person might here be led to this conclusion, that he ought not to judge in respect to an evil man, that he is evil; whereas from doctrine it appears, that it is lawful to judge, if it be done righteously; for the Lord says, "Judge righteous judgment" (John vii. 24). Again, the Lord saith, "Be not ye called Rabbi, for one is your master, even Christ;—and call no man your father upon earth, for one is your Father who is in heaven; neither be ye called masters, for one is your Master, even Christ" (Matt. xxiii. 8, 9, 10). These words, unexplained by doctrine, would seem to imply, that it is not lawful to call any person teacher, father, o master: whereas by doctrine we learn that this is lawful in a natural sense, though it be unlawful in a spiritual sense. Again: Jesus said to his disciples, "When the Son of Man shall sit in the throne of his glory, ye also shall sit upon twelve thrones, judging the twelve tribes of Israel" (Matt. xix. 28). From these words it might concluded, that the disciples of the Lord are to sit hereafter in judgment; when the truth is, that they cannot judge any person: doctrine therefore must explain how this mystery is to be understood: and this unfolds it, by teaching that the Lord alone, who is omniscient, and knows all hearts, will sit in judgment, and is able to judge; and that His twelve disciples mean the church in respect to all the truths and goods which it has from the Lord by means of the Word; from whence doctrine concludes, that those truths and goods are to judge every one; according to the words of the Lord in John (iii. 17, 18; xii. 47, 48). Whoever reads the Word without doctrine, does not know how those things cohere together, which are spoken by the prophets concerning the Jewish nation and Jerusalem, where it is said that the church shall continue with that nation, and its seat abide in that city for ever; as in the following places; "Jehovah hath visited his flock, the house of Judah, and hath made them as his goodly horse in the battle; out of him shall come forth the corner, out of him the nail, and out of him the battle-bow" (Zech. x. 3, 4, 6, 7). "And I will dwell in the midst of thee,—and Jehovah shall inherit Judah, and shall choose Jerusalem again" (Zech. ii. 11, 12). "It shall come to pass in that day, the mountains shall drop down new wine, and the hills shall flow with milk—and Judah shall dwell for ever, and Jerusalem from generation to generation" (Joel iii. 18, 19, 20). "Behold the days come—in which I will sow the house of Israel and the house of Judah with the seed of man;—that I will make a new covenant with the house of Israel and with the house of Judah; and this shall be the covenant:—I will put my law in their inward parts, and write it in their heart, and will be their God, and they shall be my people" (Jerem. xxxi. 27, 31, 33). "In those days—ten men shall take hold, out of all languages of the nations, of the skirt of him that is a Jew, saying, We will go with you, for we have heard that God is with you" (Zech. viii. 22, 23): so in other places (as Isaiah xliv. 21, 26; xlix. 22, 23; lxv. 9; lxvi. 20, 22; Jerem. iii. 18; xxii. 5: l. 19, 20; Nahum ii. 1; Malachi iii. 4), where the coming of the Lord is treated of, and it is said that these things will come to pass. But the contrary is declared in many other passages, of which the following only shall be here noticed: "I will hide my face from them, I will see what their end shall be, for they are a very froward generation, children in whom is no faith;—I said, I would scatter them into corners, I would make the remembrance of them to cease from among men,—for they are a nation void of counsel, neither is there any understanding in them.—Their vine is of the vine of Sodom, and of the fields of Gomorrah; their grapes are grapes of gall, their clusters are bitter; their wine is the poison of dragons, and the cruel venom of asps. Is not this laid up in store with me, and sealed up among my treasures? To me belongeth vengeance and recompense" (Deut. xxxii. 20—35). These things are spoken concerning that nation, as are also things of a similar nature elsewhere: see Isaiah iii. 1, 2, 8; v. 3—6; Deut. ix. 5, 6; Matt. xii. 39; xxiii. 27, 28; John viii. 44; and in Jeremiah and Ezekiel throughout. Now the above passages, although they appear contradictory and irreconcileable, are nevertheless perfectly consistent with each other when viewed in their true light according to doctrine; which teaches that by Israel and Judah, in the Word, are not meant Israel and Judah, but the church in both senses; in the one sense, that it is vastated, and in the other sense, that it is to be re-established by the Lord. Several cases of a similar nature occur in the Word; whence it manifestly appears, that the Word without doctrine cannot be understood.

52. From what has been said it is very clear, that they who read the Word without doctrine, or who do not form to themselves doctrine from the Word, are in the dark concerning every truth, and that their minds must be wavering and unsettled, prone to errors, and easily betrayed into heresies; which they will even embrace with eagerness, in case they are supported by the authority and favourable opinion of mankind, and that they may do it with a safe reputation: for the Word is to them as a candlestick without a light in it, and they fancy they see many things in the dark, though they scarcely discern a single object: for doctrine is the only light which can guide them in their inquiries. I have seen such persons examined by the angels, and it was found that they could confirm any opinion they pleased, from the Word, and that they actually do so confirm all such opinions and tenets as favour their own love, and the love of those whom they study to oblige: but I afterwards saw them stripped of their garments, which is a sign that they were destitute of truth; for garments in the spiritual world are truths.

53. II. *That doctrine ought to be drawn from the literal sense of the Word, and to be confirmed thereby.* The reason of this is, because the Lord is present in that sense, enlightening and teaching man the truths of the church: for all the Lord's operations are performed in fulness, and the Word in its literal sense is in its fulness, as was shewn above: this is the true ground why doctrine ought to be drawn from the literal sense.

54. That the Word is not only intelligible by doctrine, but is also, as it were, luminous, appears from the Word's not being intelligible without doctrine, and like a candlestick without

a light, as was shewn above. The Word, therefore, is intelligible by doctrine, and is like a candlestick with a lighted candle. Man then sees more than he had seen before, and also understands such things as he had not before understood. Things dark and discordant he either sees not and passes by, or, if he sees them, he explains them so as to be consistent with doctrine. The experience of all the Christian world proves, that the Word is seen from, and explained according to, doctrine. All of the reformed church see and explain the Word from and according to their own doctrine: in like manner the Papists, from and according to theirs; nay, the Jews, from and according to theirs. Consequently, falsities arise from false doctrine, and truths from that which is true. Hence it appears, that true doctrine is like a candle in the dark, and like a directing post on the road. But doctrine is not only to be drawn from the literal sense of the Word, but it is also to be confirmed by that sense; for if it be not confirmed by it, the truth of doctrine appears as if the intellect of man only, and not the divine wisdom of the Lord, were contained in it: and thus doctrine would be like a house in the air, and not upon the earth, and therefore without foundation.

55. The doctrine of genuine truth may also be fully drawn from the literal sense of the Word. For the Word, in that sense, is like a man clothed, whose face and hands are naked. All things necessary to the life of man, and consequently to his salvation, are naked; but the rest are clothed: and in many places where they are clothed, they shine through the clothing as the face shines through a veil of thin silk. As also the truths of the Word are multiplied by the love of them, and by that are arranged in order, they shine more and more clearly through the clothing; but this, likewise, is effected by doctrine.

56. It may be imagined that the doctrine of genuine truth might be collected by means of the spiritual sense of the Word, which is learnt by the science of correspondences; but doctrine is not attainable by means of that sense, but only capable of receiving illustration and confirmation from it. For, as was observed above, n. 26, no one can come into the spiritual sense of the Word by means of correspondences, unless he be first in genuine truths derived from doctrine; but it is possible for a person to falsify the Word by some correspondences with which he is acquainted, when he connects them together, and applies them to the confirmation of particular opinions rooted in his mind, in consequence of the principles he has imbibed, unless he be principled in genuine truth. Besides, the spiritual sense of the Word is opened to man by the Lord alone, and is guarded by Him as the angelic heaven is guarded, for heaven is included in it. It it better therefore for man to study

the Word in its literal sense: it is thence, only, that doctrine is afforded.

57. III. *That genuine truth, which doctrine is to teach, is apparent, in the literal sense of the Word, to those only who are in illustration from the Lord.* Illustration comes from the Lord alone, and is afforded to those who love truths for truth's sake, and apply them to the uses of life; none else can receive illustration from the Word. The reason why illustration comes from the Lord alone, is, because he is in all things of the Word; and the reason of its being afforded only to those who love truths for truth's sake, and apply them to the uses of life, is, because they are in the Lord, and the Lord in them. For the Lord is His own Divine Truth; and when this is loved for its own sake, which is the case when it is applied to use, then the Lord is in it, and is thus present with the man. This the Lord teaches in John: "At that day ye shall know that ye are in me, and I in you. He that hath my commandments, and keepeth them, he it is that loveth me;—and I will love him, and will manifest myself to him. And my Father will love him, and we will come unto him, and make our abode with him" (xiv. 20, 21, 23). And in Matthew: "Blessed are the pure in heart, for they shall see God" (v. 8). These are they who are in illustration when they read the Word, and to whom the Word appears in its brightness and transparence.

58. The reason why the Word appears to such in its brightness and transparence, is, because there is both a spiritual and celestial sense in every part of the Word, and these senses are in the light of heaven; wherefore the Lord by these senses and their light, enters by influx into the natural sense of the Word, and into the light thereof abiding in man. Hence man acknowledges the truth from an interior perception, and afterwards sees it in his own thought, and this as often as he is in the affection of truth for truth's sake; for perception comes from affection, and thought from perception, and thence arises acknowledgment, which is called faith. But more of this shall be said in the following article concerning the conjunction of the Lord with man through the Word.

59. With these, the first thing to be done is, to collect for themselves doctrine from the literal sense of the Word, and thus to kindle a light for their further advancement; but after doctrine is collected, and thus the light is kindled, they see the Word by it. Those who do not collect doctrine for themselves, first inquire whether the doctrine collected by others, and received by common consent, agrees with the Word; and to those things which do agree, they give their assent, but dissent from those things which do not agree: thus they form their own doctrine, and, through doctrine, their faith. But this is only the case with those, who, not being too much drawn away

by the cares of the world, are able to exercise their intellectual sight; these, if they love truths for truth's sake and apply them to the uses of life, are in illustration from the Lord; others, if they are, in any degree, in a life according to truth, may learn from them.

60. The very reverse happens, where men interpret the Word by the doctrine of a false religion; and particularly where they confirm such doctrine by the Word with a view to their own glory, or to the acquirement of worldly wealth. With such persons the truths of the Word appear as in the shades of night, and falsities as in the light of day: they read truths, but they do not see them, and if they see the shadow of them, they falsify them. These are they whom the Lord describes as having eyes, and yet they see not; and ears, and yet they do not understand (Matt. xiii. 14, 15); for nothing blinds man but his own *proprium*, and the confirmation of what is false. The *proprium* of man is self-love, and the conceit of self-intelligence thence arising; and the confirmation of what is false is darkness counterfeiting light. Hence the light of these men becomes merely natural, and their sight is like that of a person who imagines he sees phantoms in the dark.

61. I have been permitted to converse with several after death, who believed they should shine as the stars in the firmament, because, as they said, they had accounted the Word holy, had often perused it, and had collected many things from it, whereby they had confirmed the tenets of their particular faith, and had acquired the reputation of being great scholars and learned men; in consequence of which they supposed they should be advanced to the dignity of a Michael or a Raphael. But on the examination of several of them, respecting the love which influenced them in their study of the Word, it was discovered that some of them had studied it from a principle of self-love, with a view to acquire rank and distinction in the church, and some from a principle of worldly love with a view to gain. On their examination, also, respecting what they had learnt from the Word, it was discovered that they did not know a single genuine truth, but only what may be called truth falsified, which, in its own proper nature, is falsity; and they were informed that this was a consequence of reading the Word only with a view to themselves and the world, without regarding the truth of faith and the good of life as the ends of their reading. For in this case, where self and the world are the ends, the mind, in reading the Word, abides in self and in the world, and hence their thoughts are constantly derived from their own *proprium*, or selfhood, and the *proprium* of man is in utter darkness respecting all things that relate to heaven and the church; so that, in such a state, it is impossible for man to be under the Lord's guidance, and to be elevated by Him into the

light of heaven; of consequence, it is impossible he should receive any influx from the Lord through heaven. I have also seen such persons admitted into heaven, but when they were discovered to be without truths, they were cast down again; yet still they remained full of the conceit that they deserved to be in heaven. The case is different with those who have studied the Word from the affection of knowing truth for truth's sake, and because it is serviceable to the uses of life, not only in respect to themselves, but also to their neighbour. I have seen such raised up into heaven, and thus into the light wherein Divine Truth there appears, and at the same time exalted into angelic wisdom and its happiness, which is life eternal.

---

## VI. THAT, BY THE LITERAL SENSE OF THE WORD, MAN HAS CONJUNCTION WITH THE LORD, AND CONSOCIATION WITH THE ANGELS.

62. THE reason that man has conjunction with the Lord by means of the Word, is, because it treats of him alone, and through it the Lord is all in all, and is called the Word, as has been shewn in the DOCTRINE RESPECTING THE LORD. The reason that such conjunction is effected by the literal sense, is, because the Word, in that sense, is in its fulness, in its holiness, and in its power, as was shewn above. This conjunction is not apparent to man, but is wrought in the affection and perception of truth, and thus in the love and faith of Divine Truth in him.

63. The reason that man has consociation with angels by means of the literal sense, is, because the spiritual and celestial senses are included in that sense, and the angels are in those senses; the angels of the Lord's spiritual kingdom in the spiritual sense of the Word, and the angels of the Lord's celestial kingdom in its celestial sense. Those two senses are evolved or unfolded from the natural or literal sense, whilst it is read by a person who accounts the Word holy. Such evolution is instantaneous; consequently, the consociation is so likewise.

64. That the spiritual angels are in the spiritual sense of the Word, and the celestial angels in its celestial sense, has been proved to me by manifold experience. It was given me to perceive, that whilst I was reading the Word in its literal sense, communication was opened with the heavens, sometimes with one society, sometimes with another: what I understood according to the natural sense, the spiritual angels understood according to the spiritual sense, and the celestial angels accord

ing to the celestial sense, and this in an instant; and as this communication has been perceived by me many thousand times, I have not a single doubt remaining as to its reality. There are spirits, also, who are below the heavens, who abuse this communication; for they read over particular passages in the literal sense of the Word, and immediately observe and note the society with which communication is effected. From these circumstances it is given me to know, by sensible experience, that the Word, as to its literal sense, is a divine medium of conjunction with the Lord, and with heaven. Concerning this conjunction by the Word, see also what is said in the work ON HEAVEN AND HELL, n. 303—310.

65. But in what manner this unfolding of those senses takes place, shall be also explained in a few words; but that it may be understood, it will be necessary to bear in mind, what was said above, n. 6, 38, concerning successive order and simultaneous order; namely, that what is celestial, spiritual, and natural, follow one after another in successive order, from the highest things which are in heaven, to the lowest which are in the world: that the same things in simultaneous order are in the lowest degree, which is the natural, one being placed in juxta-position with the other, from the most internal to the most external; and that, in like manner, the successive senses of the Word, the celestial and spiritual, are simultaneously in the natural. These things being comprehended, it may, in some measure, be explained to the undestanding, in what manner the two senses, the celestial and the spiritual, are evolved from the natural, whilst man is reading the Word; for then the spiritual angels extract and call forth its spiritual contents, and the celestial angels its celestial contents: nor can they do otherwise, because those things are to them homogeneous, and are in agreement with their nature and essence.

66. But this may first be illustrated by comparisons drawn from the three kingdoms of nature, which are called the animal, the vegetable, and the mineral. In the ANIMAL KINGDOM, for instance, when the food is turned to chyle, the blood vessels extract from thence, and call forth, their blood, the nervous fibres their juices, and the substances from whence those fibres originate, their animal spirit. In the VEGETABLE KINGDOM: a tree, with its trunk, branches, leaves, and fruits, is supported on its root; and out of the ground, by means of its root, extracts and calls forth a grosser juice for the trunk, branches, and leaves, a purer for the fleshy parts of the fruit, and the purest of all for the seeds within the fruit. In the MINERAL KINGDOM: in some places in the bowels of the earth, are minerals impregnated with gold, silver, and iron; the gold, silver, and iron, draw their respective elements from the subterraneous exhalations.

67. We will now illustrate, by instances, in what manner the spiritual angels draw forth their sense, and the celestial angels theirs, from the natural sense, in which the Word is with men. Let us take for examples five commandments of the Decalogue. THE COMMANDMENT, *Honour thy father and mother.* By father and mother, man understands a father and mother on earth, and also all those who are in the place of father and mother; and by honouring them, he understands to hold them in honour, and to obey them. But the spiritual angel understands by father the Lord, and by mother the church, and by honouring them, he understands to love them. And the celestial angel by father understands the Divine Love of the Lord, by mother His Divine Wisdom, and by honouring them, to do good from Him. THE COMMANDMENT, *Thou shalt not steal.* By stealing, man understands to rob, to defraud, and under any pretence to take from another what belongs to him: whereas, a spiritual angel, by stealing, understands to deprive others of their truths of faith and goods of charity, by means of falsities and evils: but a celestial angel, by stealing, understands to attribute to self what belongs to the Lord, and to appropriate to self His righteousness and merit. Again: *Thou shalt not commit adultery.* By committing adultery, man understands to commit whoredom, to be guilty of obscene practices, to indulge wanton discourse, and to entertain lewd thoughts: whereas a spiritual angel, by committing adultery, understands to adulterate the goods of the Word, and to falsify its truths: but a celestial angel, by committing adultery, understands to deny the Divinity of the Lord, and to profane the Word. Again: *Thou shalt not commit murder.* By murdering, man understands, not only the taking away another's life, but likewise bearing malice and hatred in the heart, and breathing a revengeful spirit against any person, even to death: whereas, by murdering, a spiritual angel understands to play the devil's part, and destroy men's souls; and a celestial angel, by murdering, understands to hate the Lord, and those things which are the Lord's. Lastly, *Thou shalt not bear false witness.* By bearing false witness, man understands also to tell lies, and to defame any person: whereas, a spiritual angel, by bearing false witness, understands to declare, and endeavour to persuade others, that what is false is true, and what is evil is good, and *vice versa:* but a celestial angel, by bearing false witness, understands to blaspheme the Lord and the Word. These instances may serve to shew, after what manner the spiritual and celestial senses of the Word are unfolded and extracted from the natural sense in which they are included: and, what is wonderful, the angels extract their senses without having any knowledge of a man's thoughts; but still the thoughts of angels and men make a one by correspondences, like end, cause, and effect; for ends

do actually exist in the celestial kingdom, causes in the spiritual, and effects in the natural kingdom. Such conjunction by correspondences results from the laws of creation. Hence then it is, that man has consociation with angels by means of the Word.

68. The reason that man has consociation with angels by the natural or literal sense of the Word, is likewise, because in every man from creation, there are three degrees of life, the celestial, the spiritual, and the natural: man, however, is in the natural degree, so long as he continues in this world; and, at the same time, so far in the spiritual degree, as he is principled in genuine truths, and so far in a celestial degree as he is principled in a life according to those truths; nevertheless, he is not admitted into the spiritual and celestial degrees themselves till after death. But more concerning this elsewhere.

69. From what has been said, it must appear evident, that only in the Word, by which man has conjunction with the Lord and consociation with the angels, there is spirit and life; as the Lord says, "The words that I speak unto you, they are spirit and they are life" (John vi. 63). "The water that I shall give him, shall be in him a well of water springing up unto everlasting life" (John iv. 14). "Man shall not live by bread alone, but by every word that proceedeth out of the mouth of God" (Matt. iv. 4). "Labour not for the meat which perisheth, but for that meat which endureth unto everlasting life, which the Son of Man shall give unto you" (John vi. 27).

---

## VII. THAT THE WORD IS IN ALL THE HEAVENS, AND THAT THE WISDOM OF THE ANGELS IS THENCE DERIVED.

70. THAT the Word is in the heavens, has remained a secret to mankind unto this day, nor could it be made known so long as the church was ignorant that angels and spirits are men like men in this our world, and that they resemble them in every particular, with this only difference, that they themselves are spiritual beings, and that all things which they have amongst them are from a spiritual origin; whereas men on earth are natural beings, and all things amongst them are from a natural origin. So long as this remained concealed, it could never be known that the Word is also in the heavens, and that it is there read by the angelic inhabitants; and also by the spirits who are beneath the heavens. But that this truth might not remain for ever a secret, it has been granted me to be in fellowship with angels and spirits, and to converse with them, and to see what is in their world, and afterwards to relate to mankind many of the things which I have seen and heard: this I have

done in a work concerning HEAVEN AND HELL; from which work it will appear, that angels and spirits are men, and that they have amongst them an abundance of all such things as exist amongst men on earth. That angels and spirits are men, may be seen in that work, n. 73—77, and n. 453—456; that similar things exist amongst them that exist here amongst men, n. 170—190; also, that they have divine worship amongst them, and have preaching in their temples, n. 221—227; likewise writings and books, n. 258—264; and also the Holy Scriptures or Word, n. 259.

71. The Word in heaven, is written in a spiritual style, which differs entirely from a natural style: a spiritual style consists of mere letters, each involving some particular sense; and there are marks above the letters, which exalt the sense. The letters in use amongst the angels of the spiritual kingdom, are like the letters used in printing amongst men; and the letters in use amongst the angels of the celestial kingdom, each of which in itself involves some entire sense, are like the Hebrew old letters, but inflected above and beneath, with marks above, between, and within them. As their writing is of such a nature, there are not any names of persons and places in their Word, as in ours, but instead of names are the things which they signify; thus instead of Moses is mentioned the historical Word; instead of Elias, the prophetic Word; instead of Abraham, Isaac, and Jacob, the Lord with respect to His Divine-celestial, His Divine-spiritual, and His Divine-natural; instead of Aaron, the priestly office; instead of David, the kingly office, each in relation to the Lord; instead of the names of the twelve sons of Jacob, or the tribes of Israel; and instead of the names of the Lord's twelve disciples, various things respecting heaven and the church; instead of Zion and Jerusalem, the church as to doctrine derived from the Word; instead of the land of Canaan, the church itself; instead of the places and cities therein, on this side the river Jordan, and beyond it, various things relating to the church and its doctrine. The case is the same in respect to numbers; they do not occur in the copies of the Word written in heaven, but instead of them are expressed the things with which the numbers correspond. It may hence be seen, that the Word in heaven corresponds to our Word, and that consequently they are one, for correspondences make things one.

72. It is a wonderful circumstance, that the Word in heaven is so written, that the simple may understand it in simplicity, and the wise in wisdom; for there are various points and marks over the letters, which, as we observed, exalt the sense, but to which the simple do not attend, nor understand their meaning; whereas, the wise are attentive to them, every one in proportion to his wisdom, even to its highest degree. A

copy of the Word, written by angels under the Lord's inspiration, is kept by every considerable society, in a sacred repository appointed for that purpose, to preserve it from any alteration in any of its points or marks. The Word in our world is so far similar to that in heaven, that the simple understand it in simplicity, and the wise in wisdom; but yet this difference of understanding in our world arises from a different ground, and is effected in a different manner.

73. The angels themselves confess that they derive all their wisdom from the Word, for in proportion to their understanding of the Word, is the degree of light in which they dwell: the light of heaven is Divine Wisdom, which appears before the eyes of the angels as light. In the sacred repository, where the copy of the Word is kept, the light is bright and flaming, exceeding every degree of light that shines in the other parts of heaven without: the cause has already been mentioned—that the Lord is in the Word.

74. The wisdom of the celestial angels exceeds the wisdom of the spiritual angels almost as much as the wisdom of the spiritual angels exceeds the wisdom of men; and this because the celestial angels are in the good of love from the Lord, and the spiritual angels in the truths of wisdom from the Lord; and wherever the good of love is, there wisdom resides at the same time; but where truths are, there no more wisdom resides, than in proportion to the good of love by which it is attended. This is the reason why the Word, in the Lord's celestial kingdom, is differently written from the Word in His spiritual kingdom; for in the Word of the celestial kingdom the goods of love are the things expressed, and the marks denote affections; but in the Word of the spiritual kingdom the truths of wisdom are the things expressed, and the marks denote perceptions.

75. From what has been observed we may conclude, how great the wisdom must be which lies concealed in the Word we have here on earth; for in this all angelic wisdom, which is inexpressible, is hidden; and every man who is made an angel by the Lord by means of the Word, comes into this wisdom after death.

---

## VIII. THAT THE CHURCH EXISTS FROM THE WORD, AND THAT, WITH MAN, THE QUALITY OF THE CHURCH IS ACCORDING TO HIS UNDERSTANDING OF THE WORD.

76. THAT the church exists from the Word, cannot possibly be a matter of doubt; for the Word is Divine Truth itself (n. 1—4); the doctrine of the church is derived from the Word (n.

50—61); and conjunction with the Lord is effected by means of the Word (n. 62—69). But that the understanding of the Word constitutes the church, may be made a matter of doubt; as there are some who believe that they belong to the church, merely because they are in possession of the Word, and read it, or hear it from the minister, and have some knowledge of its literal sense; although, at the same time, they are totally ignorant of its meaning, and how it is to be understood in different passages; which some make a matter of small account. It will be necessary to prove, then, that it is not merely the Word which constitutes the church, but the right understanding of it, and that the quality of the church is determinable by the understanding of the Word amongst its members. This is confirmed from these circumstances.

77. The Word is properly the Word according to the understanding of it with men, that is, as it is understood: if it is not understood, it indeed is called the Word, but in reality it is not such with man. The Word is truth, according to the understanding of it; for the Word may be not the truth, inasmuch as it may be falsified. The Word is spirit and life according as it is understood; for the mere letter, without the understanding of it, is dead. Since, therefore, man has truth and life according to his understanding of the Word, so also he has faith and love according to it; for truth has relation to faith, and love to life. Now because it is by faith and love, and according to them, that the church exists, it follows, that by the understanding of the Word, and according, to it the church is a church;—a noble church if grounded in genuine truths, an ignoble one if not in genuine truths, and a ruined one if in falsified truths.

78. Moreover, the Lord is present and in conjunction with man through the Word, seeing that the Lord is the Word, and, as it were, converses in it with man, because the Lord is Divine Truth itself, and the Word is Divine Truth also. From hence it plainly appears, that the Lord is present with man, and in conjunction with him, according to his understanding of the Word: for, according to it man has truth, and from thence faith, and also love, and thence life. The Lord is also present with man through the reading of the Word; but he is in conjunction with him through the understanding of truth derived from the Word, and according to it; and in proportion as the Lord is in conjunction with man, so much of the church is in man. The church is properly in man; the church without him is the church with many others in whom the church is. This is meant by the Lord's answer to the Pharisees, on their inquiring when the kingdom of God should come: "The kingdom of God is within you" (Luke xvii. 21): by the kingdom of God is here meant the Lord, and the church from Him.

79. Many parts of the prophetical writings, where the church is treated of, treat also of the understanding of the Word, and it is taught that the church cannot exist but where there is a just understanding of the Word, and that the state and nature of the church is always to be determined by the manner in which the Word is understood by those who belong to the church. The prophets, in many parts of their writings, describe the Israelitish and Jewish church as totally destroyed and annihilated, in consequence of falsifying the meaning or understanding of the Word; for the destruction of the church proceeds from no other source than this. The understanding of the Word, both true and false, is described in the prophetic writings, particularly in the prophet Hosea, by EPHRAIM; for the understanding of the Word in the church is signified in the Word by Ephraim. As the understanding of the Word constitutes the church, therefore Ephraim is called "a dear son and a pleasant child" (Jerem. xxxi. 20); "the first-born" (Jerem. xxxi. 9); "the strength of the head of Jehovah" (Psalm lx. 7; cviii. 8); "a mighty man" (Zech. x. 7); "he that filleth the bow" (Zech. ix. 13); and the children of Ephraim are called "armed and shooters with the bow" (Psalm lxxviii. 9); for by a bow is signified doctrine derived from the Word combating with falsities. For the same reason, also, Israel stretched out his right hand upon Ephraim, and blessed him (Gen. xlviii. 14); and he was also accepted in lieu of Reuben (ver. 5); and for the same reason, Ephraim, with his brother Manasseh, under the name of their father Joseph, was exalted by Moses, in his blessing of the children of Israel, above all the rest (Deut. xxxiii. 13—17). But the state and nature of the church when the understanding of the Word is destroyed, is also described in the writings of the prophets by Ephraim, particularly in Hosea; as in these passages: "Israel and Ephraim shall fall in their iniquity; Ephraim shall be desolate; Ephraim is oppressed and broken in judgment; I will be unto Ephraim as a lion: I, even I, will tear and go away, I will take away, and none shall rescue him" (v. 5, 9, 11, 14). "O Ephraim, what shall I do unto thee? For thy goodness is as a morning cloud, and as the early dew it goeth away" (Hos. vi. 4). "They shall not dwell in the land of Jehovah, but Ephraim shall return to Egypt, and shall eat unclean things in Assyria" (Hosea ix. 3). The land of Jehovah is the church; Egypt is the scientific principle of the natural man Assyria is reasoning founded on it; therefore it is said, that Ephraim shall return into Egypt, and shall eat unclean things in Assyria. "Ephraim feedeth on wind, and followeth after the east wind; he daily increaseth lies and desolations; and they do make a covenant with the Assyrians, and oil is carried into Egypt" (Hos. xii. 1). To feed on wind, to follow after the east wind,

to increase lies and desolations, is to falsify truths, and so to destroy the church. The same is also signified by the whoredom of Ephraim, for whoredom signifies the falsification of the understanding of the Word, that is, of its genuine truth; as in these passages: "For now, O Ephraim, thou committest whoredom, and Israel is defiled" (Hosea v. 3). "I have seen a horrible thing in the house of Israel; there is the whoredom of Ephraim, Israel is defiled" (Hosea vi. 10). Israel means the church itself, and Ephraim the understanding of the Word, which determines the state and quality of the church; wherefore it is said, "Ephraim committed whoredom, and Israel is defiled." But as the church amongst the children of Israel and Judah was totally destroyed by falsifications of the Word, therefore it is thus said of Ephraim: "Shall I give thee up, Ephraim? shall I deliver thee, Israel? How shall I make thee as Admah? How shall I set thee at Zeboim" (Hosea xi. 8). Now since the prophet Hosea, from the first chapter to the last, treats of the falsification of the Word, and of the consequent destruction of the church; and because the falsification of the Word is there signified by whoredom; therefore he was commanded, for the purpose of representing that state of the church, "to take unto himself a wife of whoredoms, and children of whoredoms" (i. 1). And again: "to take to himself an adulteress" (iii. 1). We have quoted these passages, for the sake of shewing and proving from the Word, that the quality of the church is always determined by its understanding of the Word; and that it is excellent and precious, if its understanding be grounded on the genuine truths of the Word; but that it is ruined, yea, filthy, if it be grounded on truths falsified. For a further confirmation, that by Ephraim is signified the understanding of the Word, and, in a contrary sense, the falsification of it, and that thence proceeds the destruction of the church, the other passages which treat of Ephraim may be referred to; as in Hosea iv. 17, 18; vii. 1, 11; viii. 9, 11; ix. 11, 12, 13, 16; x. 11; xi. 3; xii. 1, 9, 15; xiii. 1, 12; Isaiah xvii. 3; xxviii. 1; Jerem. iv. 15; xxxi. 6, 18; l. 19; Ezekiel xxxvii. 16; xlviii. 5; Obad. 9; Zech. ix. 10.

---

## IX. THAT THERE IS A MARRIAGE OF THE LORD AND THE CHURCH, AND THENCE A MARRIAGE OF GOOD AND TRUTH, IN EVERY PART OF THE WORD.

80. That there is a marriage of the Lord and the church, and thence a marriage of good and truth, in every part of the Word, has never yet been discovered; neither could it be dis-

covered, so long as the spiritual sense of the Word remained unknown: for this sense alone can make manifest such a marriage. There are two senses contained in the Word, which lie concealed in its literal sense, and which are called spiritual and celestial: what belongs to the spiritual sense of the Word has more particular relation to the church; and what belongs to the celestial sense, to the Lord: the contents also of the spiritual sense have relation to Divine Truth, and the contents of the celestial sense to Divine Good; and this is the ground of the above-mentioned marriage in the Word. But this is only apparent to those who, by virtue of the spiritual and celestial sense of the Word, are acquainted with the signification of its names and expressions; for some particular names and expressions are predicated of good, and some of truth, and some include both; wherefore, without the knowledge of such signification, it is impossible to see how such a marriage exists in every part of the Word; and this is the reason why this arcanum was never discovered before.

81. Inasmuch as there is such a marriage in every part of the Word, therefore we frequently find in the Word two expressions which appear like repetitions of one and the same thing: they are, however, not repetitions; but one has relation to good, and the other to truth, and both, taken together, effect the conjunction of good and truth, and consequently make them one. This, also, is the true ground of the divinity of the Word and its sanctity; for in every divine work there is a conjunction of good with truth, and of truth with good.

82. The reason why we assert the marriage of good and truth in the Word to be a consequence of the marriage of the Lord and the church therein, is, because wherever there is a marriage of the Lord and the church, there also is a marriage of good and truth, the latter marriage being derived from the former: for when the church, or any member of it, is principled in truths, then the Lord flows-in by good into those truths, and communicates life to them; or, what amounts to the same, when the church, or any member of the church, is in the understanding of truth, then the Lord flows-in, by the good of love and charity, into that understanding, and thus infuses life into it.

83. There are two faculties of life in every man, which are called understanding and will: the understanding is the receptacle of truth, and thence of wisdom; and the will is the receptacle of good, and thence of charity. These two faculties ought to be united, and make a one, in order that man may be a member of the church; and they are so united, when a man forms his understanding by genuine truths, which is done to all appearance as of himself, and when his will is replenished with the good of love, which is effected by the Lord. Hence

man derives the life of truth and the life of good; the life of truth in his understanding, from his will, and the life of good in his will, by his understanding. In this consists the marriage of good and truth in man, as well as the marriage of the Lord and the church with man. Concerning this reciprocal conjunction, which is here called a marriage, more may be seen in the works entitled, ANGELIC WISDOM, CONCERNING THE DIVINE LOVE AND DIVINE WISDOM, and CONCERNING THE DIVINE PROVIDENCE.

84. That there frequently are two expressions used in the Word, which appear like repetitions of the same thing, must be evident to every attentive reader; as, for instance, brother and companion, poor and needy, wilderness and desert, vacuity and emptiness, foe and enemy, sin and iniquity, anger and wrath, nation and people, joy and gladness, mourning and weeping, justice and judgment, &c. These appear to be synonymous expressions, when in fact they are not; for the terms brother, poor, wilderness, vacuity, foe, sin, anger, nation, joy, mourning, and justice, are predicated of good, and, in the opposite sense, of evil; whereas the terms companion, needy, desert, emptiness, enemy, iniquity, wrath, people, gladness, weeping, and judgment, are predicated of truth, and, in the opposite sense, of what is false: and yet it must appear to the reader who is unacquainted with this arcanum, as if the terms poor and needy, desert, and wilderness, vacuity, and emptiness, &c., meant the same thing, whereas, they do not, but yet form one thing by conjunction. In the Word, also, we frequently find two things joined together, as fire and flame, gold and silver, brass and iron, wood and stone, bread and wine, purple and fine linen, &c., because fire, gold, brass, wood, bread, and purple, are predicated of good; but flame, silver, iron, stone, water, wine, and fine linen, are predicated of truth. In like manner it is said, that God is to be loved with all the heart, and with all the soul; and also, that God will create in man a new heart and a new spirit; for the heart is predicated of the good of love, and the soul and spirit of the truths of faith from that good. There are some expressions, also, which in consequence of partaking alike both of good and truth, are used by themselves, without the adjunction of others. But these, and many things besides, are apparent only to the angels, and to those who see into the spiritual sense of the Word, whilst they are reading the natural sense.

85. It would be tedious to shew from the Word, that two expressions of this nature are used, for it would fill a volume to quote all the particular cases where such double expressions occur; I shall, however, in order to remove all doubt on this subject, produce some passages where the terms judgment and justice, nation and people, joy and gladness, are used togethe

Judgment and justice are mentioned together in these places: "The city was full of *judgment, justice* lodged in it" (Isaiah i. 21). "Zion shall be redeemed with *judgment*, and her converts with *justice*" (Isaiah i. 27). "Jehovah of hosts shall be exalted in *judgment*, and God that is holy shall be sanctified in *justice*" (Isaiah v. 16). "He shall sit upon the throne of David, and his kingdom, to establish it with *judgment* and with *justice*" (Isaiah ix. 7). "Jehovah shall be exalted, for He dwelleth on high, He hath filled Zion with *judgment* and *justice*" (Isaiah xxxiii. 5). "Thus saith Jehovah, Keep ye *judgment*, and do *justice;* for my salvation is near to come, and my *justice* to be revealed" (Isaiah lvi. 1). "As a nation that did *justice*, and forsook not the *judgments* of their God: they ask of me the *judgments* of *justice*" (Isaiah lviii. 2). "And thou shalt swear Jehovah liveth, in truth, in *judgment* and in *justice*" (Jerem. iv. 2). "Let him that glorieth glory in this, that Jehovah doth *judgment* and *justice* in the earth" (Jerem. ix. 24). "Execute ye *judgment* and *justice.* Woe unto him that buildeth his house without *justice* and his chambers without *judgment.* Did not thy father do *judgment* and *justice*, and then it was well with him?" (Jerem. xxii. 3, 13, 15). "I will raise unto David a righteous branch, and a king shall reign, and shall execute *judgment* and *justice* in the earth" (Jerem. xxiii. 5; xxxiii. 15). "If a man be just, and do *judgment* and *justice*" (Ezek. xviii. 5). "If the wicked man turn from his sin, and do *judgment* and *justice*,—none of his sins—shall be mentioned unto him; he hath done *judgment* and *justice*, he shall surely live" (Ezek. xxxiii. 14, 16, 19). "I will betroth thee unto me for ever,—in *judgment* and *justice*, and in loving-kindness and in mercies" (Hosea ii. 19). "Let *judgment* run down as waters and *justice* as a mighty stream" (Amos v. 24). "Ye have turned *judgment* into gall, and the fruit of *justice* into hemlock" (Amos vi. 12). "Jehovah shall plead my cause, and execute *judgment* for me: He will bring me forth to the light, and I shall behold His *justice*" (Micah vii. 9). "Thy *justice* is like the great mountains, and thy *judgments* are a great deep" (Psalm xxxvi. 6). "Jehovah shall bring forth thy *justice* as the light, and thy *judgment* as the noon-day" (Psalm xxxvii. 6). "He shall judge thy people with *justice* and thy poor with *judgment*" (Psalm lxxii. 2). "*Justice* and *judgment* are the habitation of His throne" (Psalm xcvii. 2). "When I shall have learnt the *judgment* of thy *justice.* Seven times a day do I praise thee, because of the *judgments* of thy *justice*" (Psalm cxix. 7, 164). "He executed the *justice* of Jehovah and His *judgments* with Israel" (Deut. xxxiii. 21). "He shall reprove the world of sin, of *justice* and of *judgment*" (John xvi. 8, 10; and elsewhere). The reason why judgment and justice are so often mentioned together, is, because judgment is predicated of truth, and jus tice of good; wherefore by executing judgment and justice, is also meant to act from a principle of truth and good. The reason why judgment is predicated of truth, and justice of good, is, because the government of the Lord in the spiritual kingdom is called *judgment*, and the government of the Lord in the celestial kingdom is called *justice;* concerning which more may be seen in the treatise ON HEAVEN AND HELL, n. 214, 215. Because judgment is predicated of truth, therefore, in many places, mention is made of truth and justice, as in Isaiah xi. 5; and Psalms lxxxv. 12; and in other places.

86. The reason why repetitions as it were of the same thing are used in the Word, on account of the marriage of good and truth, may be more clearly seen in those places where the terms nation and people are used; as in the following: "Ah! sinful *nation*, a *people* laden with iniquity" (Isaiah i. 4). "The *people* that walked in darkness, have seen a great light; —thou hast multiplied the *nation*" (Isaiah ix. 2, 3). "O Assyrian, the rod of mine anger,—I will send him against a hypocritical *nation*, and against the *people* of my wrath will I give him a charge" (Isiah x. 5, 6). "In that day there shall be a root of Jesse, which shall stand for an ensign of the *people;* to it shall the *nations* seek" (Isaiah xi. 10). "He who smote the *people* in wrath with a continual stroke: He that ruled the *nations* in anger" (xiv. 6). "In that time shall the present be brought unto Jehovah of hosts, of a *people* scattered and peeled—a *nation* meted out and trodden under foot" (Isaiah xviii. 7). "Therefore shall the strong *people* glorify thee, the city of terrible *nations* shall fear thee" (Isaiah xxv. 3). "Jehovah will destroy in this mountain the face of the covering cast over all *people*, and the veil that is spread over all *nations*" (Isaiah xxv. 7). "Come near, ye *nations*, to hear: and hearken, ye *people*" (Isaiah xxxiv. 1). "I have called thee for a covenant of the *people*, for a light of the *nations*" (Isaiah xlii. 6). "Let all the *nations* be gathered together, and let the *people* be assembled" (Isaiah xliii. 9). "Behold, I will lift up my hand to the *nations*, and set up my standard to the *people*" (Isaiah xlix. 22). "Behold, I have given him for a witness to the *people*, a leader and a commander to the *nations*" (Isaiah lv. 4). "Behold, a *people* cometh from the north country, and a great *nation*—from the sides of the earth" (Jerem. vi. 22). "Neither will I cause men to hear in thee the shame of the *nations* any more, neither shalt thou bear the reproach of the *people* any more" (Ezek. xxxvi. 15). "All *people* and *nations* shall serve him" (Dan. vii. 14). "Spare thy *people*, O Jehovah, and give not thine heritage to reproach; that the *nations* should rule over them" (Joel ii. 17). "The residue of my *people* shall spoil them, and the remnant of my *nation* shall possess them" (Zeph. ii. 9). "Many *people*, and strong *nations*, shall come to seek

Jehovah in Jerusalem" (Zech. viii. 22). "Mine eyes have seen thy salvation, which thou hast prepared before the face of all *people*, a light to lighten the *nations*" (Luke ii. 30, 31, 32). "Thou hast redeemed us by thy blood out of every *people* and *nation*" (Apoc. v. 9). "Thou must prophesy again before many *people* and *nations*" (Apoc. x. 11). "Thou hast made me the head of the *nations*, a *people* whom I have not known shall serve me" (Psalms xviii. 43). "Jehovah bringeth the counsel of the *nations* to nought; He maketh the devices of the *people* of none effect" (Psalms xxxiii. 10). "Thou makest us a by-word among the *nations*, a shaking of the head among the *people*" (Psalms xliv. 14). "Jehovah shall subdue the *people* under us, and the *nations* under our feet. God reigneth over the *nations*, the princes of the *people* are gathered together, even the *people* of the God of Abraham" (Psalms xlvii. 3, 8, 9). "Let the *people* praise thee,—let the *nations*—sing for joy; for thou shalt judge the *people* righteously, and govern the *nations* upon earth" (Psalms lxvii. 3, 4). "Remember me, O Jehovah, with the favour that thou bearest unto thy *people*, that I may rejoice in the gladness of thy *nations*" (Psalm cvi. 4, 5); not to mention several other places. The reason why people and nations are expressed at the same time, is, because by nations are meant those who are in good, and, in the opposite sense, those who are in evil, and by people, those who are in truths, and, in the opposite sense, those who are in falsities. For this reason they who are of the Lord's spiritual kingdom are called people, and they who are of His celestial kingdom are called nations; for all in the spiritual kingdom are in truths, and thereby in wisdom, but all in the celestial kingdom are in good, and thereby in love.

87. The case is the same with many other expressions; as with *joy* and *gladness*, which frequently occur together, as may be seen in the following passages: "And behold *joy* and *gladness*, slaying oxen, and killing sheep" (Isaiah xxii. 13). "They shall obtain *joy* and *gladness*, and sorrow and mourning shall flee away" (Isaiah xxxv. 10; li. 11). "*Joy* and *gladness* are cut off from the house of our God" (Joel i. 16). "The fast of the tenth month shall be to the house of Judah *joy* and *gladness*" (Zech. viii. 19). "That we may *rejoice* and be *glad* all our days" (Psalm xc. 14). "*Rejoice* ye with Jerusalem, and be *glad* with her—*rejoice* in her *joy*" (Isaiah lxvi. 10). "*Rejoice* and be *glad*, O daughter of Edom" (Lament. iv. 21). "Let the righteous be *glad*, let them *rejoice* before God" (Psalm lxviii. 3). "Make me to hear *joy* and *gladness*" (Psalm li. 8). "*Joy* and *gladness* shall be found in Zion, thanksgiving and the voice of melody" (Isaiah li. 3). "And thou shalt have *joy* and *gladness*, and many shall rejoice at His birth" (Luke i. 14). "Then will I cause to cease—the voice of *joy* and the voice of *gladness*,

the voice of the bridegroom and the voice of the bride" (Jerem. vii. 34; xvi. 9; xxv. 10). "Again there shall be heard in this place—the voice of *joy* and the voice of *gladness*, the voice of the bridegroom and the voice of the bride" (Jerem. xxxiii. 10, 11); and in many other places. The reason why mention is made, in these passages, both of joy and gladness, is, because joy is predicated of good, and gladness of truth; or joy of love, and gladness of wisdom: for joy belongs to the heart, and gladness to the spirit; or joy belongs to the will, and gladness to the understanding. That there is also a marriage of the Lord and the church in these two, is evident from this circumstance, that mention is made of "the voice of joy and the voice of gladness, the voice of the bridegroom and the voice of the bride" (Jerem. vii. 34; xvi. 9; xxv. 10; xxxiii. 10, 11); and the Lord is the bridegroom, and the church is the bride. That the Lord is the bridegroom, may be seen, Matt. ix. 15; Mark ii. 19, 20; Luke v. 35; and that the church is the bride, may be seen, Apoc. xxi. 2, 9; xxii. 17; wherefore John the Baptist said of Jesus, "He that hath the bride is the bridegroom" (John iii. 29).

88. By reason of the marriage of the Lord with the church, or, what is the same thing, the marriage of Divine Good and Divine Truth, in every part of the Word, the expressions Jehovah and God so frequently occur: also, Jehovah and the Holy One of Israel; as if they were two, when nevertheless they are one; for by Jehovah is meant the Lord as to Divine Good and by God, and the Holy One of Israel, is meant the Lord as to Divine Truth. That the expressions Jehovah and God, and Jehovah and the Holy One of Israel, also occur in many parts of the Word, and yet signify one, may be seen in the DOCTRINE RESPECTING THE LORD, n. 34, 38, 46.

89. Since then there is a marriage of the Lord and the church in all and every part of the Word, it is evident, that all and every particular of the Word treats of the Lord, as is demonstrated in the DOCTRINE RESPECTING THE LORD, n. 1—7. The church too, of which it treats, is the Lord also; for the Lord Himself teaches that a man of the church is in Him, and He in him (John vi. 56; xiv. 20, 21; xv. 5, 7).

90. Because the divinity and sanctity of the Word are here treated of, it may be proper to add a MEMORABLE RELATION to what has been already said. There was once sent me down from heaven a small piece of paper, covered with Hebrew characters, but written as they used to be amongst the ancients, with whom those letters, which are at this day partly linear, were inflected, with little bendings upwards; and the angels who were then with me declared, that they could discover entire and complete senses by the very letters, and that they discovered them particularly by the flexures of the lines, and of the apices

of each letter: and they explained what was their signification both separately and conjointly, telling me that the *h* which was added to the names of Abram and Sarai, signified infinite and eternal. They also explained to me the meaning of the Word in Psalm xxxii. 2, by the letters or syllables only, and informed me, that their purport, when summed up, was this: That the Lord is ever merciful to those who do evil. They informed me, that the writings in the third heaven consisted of letters inflected, and variously curved, each of which contained some particular meaning; and that the vowels there used were to express a sound which should correspond with affection: they added, that, in that heaven, they were not able to express the vowels *i* and *e*, but instead of them *y* and *eu*, and that the vowels, *a*, *o*, and *u*, were in use amongst them, because they give a full sound; also, that they did not express any consonants roughly, but softly, and that it was from this ground, that some Hebrew letters are pointed within, as a mark that their pronunciation should be soft. They said, likewise, that harshness in letters was in use in the spiritual heaven, by reason that the spiritual angels are principled in truths, and truth admits of harshness; whereas good, wherein the angels of the Lord's celestial kingdom, or of the third heaven, are principled, admits of no harshness. They declared further, that they had the written Word amongst them composed of letters inflected with significative little bendings and apices; from whence it appeared what those words of the Lord signify, "One jot or one tittle shall in no wise pass from the law, till all be fulfilled" (Matt. v. 18). And again: "It is easier for heaven and earth to pass away, than one tittle of the law to fail" (Luke xvi. 17).

---

## X. THAT HERETICAL OPINIONS MAY BE COLLECTED AND IMBIBED FROM THE LETTER OF THE WORD, BUT THAT TO CONFIRM SUCH OPINIONS IS HURTFUL.

91. It was shewn above, that the Word cannot be understood without doctrine, and that doctrine is as a lamp for the discovery of genuine truths; and that this is a consequence of the Word's being written by mere correspondences. Hence it is that many passages are appearances of truth, and not naked truths: thus many things are written according to the apprehensions of the merely natural man, yet in such a manner, that the simple may understand them in simplicity, the intelligent in intelligence, and the wise in wisdom. Now since the Word is of such a nature, the appearances of truth, which are truths clothed, may be taken for naked truths; and such appearances,

when they are confirmed, become falsities. But this is done by those who believe themselves to be superior to others in wisdom, when yet they are not wise: for wisdom consists in seeing whether a thing be true before it is confirmed, but not in confirming whatever one pleases. The latter is the case with those who possess a talent for confirmation and are in the pride of self-intelligence: but the former with those who love truths, and are affected by them because they are truths, and who apply them to the purposes of life. These are in illumination from the Lord, and see truths by the light of truth: but the others are in illumination from themselves, and see falsities in the light of falsities.

92. All the heresies which ever did, or do still, exist in Christendom, have sprung from this circumstance, that men have taken appearances of truth for genuine truths, and as such have confirmed them. Heresies themselves do not occasion man's condemnation; but an evil life, together with confirmations of the falsities contained in any heresy by misapplication of the Word, and by reasonings that originate in the natural man, are what condemn him. For every one by birth is introduced into the religion of his country, or of his parents, is initiated into it from his earliest years, and afterwards continues in the same persuasion, nor is it in his power to extricate himself from its falsities, being prevented by his engagements in the world; but to live in evil, and to confirm falsities so as to destroy genuine truths, this it is which causes condemnation. For he who simply abides in the religion of his country, who believes in God, and (in case he be of the Christian Church) believes in the Lord, esteems the Word to be holy, and lives according to the commandments of the Decalogue from a religious motive; such a one does not bind himself to the falsities of the religion he professes: when therefore truths are proposed to him, and he perceives them according to the measure of light which he has attained, he has a capacity to embrace them, and thus to be extricated from falsities. But it is not so with him who has confirmed the falsities of his religion: these, when confirmed, are made permanent, and cannot be extirpated: for when a man has confirmed himself in what is false, he is as if he had sworn to maintain it; especially if self-love, or the pride of his own understanding, be engaged in its favor.

93. I have conversed in the spiritual world with some who lived many ages ago, and had confirmed themselves in the falsities of their particular religious persuasions; and I found that they still continued rooted in the same: I have likewise conversed, in that world, with others, who had been of the same religious persuasion, and had entertained the same notions with the former, but yet had not confirmed their falsities in themselves: and I found that, when they were instructed by the

angels, they rejected falsities, and received truths; the consequence was, that the latter were saved, but the former were not. Every man, after death, is instructed by angels, and they are received into heaven who discern truths, and thence falsities; for opportunity is given to every man after death to discern truths spiritually, but they only have the capacity of doing this, who have not confirmed themselves in falsities; for they who have so confirmed themselves are not willing to see truths, and in case they do see them, they turn their backs upon them, and then either ridicule or falsify them.

94. But we will illustrate what we mean by an example. In many passages of the Word we find anger, wrath and vengeance, attributed to God, and it is said that He punishes, casts into hell, tempts, with many other expressions of a like nature: now where all this is believed in a child-like simplicity, and made the ground of the fear of God, and of care not to offend Him, no man incurs condemnation by such a simple belief. But where a man confirms himself in such notions, so as to be persuaded that anger, wrath, vengeance, belong to God, and that He punishes mankind, and casts them into hell, under the influence of such anger, wrath, and vengeance; in this case his belief is condemnatory, because he has destroyed genuine truth, which teaches that God is love itself, mercy itself, and goodness itself, and being these, that He cannot be angry, wrathful, or revengeful. Where such evil passions then are attributed in the Word to God, it is owing to appearance only. It is the same in many other instances.

95. That several expressions in the literal sense of the Word are but appearances of truth, in which genuine truths lie concealed, and that no hurt is incurred by thinking, or even speaking, in simplicity, according to such appearances, but that it is hurtful to confirm them so as to destroy the Divine Truth concealed within, may also be illustrated by an example from nature; which shall here be introduced, because natural considerations instruct and convince the mind more clearly than spiritual. It appears to the bodily eye as if the sun performed a daily and an annual revolution about the earth; hence it is common to say, that the sun rises and sets, that it causes morning, noon, evening, and night, and also the seasons of the year, as spring, summer, autumn, and winter, and consequently days and years; when nevertheless the sun continues immoveable, being an ocean of fire, whilst it is the earth which moves, revolving daily round her own axis, and annually round the sun. A person now, who in simplicity and ignorance supposes that the sun revolves about the earth, does not destroy this natural truth respecting the earth's daily rotation round her own axis, and her annual revolution in the ecliptic; but whoso confirms the sun's apparent motions by the reasonings of the natural

man, particularly if he supports such an opinion by the authority of the Word, which speaks of the sun's rising and setting, invalidates the truth and destroys it. That the sun moves, is then an apparent truth, but that it does not move, is a genuine truth: nevertheless, every one may speak according to the apparent truth, and, indeed, does so speak; but to think, in conformity to such a mode of expression, that the fact is really so, and to confirm such a thought, dulls and darkens the rational understanding. It is similar with the stars of the firmament; it is an apparent truth that they also are borne round daily with the sun, wherefore it is also said of the stars that they rise and set; but it is a genuine truth that the stars are fixed, and that their firmament is immoveable: nevertheless, every one may speak according to the appearance.

96. That it is hurtful to confirm the appearances of truth that occur in the Word, so as to destroy the genuine truth which lies within, may be evident from this consideration. All and every part of the literal sense of the Word has communication with, and opens heaven, according to what was said above, n. 62—69. When therefore man applies that sense to the confirmation of worldly loves, which are contrary to heavenly loves, then the internal of the Word is rendered false [that is, a false meaning is introduced into the words]; wherefore, when the external, which is the literal sense, whose internal is false, has communication with heaven, then heaven is closed, for the angels who are in the internal sense of the Word reject it. Hence it appears, that a false internal, or falsified truth, prevents communication with heaven, and closes it up. This is the reason why it it is hurtful to confirm any false heretical opinions. The Word is like a garden which may be called a heavenly paradise, containing delicacies and delights of every kind, delicacies of fruits and delights of flowers, in the midst of which are trees of life, and beside them fountains of living water; and forest trees round about the garden. Whosoever, being instructed by doctrine, is principled in divine truths, is in the midst of the garden, amongst the trees of life, and in the actual enjoyment of its delicacies and delights: where a man is not principled in truths by virtue of doctrine, but only from the literal sense, he abides in the boundaries of the garden and sees nothing but the forest scenery: but where a man is in the doctrine of a false religion, and has confirmed its falsities in his mind, he is not even in the forest, but in a sandy plain without, where there is not even grass. That these are also the respective states of such persons after death will be confirmed in its proper place.

97. It is moreover to be observed, that the literal sense of the Word is a guard to the genuine truths concealed in it: and it operates as a guard thus, that the literal sense can be turned

in every direction, and be explained according to the reader's apprehension, without its internal being hurt and violated: for no hurt ensues from the literal sense being understood differently by different persons: but the danger is, if the divine truths, which lie concealed within, should be perverted: from this the Word suffers violence; to prevent which the literal sense is its guard; and it operates as such a guard with those who are in falsities from a principle of religion, and yet do not confirm them: from these persons the Word suffers no violence. The literal sense of the Word acting as a guard, is signified in the Word by the cherubs, and is also described by them. This guard is signified by the cherubs, which, after the expulsion of Adam and his wife from the garden of Eden, were placed at the entrance; of which it was written, that, When Jehovah God had driven out the man, he placed at the east end of the Garden of Eden, cherubs, and a flaming sword, which turned this way and that, to keep the way of the tree of life (Gen. iii. 23, 24). By cherubs is signified defence; by the way of the tree of life is signified admission to the Lord, which men have by means of the truths contained in the Word; Divine Truth in its ultimates is represented by the flaming sword, which turned every way, which is like the Word in its literal sense, thus capable of being so turned. The like is meant by the CHERUBS MADE OF GOLD, over the two extremities of the mercy-seat which was above the ark in the tabernacle (Exod. xxv. 18—21). This being the signification of the cherubs, therefore the Lord talked with Moses from between them (Exod. xxv. 22; Numb. vii. 89). As the Lord never speaks with man but in fulness, and the Word, in the literal sense, is Divine Truth in its fulness (as was shewn above, n. 37—49), therefore he spake with Moses from between the cherubs. The like is understood by THE CHERUBS upon the curtains of the tabernacle, and upon the vail (Exod. xxvi. 31): for the curtains and vails of the tabernacle signified the ultimates of heaven and the church, and consequently of the Word (see above, n. 46): and also by the CHERUBS carved over the walls and doors of the temple at Jerusalem (1 Kings vi. 29, 32, 35); and also by the *cherubs* in the new temple (Ezek. xli. 18, 19, 20;—see above, n. 47). Since by cherubs a guard was signified, to provide that the Lord, heaven, and Divine Truth, which constitute the internal of the Word, should not be approached immediately, but by the mediation of ultimates, it is therefore said of the king of Tyre, "Thou sealest up the sum, full of wisdom, and perfect in beauty; thou hast been in Eden, the garden of God; every precious stone was thy covering;—thou art the anointed *cherub* that covereth;—I will destroy thee, *O covering cherub*, from the midst of the stones of fire" (Ezek. xxviii. 12, 13, 14, 16). Tyre signifies the church in respect to the knowledges of truth and good, and hence the king of Tyre is the Word, where those knowledges are, and from whence they are derived. That the Word, in its ultimate, which is the literal sense, is in this place signified by the king of Tyre, and by the term cherub, a guard, is plain from this circumstance, that it is said, "Thou that sealest up the sum, every precious stone was thy covering;" "Thou art the anointed *cherub* that coverest;" and "O covering *cherub*." That whatsoever belongs to the literal sense of the Word, is signified by the precious stones, which are also mentioned in the same chapter, may be seen above (n. 45). Inasmuch as Divine Truth in its ultimates is signified by cherubs, and also a guard, it is therefore written in the Psalms of David, "Jehovah bowed the heavens also, and came down;—and he rode upon a *cherub*" (xviii. 9, 10). "O Shepherd of Israel, thou that dwellest upon the *cherubim*, shine forth" (lxxx. 1). "Jehovah sitteth between the *cherubim*" (xcix. 1). To ride on the cherubs, and to sit upon them, means, on the ultimate sense of the Word. Divine Truth in the Word, with its nature and quality, is described by the cherubs in Ezekiel, chap. i. ix. and x.; but as no one can know what is signified by the particulars in the description of them, unless the spiritual sense be opened, it has, therefore, been discovered to me what is generally signified by all those things which are said concerning the cherubim in the first chapter of Ezekiel; which are these: The divine external sphere of the Word is described, verse 4. Is represented as a man, verse 5. Its conjunction with spiritual and celestial things, verse 6. The natural sense of the Word, its quality, verse 7. The spiritual and celestial sense of the Word conjoined with the natural, its quality, verses 8, 9. Divine love of goodness and truth, celestial, spiritual, and natural, therein, distinct and united, verses 10, 11. That they regard one end, verse 12. The sphere of the Word is from the Divine Good and the Divine Truth of the Lord, from which the Word lives, verses 13, 14. The doctrine of goodness and truth in the Word and from it, verses 15—21. The Divine Essence of the Lord above it and in it, verses 22, 23. And from it, verses 24, 25. That the Lord is above the heavens, verse 26. And that he is Divine Love and Divine Wisdom itself, verses 27, 28. These summaries also have been compared with the Word in heaven, and are in conformity with it.

---

## XI. THAT THE LORD CAME INTO THE WORLD THAT HE MIGHT FULFIL ALL THINGS CONTAINED IN THE WORD, AND THEREBY BECOME DIVINE TRUTH OR THE WORD IN ITS ULTIMATES.

98. THAT the Lord came into the world that He might fulfil all things contained in the Word, may be seen in the DOCTRINE OF THE LORD, n. 8—11; and that He thus became Divine Truth, or the Word, even in ultimates, is understood by these words in John: "And the Word was made flesh, and dwelt among us, and we beheld His glory, the glory as of the only begotten of the Father, full of grace and truth" (i. 14). To be made flesh, is to be made the Word in ultimates. What the Lord's appearance is, as the Word in ultimates, He exhibited to His disciples at His transfiguration, Matt. xvii. 2, &c.; Mark ix. 2, &c.; Luke ix. 28. It is there said, that Moses and Elias appeared in glory; that by Moses and Elias is meant the Word, may be seen above, n. 43. The Lord, as the Word in ultimates, is also described by John in the Apocalypse (i. 13—16); where all parts of the description given of Him signify the ultimates of Divine Truth, or of the Word. The Lord, indeed, before His incarnation, was the Word, or Divine Truth, but only in first principles; for it is said, "In the beginning was the Word, and the Word was with God, and *the Word was God*" (John i. 1, 2): but when the Word was made flesh, then the Lord became the Word in ultimates also; and it is from this circumstance that He is called *the First and the Last* (Apoc. i. 8, 11, 17; ii. 8; xxi. 6; xxii. 12, 13).

99. By reason, also, of the Lord's becoming the Word in its ultimates, the state of the church was entirely changed. All the churches which were before His advent, were representative churches, which could not see Divine Truth but as it were in the shade; but after the advent of the Lord into the world, a church was instituted by Him, which saw Divine Truth in the light. The difference between the churches is similar to evening and morning. The state of the church, previous to the Lord's coming, is also called evening; and the state of the church after His coming, is called morning. The Lord, previous to His coming into the world, was indeed present with the men of the church, but it was mediately through heaven: but since His advent in the world he is immediately present with the men of the church. For in the world He put on also the Divine Natural, in which He is present with men. The glorification of the Lord is the glorification of His Humanity, which He took in the world; and the humanity of the Lord glorified, is the Divine Natural.

100. Few people understand in what sense the Lord is the Word; for it is generally thought, that the Lord, by means of

the Word, may enlighten and teach mankind, and yet that this is no reason why He should be called the Word. But let it be known, that every individual man is his own particular love, and thence his own particular good and his own particular truth: man is man only by virtue of these his constituent parts, and nothing else in his constitution can be called man. On the same ground that man is his own particular good and his own particular truth, angels and spirits are men; for all goodness and truth proceeding from the Lord, is, in its own particular form, man. But the Lord is essential Divine Good, and essential Divine Truth; so also is He the essential man, from whom every man receives what constitutes him a man. That all Divine Good and Divine Truth is, in its form, man, may be seen in the treatise on HEAVEN AND HELL, n. 460; and it is more clearly explained in the works which treat of ANGELIC WISDOM.

---

## XII. THAT PREVIOUS TO THE WORD WHICH THE WORLD NOW POSSESSES, THERE EXISTED A WORD WHICH IS LOST.

101. THAT previous to the Word which was given by Moses and the prophets to the people of Israel, men were acquainted with sacrificial worship, and prophesied from the mouth of Jehovah, may appear from what is recorded in the books of Moses. *That they were acquainted with sacrificial worship*, is evident from these circumstances: that the children of Israel were commanded to destroy the altars of the Gentiles, to break their images, and cut down their groves (Exodus xxxiv. 13; Deut. vii. 5; xii. 3): that Israel in Shittim began to commit whoredom with the daughters of Moab, and called the people unto the *sacrifices* of their gods, and that the people did eat, and bowed themselves to their gods, and chiefly joined themselves to Baal-peor, and that upon that account the anger of Jehovah was kindled against Israel (Numb. xxv. 1, 2, 3): that Balaam, who was from the land of Syria, caused altars to be built, and *sacrificed oxen and sheep* (Numb. xxii. 40; xxiii. 1, 2, 14, 29, 30); that he also *prophesied concerning the Lord*, saying, that there should come a star out of Jacob, and a sceptre should rise out of Israel (Numb. xxiv. 17); *and that he prophesied from the mouth of Jehovah* (Numb. xxii. 13, 18; xxiii. 3, 5, 8, 16, 26; xxiv. 1, 13): from all which circumstances it is very evident, that the Gentiles performed divine worship, in many respects similar to that which was instituted by Moses amongst the people of Israel. That such worship was in use also before the days of Abraham, is plain from what is written

by Moses (Deut. xxxii. 7, 8); but still plainer from what is recorded of *Melchizedek*, king of Salem; as that he brought forth *bread and wine*, and blessed Abraham, and that Abraham gave him *tithes* of all (Gen. xiv. 18, 19, 20); and that Melchizedek represented the Lord, for he is called the priest of the Most High God (Gen. xiv. 18); and it is said of the Lord by David, "Thou art a priest for ever, after the order of Melchizedek" (Psalm cx. 4): hence it was that Melchizedek brought forth bread and wine, as being the most holy things of the church, agreeably to their holiness in the Lord's Supper, and that Melchizedek could bless Abraham, and that Abraham gave him tithes of all.

102. That the Word amongst the ancients was written by mere correspondences, but that it was lost, has been related to me by the angels of heaven; and they said that the Word was still preserved amongst them, and used in heaven, by those ancients among whom that Word existed when they were in the world. Those ancients amongst whom that Word is still in use in heaven, were in parts natives of the land of Canaan and its confines, as of Syria, Mesopotamia, Arabia, Chaldea, Assyria, Egypt, Zidon, Tyre, and Nineveh; the inhabitants of all which kingdoms were initiated into representative worship, and consequently were skilled in the science of correspondences. The wisdom of those times was derived from that science, and thereby they enjoyed interior perception and communication with the heavens: they also who were internally acquainted with the correspondences of that Word, were called wise men and intelligent, and, in succeeding ages, diviners and magi. But, inasmuch as that Word was full of such correspondences as were remotely significative of celestial and spiritual things, in consequence whereof it began to be generally falsified; then, by the divine providence of the Lord, in process of time it was removed, and at last was lost, and another Word, written by correspondences less remote, was given, which was the Word published by the prophets amongst the children of Israel. Yet in this Word are retained several names of places which were in the land of Canaan, and in the neighbouring kingdoms of Asia, by which are signified things similar to what were in the ancient Word. It was on this account that Abraham was commanded to go into that land, and that his posterity, out of the loins of Jacob, were introduced into it.

103. That the ancients had a Word, is evident from the writings of Moses, who mentions it, and also gives quotations from it (Numb. xxi. 14, 15, 27—30); and that the historical parts of that Word were called *the Wars of Jehovah*, and the prophetical parts, *Enunciations*. From the historical parts of that Word Moses has given this quotation: "Wherefore it is said in *the book of the Wars of Jehovah*, what He did in the

Red Sea, and in the brooks of Arnon, and at the stream of the brooks that goeth down to the dwelling of Ar, and lieth upon the border of Moab" (Numb. xxi. 14, 15). By the wars of Jehovah, mentioned in that Word, as in ours, the Lord's combats with the hells are meant and described, and His victories over them, when He should come into the word: the same combats are also meant and described in many passages in the historical part of our Word, as in the wars of Joshua with the inhabitants of the land of Canaan, and in the wars of the judges and of the kings of Israel. From the prophetical parts of that Word Moses has given this quotation: "Wherefore say the *enunciators*, Come unto Heshbon; let the city of Sihon be built and prepared; for there is a fire gone out of Heshbon, a flame from the city of Sihon; it hath consumed Ar of Moab, and the lords of the high places of Arnon. Woe to thee, Moab! thou art undone, O people of Chemosh! He hath given his sons that escaped, and his daughters, into captivity unto Sihon, king of the Amorites; we have shot at them. Heshbon is perished even unto Dibon, and we have laid them waste even unto Nophah, which reacheth unto Medebah" (Numb. xxi. 27—30). The translators render it, *they that speak in proverbs*, but they are more properly callled *enunciators*, and their compositions *prophetical enunciations*, as may appear from the signification of the word *moshalim* in the Hebrew tongue, which not only means proverbs, but also prophetical enunciations; as in Numb. xxiii. 7, 18; xxiv. 3, 15: it is there said, that Balaam uttered *his enunciation*, which was also a prophecy concerning the Lord; his enunciation is called *moshal* in the singular number: it may be further observed, that the passages thence quoted by Moses, are not proverbs, but prophecies. That that Word, like ours, was divinely inspired, is plain from a passage in Jeremiah, where nearly the same expressions occur: "A fire shall come forth out of Heshbon, and a flame from the midst of Sihon, and shall devour the corner of Moab, and the crown of the head of the sons of Shaon. Woe be unto thee, O Moab! the people of Chemosh perisheth; for thy sons are taken captive and thy daughters captive" (xlviii. 45, 46). Besides these, mention is also made of a prophetical book of the ancient Word, called *the book of Jasher*, or the book of the Upright, by David and by Joshua; by David in the following passage: "David lamented—over Saul and over Jonathan; also he bade them teach the children of Judah the bow; behold it is written in the *book of Jasher*" (2 Sam. i. 17, 18): and by Joshua in this passage: "Joshua said, Sun, stand thou still upon Gibeon, and thou, moon, in the valley of Ajalon; is not this written in the *book of Jasher?*" (Josh. x. 12, 13). Moreover, it has been told me that the seven first chapters of Genesis are extant in that ancient Word, and that not the least word is wanting.

## XIII. THAT BY MEANS OF THE WORD, LIGHT IS COMMUNICATED TO THOSE WHO ARE OUT OF THE PALE OF THE CHURCH, AND ARE NOT IN POSSESSION OF THE WORD.

104. THERE is no possibility of conjunction with heaven, unless there be, in some part or other of the earth, a church which is in possession of the Word, and is thus acquainted with the Lord; for the Lord is the God of heaven and earth, and without Him there is no salvation. It is enough that there be a church which is in possession of the Word, although it may consist of very few persons in respect to the whole race of mankind; for still, by means of the Word so possessed, the Lord is present in every country on the face of the earth, inasmuch as by that means heaven is in conjunction with mankind. That conjunction is effected by the Word, may be seen above, n. 62—69.

105. But in what manner the presence and conjunction of the Lord and of heaven is effected in all countries by means of the Word, shall now be shewn. The universal heaven is, in the Lord's sight, as a single man; and so also is the church on earth: that they have, moreover, the actual appearance of a man, may be seen in the treatise concerning HEAVEN AND HELL, n. 59—87. In this man, the church, where the Word is read, and where the Lord is thereby known, is as the *heart* and as the *lungs;* the celestial kingdom as the heart, and the spiritual kingdom as the lungs. Now as from these two fountains of life in the human body, all the other members, viscera, and organs, subsist and live; so also do all those people, in every part of the earth, who have any religion, who worship one God, lead good lives, and thus make a part of this man, subsist and live from the conjunction of the Lord and heaven with the church by means of the Word; resembling in this respect the members and viscera without the thorax, wherein the heart and lungs are contained. For the Word in the church, although it may consist of but few persons, is life to all the rest from the Lord through the heavens; just as the members aud viscera of the whole body receive life from the heart and the lungs. The communication also is similar; which is the reason why those Christians among whom the Word is read, constitute the breast of the fore-mentioned man,—they are also in the middle or centre of all the rest; next to them are the Roman Catholics; beyond these are the Mahometans, who acknowledge the Lord as a very great prophet, and as a son of God; after these come the Africans; and the last circumference is occupied by the people and nations in Asia and the Indies. Concerning which arrangement of these people, something may be seen in the CONTINUATION OF THE LAST JUDGMENT, n. 58. For all who are in that man, look towards the centre, where the Christians are situated.

106. In the centre, where the Christians are situated, who are in possession of the Word, is the greatest light; for light in the heavens is Divine Truth, proceeding from the Lord as the sun there; and inasmuch as the Word is Divine Truth, the greatest light is with those who are in possession of the Word. Light thence, as from its centre, spreads itself around through all the circumferences, quite to the extremities: hence the illumination of the nations and people without the church is also through the Word. That the light in the heavens is Divine Truth proceeding from the Lord, and that that light gives intelligence, not only to the angels, but to men also, may be seen in the treatise concerning HEAVEN AND HELL, n. 126—140.

107. That this is the case in the universal heaven, may be concluded from a similarity of circumstances in every particular society there; for every particular society is a heaven in a lesser form, and is likewise as a man: this may be seen in the treatise concerning HEAVEN AND HELL, n. 41—87. In every society of heaven, they who are in the middle, in like manner, represent the heart and the lungs, and enjoy the greatest degree of light: this light, and the perception of truth thence arising, diffuse themselves from the centre in every direction towards the circumferences, consequently to all who are in the society, and cause their spiritual life. It was shewn me, that when they who were in the centre, and who constituted the province of the heart and of the lungs, and enjoyed the greatest degree of light, were removed, immediately they who were in the neighbourhood around them had their understandings obscured, and were reduced to so faint a perception of truth, as scarcely to have any; but as soon as ever the others were replaced, the light re-appeared, and their former perception of truth was restored.

108. The same may also be illustrated by this experience. There were certain African spirits from Abyssinia with me, whose ears, on a certain occasion, were opened, that they might hear singing in a church of the world, from the Psalms of David; by which they were affected with such delight, that they joined in the singing: after that, however, their ears were closed, so that they could not hear any thing thence; but they were then affected with a greater degree of delight, because it was spiritual, and were at the same time filled with intelligence; for that psalm treated of the Lord, and concerning redemption. The reason of such an increase of delight was, that there was then granted them a communication with that society in heaven, which was in conjunction with those who were singing that psalm in the world. From this and much other experience, it was made clear to me, that communication with the universal heaven is granted through the Word. For which reason, by the divine providence of the Lord, the kingdoms of Europe

and especially those in which the Word is read, have a universal intercourse with the nations without the pale of the church.

109. This may be illustrated by comparison with the heat and light flowing from the sun of this world, which cause vegetation in trees and shrubs, even in such as are not exposed to their direct influence, but are planted in shady places; which yet never fail to grow, if the sun be only risen above the horizon. So it is with the light and heat of heaven, proceeding from the Lord as the sun of heaven, which light is Divine Truth, whence angels and men derive all intelligence and wisdom; it is therefore said of the Word, that it "was with God, and was God;" "that it enlighteneth every man that cometh into the world;" and that this light also "shineth in darkness" (John i. 1, 5, 9): by the Word is there meant the Lord as to Divine Truth.

110. From these circumstances it may evidently appear, that the Word, which is read in the Protestant Church, enlightens all nations and people by spiritual communication; and further, that is provided by the Lord, that there should always be a church on earth, where the Word is read, and where the Lord in consequence is known: when therefore the Word was almost totally rejected by the Romish Church, through the divine providence of the Lord the Reformation took place, and the Word was again received. It was also provided that the Word should be accounted holy by an eminent nation among the papists.

111. Seeing that without the Word there can be no knowledge of the Lord, and thus no salvation, therefore when the Word was entirely falsified and adulterated by the Jewish nation, and thus rendered in a manner null, it pleased the Lord to descend from heaven, and to come into the world to fulfil the Word, and thus renew and restore it, and give light again to the inhabitants of the earth; according to these words of the Lord: "The people that walked in darkness have seen a great light; they that dwell in the land of the shadow of death, upon them hath the light shined" (Isaiah ix. 2; Matt. iv. 16).

112. It having been foretold, that at the end of the present church, also, darkness would arise, in consequence of its members not knowing and acknowledging the Lord as the God of heaven and earth, and separating faith from charity; therefore, lest the genuine understanding of the Word, and consequently the church, should perish, it has pleased the Lord now to reveal the *spiritual sense of the Word*, and to shew that the Word in that sense, and from this in the natural sense, treats of the Lord and the church, and of them only; with many other discoveries, by which the light of truth derived from the Word

that was well nigh extinguished, may be restored. That the light of truth would be almost wholly extinguished at the end of the present church, is foretold in many passages of the Apocalypse, and is also meant by these words of the Lord: "Immediately after the tribulation of those days shall the sun be darkened, and the moon shall not give her light, and the stars shall fall from heaven, and the powers of the heavens shall be shaken; and then—they shall see the Son of Man coming in the clouds of heaven with power and great glory" (Matt. xxiv. 29, 30). By the sun, is there meant the Lord in respect to love; by the moon, the Lord as to faith; by the stars, the Lord as to the knowledges of good and truth; by the Son of Man, the Lord as to the Word; by clouds, the literal sense of the Word; by glory, its spiritual sense, and its transparence through the literal sense.

113. It has been given me to know, by much experience, that man has communication with heaven by means of the Word. Whilst reading the Word, from the first chapter of Isaiah to the last of Malachi, with the Psalms of David, and keeping my thought fixed on the spiritual sense of each passage, it was given me to perceive clearly, that every verse communicates with some particular society in heaven, and thus that the whole Word communicates with the universal heaven.

---

## XIV. THAT WITHOUT THE WORD, NO ONE WOULD HAVE ANY KNOWLEDGE OF GOD, OR OF HEAVEN AND HELL, OR OF A LIFE AFTER DEATH, AND MUCH LESS OF THE LORD.

114. THIS follows as a common conclusion from all that has been said and shewn; as, that the Word is Divine Truth itself, n. 1—4: that the Word is the medium of conjunction with the angels of heaven, n. 62—69: that everywhere in the Word there is a marriage of the Lord and the Church, and consequently a marriage of goodness and truth, n. 80—89; that the state of the church is according to its understanding of the Word, n. 76—79: that the Word is also in the heavens, and that from thence the angels derive their wisdom, n. 70—75: that through the Word also the nations and people without the pale of the church derive their spiritual light, n. 104—113: beside many other things: from which it may be concluded, that without the Word no one can have spiritual intelligence, which consists in the knowledge of the Lord, of heaven and hell, and a life after death; nor, moreover, could know any thing of the Lord, of faith and love to Him, nor, consequently, any thing of redemption, by which nevertheless we have our

salvation. The Lord also says to His disciples, "Without me ye can do nothing" (John xv. 5). "Man can receive nothing except it be given him from heaven" (John iii. 27).

115. But there are persons who insist, and confirm themselves in the opinion, that man, without the Word, might know the existence of a God, and likewise of heaven and hell, with other points which the Word teaches, and who by that means derogate from the authority and holiness of the Word, if not with their mouth, yet in their heart; and it would not be proper to reason with such persons from the Word, but from the natural light of reason; for they do not believe the Word, but themselves. Inquire then of the light of reason, and you will find that there are two faculties of life in man, called understanding and will, and that the understanding is subject to the will, and not the will to the understanding; for the understanding only teaches and points out the way. Inquire further, and you will find that the will of man is his *proprium*, or selfhood: that this, considered in itself, is evil: and that in consequence of this his understanding is full of false apprehensions. When you have made these discoveries, you will see, that man of himself is not willing to understand any thing but what comes from the *proprium* or selfhood of his will, nor would be able unless there were some other source of knowledge. Man, from the *proprium* of his will, is not desirous of understanding any thing but what regards himself and the world. Every thing of a higher nature is in darkness to him. When he saw the sun, the moon, and the stars, if by chance he should reflect on their origin, he would not be able to refer them to any other creative power than their own; for could he proceed farther than many very learned men in the world have done, who, although they were informed by the Word that God created all things, have yet ascribed creation to nature? What then would have been their sentiments in case they had received no information from the Word? Is it credible, that the ancient philosophers, as Aristotle, Cicero, Seneca, and others, who have written about God, and the immortality of the soul, received their first information on those subjects from their own understanding? No, surely, but from others, to whom the information was successively handed down from those who had it originally from the Word. In like manner, the writers on natural religion do not derive their knowledge on the subject from themselves, but only confirm, by rational deductions, the truths they have learnt from the church, which is in possession of the Word; and it is possible there may be some amongst them who confirm such truths, and yet do not believe them.

116. It has been permitted me to see people, born in remote islands, who were possessed of rationality so far as relates to civil concerns, and yet had no knowledge at all concerning

God. Such persons, in the spiritual world, have the appearance of apes; but whereas they are men of birth, and consequently enjoy the capacity of receiving spiritual life, they are instructed by angels, and by means of knowledges concerning the Lord as to His human character, are made alive. What man of himself is, clearly appears from those who are in hell, some of whom have been ranked among the learned and distinguished: these are unwilling to hear any thing of God, and on that account cannot pronounce the word "God." I have seen them, and conversed with them; and I have also conversed with some who have burst into the most violent wrath and anger at the bare mention of God. Consider, therefore, what sort of a creature man would have been, supposing him to have received no information about God, when some, who have spoken about God, have written about God, and have preached about God, are in such a state. There are many such from among the Jesuits. The reason,why they are in such a state, is, because their wills are evil, and the will, as before observed, leads the understanding, and robs it of the truths which it had received from the Word. If man could have known, of himself, that there is a God, and a life after death, how comes it to pass that he never discovered that man is a real man after death? Why does he imagine that his soul, or spirit, is like a puff of wind, or ether, which has neither eyes to see, nor ears to hear, nor mouth to speak, until it is re-united with its dead body and its skeleton? Supposing therefore a doctrine on the subject of worship to be framed from the light of reason alone, would it not establish the worship of self; as was the case in former ages, and is also still the case with many who yet are instructed by the Word, that God alone is to be worshipped? It is not possible that any other worship but that of self should proceed from the *proprium* or selfhood of man, not even the worship of the sun and the moon.

117. The prevalence of religious worship from the most early ages of the world, and the universal knowledge of a God amongst the inhabitants of the globe, with some notion of a life after death, are not to be ascribed to men, nor to their self-derived intelligence, but to the ancient Word mentioned above, n. 101, 102, 103; and, in succeeding times, to the Israelitish Word. From these two sources, religious knowledge was propagated through all parts of India, with its islands; through Egypt and Ethiopia into the kingdoms of Africa; from the maritime parts of Asia into Greece; and from thence into Italy. But as the Word could not be written otherwise than by representatives, which are such earthly existences as correspond with heavenly ones, and are consequently significative of them, therefore the religious notions of the Gentiles were changed into idolatry, and in Greece were turned into fables;

and the divine properties and attributes were considered as so many separate gods, governed by one supreme Deity, whom they called Jove, from Jehovah. That they had a knowledge of paradise, of the flood, of the sacred fire, of the four ages, beginning with that of gold and ending with that of iron, by which in the Word are signified the four states of the church, as in Daniel, chap. ii. 31—35, is well known. That the Mahometan religion, which succeeded and destroyed the former religious persuasions of many nations, was taken from the Word of both Testaments, is also well known.

118. Lastly, I will mention what is the state of those after death who ascribe all things to their own understanding, and very little, if any thing, to the Word. They first become like persons intoxicated, afterwards like idiots, and lastly they sink into stupidity and sit in darkness. Let every one therefore take heed to himself how he falls into such insanity.

THE END.

# THE DOCTRINE

OF

# FAITH

OF

# THE NEW JERUSALEM

THE

# DOCTRINE

OF

# THE NEW JERUSALEM

RESPECTING

# FAITH.

---

BY EMANUEL SWEDENBORG,

*Servant of the Lord Jesus Christ.*

---

BEING A TRANSLATION OF HIS WORK ENTITLED

"DOCTRINA NOVÆ HIEROSOLYMÆ DE FIDE." Amstelodami, 1763.

NEW YORK:

AMERICAN SWEDENBORG PRINTING AND PUBLISHING SOCIETY.

1873.

# THE DOCTRINE

OF

# FAITH

OF

# THE NEW JERUSALEM.

---

## I. THAT FAITH IS AN INTERNAL ACKNOWLEDGMENT OF TRUTH.

1. THE idea attached to the term faith at the present day, is this, that it consists in thinking a thing to be so, because it is taught by the church, and because it does not fall within the scope of the understanding. For it is usual with those who inculcate it to say, "You must believe, and not doubt." If you answer, "I do not comprehend it," it is replied, that is the very circumstance which makes a doctrine an object of faith. Thus the faith of the present day is a faith in what is not known, and may be called a blind faith: and as being the dictate of one person abiding in the mind of another, it is an historical faith [or a faith that depends on the authority of the relater]. That this is not spiritual faith will be seen in what follows.

2. Genuine faith, however, is an acknowledgment that a thing is so, because it is true. For he who is in genuine faith thinks and speaks to this effect: "This is true; and therefore I believe it." For faith is the assurance with which we embrace that which is true; and that which is true is the proper object of faith. A person of this character also, if he does not comprehend a sentiment, and see its truth, will say, "I do not know whether this is true or not, therefore I do not yet believe it. How can I believe what I do not comprehend? Perhaps it may be false."

3. But the common language is, that nobody can comprehend things of a spiritual or theological nature, because they transcend our natural faculties. Spiritual truths, however, are as capable of being comprehended as natural truths, and when the comprehension of them is not altogether clear, still, when

they are heard, they fall so far within the perception of the hearer, that he can discern whether they are truths or not, especially if he be a person who is affected with truths. This it has been granted me to know from repeated experience. Opportunities have been given me of conversing with the ignorant, the dull, the stupid; and also with persons who had been born within the church, and had heard something of the Lord, of faith, and of charity, but who nevertheless were immersed in falses and in evils. It was given me to relate the arcana of wisdom, and they comprehended them all, and acknowledged their truth; but they were then in that light of the understanding which is proper to every man, and at the same time in the glory of being thought intelligent. But this occurred in my intercourse with spirits. Many who were present were thus convinced, that spiritual things may be comprehended as well as natural things, that is; when they are heard or read; but it is more difficult for a man to discover them by unassisted reflection. The reason that spiritual things admit of being comprehended, is, because man, as to his understanding, is capable of being elevated into the light of heaven, in which light no other objects appear than such as are spiritual, which are the truths of faith; for the light of heaven is spiritual light.

4. Hence now it is that those who are in the spiritual affection of truth, enjoy an internal acknowledgment of it. As the angels are in that affection, they utterly reject the tenet, That the understanding ought to be kept in subjection to faith: for they say, "How can you believe a thing, when you do not see whether it is true or not?" And should any one affirm that what he advances must nevertheless be believed, they reply, "Do you think yourself a god, that I am to believe you? Or, that I am mad, that I should believe an assertion in which I do not see any truth? If I must believe it, cause me to see it." The dogmatizer is thus constrained to retire. Indeed, the wisdom of the angels consists solely in this, that they see and comprehend what they think.

5. There is a spiritual idea of which few have any knowledge, which enters by influx into the minds of those who are in the affection of truth, and dictates interiorly, whether the thing which they are hearing or reading, is true or not. In this idea are those who read the Word in illumination from the Lord. To be in illumination is to be in perception, and thence in an internal acknowledgment, that "This is true; and this." Those who are in this illumination, are said to be "taught of Jehovah" (Isaiah liv. 13; John vi. 45); and of them it is said in Jeremiah, "Behold, the days come,—that I will make a new covenant:—this shall be the covenant;—I will put my law in their inward parts, and write it in their hearts; and they shall no more teach every man his neighbour, and every man his

brother, saying, Know ye Jehovah; for they shall all know Me" (xxxi. 31, 33, 34).

6. From these considerations it is plain, that faith and truth are a one. This also is the reason that the ancients, who were more accustomed to think of truth from affection than the moderns, instead of faith used the word truth: and for the same reason in the Hebrew language, truth and faith are expressed by one and the same word, namely, Amuna or Amen.

7. The reason why faith is mentioned by the Lord in the Evangelists and in the Apocalypse, is, because the Jews did not believe it to be true, that the Lord was the Messiah foretold by the prophets: and where truth is not believed, there faith is mentioned. But still it is one thing to have faith and believe in the Lord, and another to have faith in, or believe, any man. The difference shall be explained below.

8. Faith separated from truth entered and invaded the church together with the dominion of popery, because the chief security of that religion was ignorance of the truth. For which reason also they forbade the reading of the Word: otherwise they could not have been worshipped as deities, nor their saints invoked, nor idolatry introduced to such an extent, as that their carcases, bones, and sepulchres, should be thought holy, and be converted into sources of lucre. Hence it is plain what enormous falsities a blind faith is capable of producing.

9. A blind faith continued also afterwards among many of the Reformed, owing to their separating faith from charity: for those who do this cannot but be in ignorance of the truth, and will give the name of faith to the mere thought that a thing is so, without having any internal acknowledgement that so it is. Among these also, ignorance is the security of their tenets; for so long as ignorance reigns, with the persuasion that things of a theological nature are too high for the understanding, they can talk without being contradicted; and others suppose their notions are true, and that they themselves know what they mean.

10. The Lord said to Thomas, "Because thou hast seen me, thou hast believed; blessed are they that have not seen and yet have believed" (John xx. 29): by which is not meant a faith separate from the internal acknowledgment of truth, but that those are blessed who do not see the Lord with their *eyes*, as Thomas did, and yet believe that HE IS: for this is seen in the light of truth which is from the Word.

11. Since the internal acknowledgment of truth is faith, and faith and truth are a one, as was observed above (n. 2, 4, 5, 6), it follows that an external without an internal acknowledgment is not faith; and also, that a persuasion of what is false is not faith. An external without an internal acknow-

ledgment is a faith in what is not known; and faith in what is not known is only knowledge [scientia], which is a thing of the memory, and which, if confirmed, becomes a persuasion. Those who are principled herein think that a tenet is true, because another says so; or they think it is true in consequence of having confirmed it: and yet a false sentiment may be as easily confirmed as a true one, and sometimes more strongly. By thinking that a tenet is true in consequence of having confirmed it, is meant, to think that what another says is true, and to confirm it without previous investigation.

12. If any one thinks with himself, or says to another, "Who can have that internal acknowledgment of truth, which is faith? I cannot:" I will tell him how he may: "Shun evils as sins, and apply to the Lord: then you will have as much as you desire." That he who shuns evils as sins is in the Lord, may be seen in the DOCTRINE OF LIFE FOR THE NEW JERUSALEM, n. 18—31. That he loves truth and sees it, n. 32—41, of the same; and, that he has faith, n. 42—52, of the same.

---

## II. THAT AN INTERNAL ACKNOWLEDGMENT OF TRUTH, WHICH IS FAITH, CANNOT EXIST WITH ANY BUT SUCH AS ARE IN CHARITY.

13. WHAT faith is, has been explained above; here we will explain what charity is.

Charity in its origin is the affection of good: and as good loves truth, the affection of good produces the affection of truth; and, by the affection of truth, the acknowledgment of truth, which is faith. By these in their series, the affection of truth exists, and becomes charity. This is the progression of charity, from its origin, which is the affection of good, through faith, which is the acknowledgment of truth, to its end, which is charity. Its end is action. Hence it appears how love, which is the affection of good, produces faith, which is the same as the acknowledgment of truth, and by this produces charity, which is the same as the act of love through faith.

14. But to set this in a clearer light. Good is nothing else but *use*; wherefore charity in its origin is the affection of use: and as use loves the means necessary for its existence, charity produces the affection of means, whence results the knowledge of what they are. Through these in their series the affection of use exists and becomes charity.

15. Their progression is like the progression of all things that belong to the will, through the understanding, into acts in the body. The will produces nothing of itself without the un-

derstanding, nor does the understanding produce any thing of itself without the will; they must act in conjunction that any thing may exist. Or, what amounts to the same, affection, which is of the will, produces nothing of itself except by means of thought, which is of the understanding, and *vice versa:* they must act in conjunction that any thing may exist. For consider: if from thought you remove affection proceeding from some love or other, can you think? Or if from affection you remove thought, can you be affected by any thing? Or, what amounts to the same, if from thought you remove affection, can you speak? Or if from affection you remove thought or understanding, can you do any thing? It is the same with charity and faith.

16. These truths may be illustrated by comparison with a tree. A tree, in its origin, is a seed, in which there is an effort [conatus] to produce fruit. This effort being excited by heat, first produces a root, and from it a stem or stalk with branches and leaves, and lastly fruit; and thus the effort to fructify comes into existence. From this it is plain, that the effort to produce fruit is perpetual in the whole of the progression, until it comes into existence or effect; for if it were to cease, the faculty of vegetating would instantly perish. This is the application. The tree is man; the effort to produce means, is, with man, from his will in his understanding; the stem or stalk with its branches and leaves, are, in man, the instrumental means, and are called the truths of faith; fruits, which are the ultimate effects of the effort in a tree to fructify, are, in man, uses: in these his will comes into existence. Hence it may be seen, that the will of producing uses, by means of the understanding is perpetual through the whole progression, until it comes into existence. Respecting the will and the understanding, and their conjunction, see the DOCTRINE OF LIFE FOR THE NEW JERUSALEM, n. 43.

17. From what has now been said it is evident, that charity, so far as it is the affection of good or of use, produces faith, as the means whereby it may exist; consequently, that charity and faith, in effecting uses, act in conjunction: also, that faith does not produce good or use from itself, but from charity; for faith is charity as to its means of operation. It is therefore a fallacy to suppose that faith produces good as a tree does fruit,—the tree is not faith, but the tree is man.

18. It should be known, that charity and faith form a one, as do the will and the understanding; since charity is of the will, and faith of the understanding. In like manner, charity and faith form a one, as do affection and thought; since affection is of the will, and thought of the understanding. So again, charity and faith form a one, as do goodness and truth; because good is of the affection, which is of the will, and truth of the

thought, which is of the understanding. In a word, charity and faith make a one, like essence and form; for the essence of faith is charity, and the form of charity is faith. Hence it is evident, that faith without charity is like a form without an essence, which is not any thing; and that charity without faith is like an essence without a form, which likewise is not any thing.

19. It is with charity and faith in man just as it is with the motion of the heart, which is called its systole and diastole, and the motion of the lungs, which is called respiration. There is also an entire correspondence of these with the will and understanding of man, and thus with charity and faith: wherefore also the will and its affection are meant by the heart, when mentioned in the Word, and the understanding and its thought by the soul, and also by the spirit. It may here be necessary to apprize the unlearned reader, that the primary meaning of the words for soul and spirit, in the Hebrew and Greek languages, as also in the Latin, is breath, by which word, likewise, they are frequently translated. It is only in a secondary and figurative sense that these words are used to denote that part of man which lives after death. Hence to yield the breath is to retain animation no longer [emittere *animam*, est non amplius *animare*]; and to give up the ghost is to respire no longer [et emittere *spiritum*, est non amplius *respirare*]. From which it follows that there can be no faith without charity, nor charity without faith; and that faith without charity is like the respiration of the lungs without a heart, which cannot take place in any living thing, but in an automaton only; and that charity without faith is like a heart without lungs, in which case there can be no conscious life: consequently, that charity by faith accomplishes uses, as the heart by the lungs accomplishes actions. So great, indeed, is the similitude between the heart and charity, and between the lungs and faith, that in the spiritual world it is known by a person's breathing, what is the nature of his faith, and by the beating of his heart, what is the nature of his charity. For angels and spirits, as well as men, live from the heart and by respiration: thence it is that they, as well as men in this world, feel, think, act and speak.

20. Since charity is love towards our neighbour, what our neighbour is shall also be explained. Our neighbour, in a natural sense, is man, both collectively and individually. Man in the aggregate, is the church, our country, and society: and man as an individual is our fellow-citizen, who in the Word is called our brother and companion. But, our neighbour, in a spiritual sense, is good; and as use is good, our neighbour, in a spiritual sense, is use.

That use is our spiritual neighbour, every one must acknowledge. For who loves a man merely as a person, and not rather for something in him, by virtue of which he is what he is? Therefore he loves him for his quality; for that is the man. This quality which is love is his use, and is called good; wherefore this is our neighbour. As the Word in its bosom is spiritual, therefore, in its spiritual sense, this love of good is what is signified by loving our neighbour.

21. But it is one thing to love our neighbour from the good or use that is in him towards ourselves, and another to love our neighbour from the good or use that is in ourselves towards him. To love our neighbour from the good or use in him to ourselves, even a bad man can do; but to love our neighbour from our own good or use towards him, can only be done by a good man: for he loves good from good, or loves use from the affection of use. The difference between these is described by the Lord in Matthew, v. 42, 43. It is said by many, "I love him because he loves me, and does me good;" but still to love him for that reason only, is not to love him interiorly, unless he that so loves is principled in good, and thence loves the good of the other. The one is in charity; but the other is only in friendship, which is not charity.

He who loves his neighbour from charity, conjoins himself with the good that is in him; and not with his person, except so far and so long as he is in good. Such a man is spiritual, and loves his neighbour spiritually. But he who loves another only from friendship, conjoins himself with his person, and at the same time with the evil that is in him. The latter after death cannot, without great difficulty, be separated from the person who is in evil: but the former can. Charity does this by faith; because faith is truth; and the man who is in charity examines and discovers, by means of truth, what ought to be beloved, and, in loving and conferring benefits, regards the quality of the other's use.

22. Love to the Lord is love properly so called, and love towards our neighbour is charity. Love to the Lord is not communicated to man except in charity. In this the Lord conjoins himself with man.

Since faith in its essence is charity, it follows, that no one can have faith in the Lord except he be in charity. From this, by means of faith, there is a conjunction; by charity, a conjunction of the Lord with man; and by faith, a conjunction of man with the Lord. That the conjunction is reciprocal, may be seen in the DOCTRINE OF LIFE FOR THE NEW JERUSALEM, n. 102—107.

23. In a word: In proportion as any one shuns evils as sins, and looks to the Lord, he is in charity, and therefore in the same proportion he is in faith. That in proportion as any one shuns evils as sins and looks to the Lord, he is in charity, may be seen in the DOCTRINE OF LIFE FOR THE NEW JERUSALEM

n. 67—73; also n. 74—91; and that in the same proportion he has faith, n. 42—52. What charity is, in a proper sense, may be seen in n. 114 of the same work.

24. From all that has been thus far said, it is manifest that a saving faith, which is an internal acknowledgement of truth, cannot be communicated to any, except to such as are in charity.

---

## III. THAT THE KNOWLEDGES [COGNITIONES] OF WHAT IS TRUE AND GOOD ARE NOT THE KNOWLEDGES OF FAITH, BEFORE A MAN IS IN CHARITY; BUT THAT THEY ARE A STORE-HOUSE, OUT OF WHICH THE FAITH OF CHARITY MAY BE FORMED.

25. MAN has the affection of knowing from his earliest childhood. By it he learns many things which will be of use to him, and many which will be of no use. When he grows up, by application to some business, he acquires the things which relate to his business: this then becomes his use,—that by which he is affected. Thus commences the affection of use, which produces the affection of the means [media], whereby he acquires his business, which is his use.

This progression takes place with every one in the world: because every one has some business, to which he proceeds, from the use which is his end, by the means to the use itself, which is the effect. Since, however, this use, together with the means of attaining it, is for the purposes of life in this world, the affection of it is natural.

26. But since every man regards not only the uses conducive to a life in this world, but will also regard the uses conducive to a life in heaven; since he will enter into this after his life in the world, and will live therein afterwards to eternity. Wherefore every one from his childhood procures for himself —from the Word, or from the doctrine of the church, or from preaching,—knowledges of what is true and good, which are for the purposes of that life, and deposits them in his natural memory; acquiring them in greater or less abundance, according to his connate affection of knowing, and according as this has been increased by various excitements.

27. But all these knowledges, whatever may be their number and quality, are only a storehouse, from which the faith of charity may be formed; and this faith is not formed, except in proportion as he shuns evils as sins. If he shun evils as sins, then these knowledges become those of the faith which has in it spiritual life: but if he do not shun evils as sins, these knowledges are knowledges only, and do not become those of a faith which has in it any spiritual life.

28. This storehouse is especially necessary, because without it faith cannot be formed; for the knowledges of truth and of good enter into faith and compose it. If there be none of these, faith does not exist; for a faith entirely empty and void is not given: if they be few, a scanty and meagre faith is formed; if they be many, a faith rich and full, according to their abundance, is formed.

29. But let it be known, that the knowledges of genuine truth and good constitute faith, and by no means the knowledges of the false; for faith is truth, as has been observed above, n. 5—11; and falsity, because it is the opposite of truth, destroys faith. Neither can charity exist where there are mere falsities; for, as was said above, n. 18, charity and faith form a one, just as good and truth form a one. Hence it also follows, that no knowledges of genuine truth and good form no faith; that a few form some faith; and that many constitute a faith which is enlightened according to their fulness. Such as is a man's faith originating in charity, such is his intelligence.

30. There are, moreover, many persons who have not an internal acknowledgment of truth, and yet have the faith of charity. They are such as in their life have had respect to the Lord. and from a principle of religion have avoided evils; but who have been kept from thinking of truths by cares and business in the world, and also from a want of truths in their teachers. Yet these interiorly, or in their spirit, are in the acknowledgment of truth, because they are in the affection of it; wherefore after death, when they become spirits, and are instructed by angels, they acknowledge truths and receive them with joy. But it is otherwise with those who in their life have not had respect unto the Lord, and have not avoided evils from a principle of religion. These interiorly, or in their spirit, are not in any affection of truth, and therefore not in any acknowledgment of it: wherefore after death, when they become spirits, and are instructed by angels, they are unwilling to knowledge truths, and therefore do not receive them. For the evil of life interiorly hates truths; but the good of life interiorly loves truths.

31. The knowledges of what is good and true which precede faith, appear to some as though they were of faith; but yet they are not. Their thinking and saying that they believe, is no proof that they really do believe Neither do such knowledges constitute faith; for they only consist in thinking that a thing is so, without any internal acknowledgment that the truths professed are truths; and faith in unknown truths is a species of persuasion remote from internal acknowledgment. As soon, however, as charity is implanted, then those knowledges become the knowledges of faith; but no farther than there

is charity in that faith. In the first state, before charity is perceived, faith appears to them to be in the first place, and charity in the second; but in the second state, when charity is perceived, faith stands in the second place, and charity in the first. The first state is called reformation; the second state is called regeneration. When a man is in this latter state, then wisdom increases in him daily; and good daily multiplies truths, and makes them fruitful. He is then like a tree which bears fruit, and in its fruit deposits seeds, from which new trees are produced, and at length a garden. Then he becomes truly a man, and after death an angel, in whom charity constitutes the life, and faith of the form, which is beautiful according to its quality; but his faith is then no longer called faith but intelligence.

From these considerations it may appear, that the all of faith is from charity, and nothing of it from itself: also, that charity produces faith, and not faith charity. The knowledges of truth, which precede, are just like the provision in a barn, which does not nourish a man, unless, having an appetite for food, he takes out the corn for use.

32. It shall also be explained, how faith is formed from charity. Every man has a natural mind and a spiritual mind; a natural mind for the world, and a spiritual mind for heaven. Man as to his understanding is in both; but not as to his will, before he shuns and turns away from evils as sins. When he does this, his spiritual mind is open also in respect to the will; and then there flows thence into the natural mind spiritual heat from heaven; which heat in its essence is charity, and gives life to the knowledges of truth and good which are therein, and out of them forms faith. The case herein is just as it is with a tree, which does not receive vegetative life before heat flows from the sun, and joins itself with the light, as occurs in the season of spring. There is, moreover, a full parallelism between the vivification of man and the vegetation of a tree, in this respect, that the one is effected by the heat of this world, and the other by the heat of heaven: wherefore also man is so often likened to a tree by the Lord.

33. From these few observations it may appear, that the knowledges of truth and good are not of faith before a man is in charity; but that they are a storehouse, out of which the faith of charity may be formed. The knowledges of truth become truths in a regenerate man, as do likewise the knowledges of good; for the knowledge of good is in the understanding, but the affection of good is in the will: and that is called truth which is in the understanding, and that is called good which is in the will.

---

## IV. A UNIVERSAL IDEA OF THE CHRISTIAN FAITH.

34. THE Christian faith in its universal idea is this: "That the Lord from eternity, who is Jehovah, came into the world to subjugate the hells, and to glorify His Humanity; that without this no mortal could be saved; and that those are saved who believe in Him."

35. This is called the Christian faith in its universal idea, because it is the universal of faith, and the universal of faith is that which enters into the whole and every part of it. It is a universal of faith, that God is one in person and essence in whom there is a trinity; and that the Lord is that God. It is a universal of faith, that no mortal could have been saved, unless the Lord had come into the world. It is a universal of faith, that He came into the world that He might remove hell from man; and He removed it by combats against it, and by victories over it; thus He subjugated it, and reduced it to order and under obedience to Himself. It is also a universal of faith, that He came into the world to glorify the Humanity, which He took upon Him in the world; that is, to unite it to the Divinity from which are all things: it is thus, that having subjugated hell, He keeps it in order and under obedience to Himself to eternity. As neither of these ends could have been effected except by temptations even to the last of them, which was His passion on the cross, therefore He endured that also. These are the universals of the Christian faith respecting the Lord.

36. The universal of the Christian faith on man's part is, to believe in the Lord; for by believing in Him, conjunction with Him is effected, whereby is salvation. To believe in Him is to have confidence that He will save: and because no one can have such confidence, but He who lives a good life, therefore this also is implied by believing in Him.

37. Of these two universals of the Christian faith, the first, which relates to the Lord, is treated of specifically in THE DOCTRINE OF THE NEW JERUSALEM CONCERNING THE LORD; and the second, which relates to man, in THE DOCTRINE OF LIFE FOR THE NEW JERUSALEM: wherefore there is no occasion to enter into any further explanation of them here.

---

## V. A UNIVERSAL IDEA OF THE FAITH GENERALLY PREVAILING.

38. THE faith generally prevailing, in its universal idea, is this: "That God the Father sent His Son to make satisfaction for the human race, and that by reason of this the Son's merit, He is moved to compassion, and saves those who believe this;"

or, according to others, "those who believe this, and at the same time do good."

39. But that it may be seen more clearly what the nature of this faith is, I will state in order the several things which it implies.

The faith of the present day,

I. Supposes God the Father and God the Son to be two; both from eternity.

II. It supposes that God the Son came into the world by the will of the Father, to make satisfaction for the human race; who otherwise would have perished in eternal death by the divine justice, which they also call vindictive justice.

III. It supposes the Son to have made satisfaction by fulfilling the law, and by the passion of the cross.

IV. It supposes the Father to have been moved to compassion by these acts of the Son.

V. It supposes the Son's merit to be imputed to those who believe this.

VI. It supposes this to take place in an instant; and that therefore it may do so, if not before, even at the point of death.

VII. It supposes somewhat of temptation, and then deliverance through that faith.

VIII. It supposes such as these, especially, to have trust and confidence.

IX. It supposes that such as these, especially, enjoy justification, the plenary grace of the Father for the Son's sake, the remission of all sins, and thus salvation.

X. The more learned suppose, that there is present with persons thus justified an effort towards good which operates secretly, and does not manifestly move the will; others suppose a manifest operation: both by the Holy Ghost.

XI. Of those who confirm themselves in this notion, that no one can do good from himself, which is really good, and which is not meritorious, and that they are not under the yoke of the law, the majority omit, and do not think of the evil and the good of life; for they say within themselves that good works do not save, neither does evil condemn, because faith alone does all things.

XII. In general, they suppose the understanding ought to be kept in subjection to this faith, calling that faith which is not understood.

40. To illustrate and investigate the truth or otherwise, of these several propositions, is unnecessary; that must appear clearly from what has been said above, and also particularly from what is proved from the Word, and at the same time rationally confirmed, in THE DOCTRINE OF LIFE FOR THE NEW JERUSALEM, and in THE DOCTRINE OF THE NEW JERUSALEM RESPECTING THE LORD.

41. But yet that it may be seen what is the nature of faith separated from charity, and what the nature of faith not separated from charity, I will communicate what I have heard from an angel of heaven. He told me that he had conversed with many of the Reformed, and had heard what the nature of their faith was; and he related what had passed between himself and one who was in faith separated from charity, and another who was in faith not separated from charity, and what he had heard from both. He stated that he questioned them, and that they replied; and as these conversations are adapted to throw light on the subject, I will here relate them.

42. The angel said that he thus conversed with him who was in faith separated from charity:

"Friend, who art thou?" He replied, "I am a Christian of the Reformed Church." "What is thy doctrine, and the religion thou derivest from it?" He replied, "It is faith." He said, "What is the nature of thy faith?" The other made answer, "My faith is, that God the Father sent His Son to make satisfaction for the sins of mankind; and that those are saved who believe this." He then asked him, "What more dost thou know respecting salvation?" To which he replied, "Salvation is obtained by that faith alone." He said further, "What dost thou know of redemption?" He answered, "It was effected by the passion of the cross, and the Son's merit is imputed through that faith." Again: "What dost thou know of regeneration?" He answered, "It is effected by faith." "What dost thou know of repentance and the remission of sins?" His reply was, "They are attained by that faith." "Tell me what thou knowest of love and charity?" His answer was, "They are that faith." "Tell me what thou knowest of good works?" He replied, "They are that faith." "Tell me what thou thinkest of all the commandments in the Word?" He made answer, "They are included in that faith." Then he said, "What then, art thou to do nothing?" His answer was, "What can I do? I cannot do good, which is really good, from myself?" He said, "Canst thou have faith from thyself?" His reply was, "I cannot." He said, "How then canst thou have faith?" He replied, "This I do not inquire into. I will have faith." At length he said, "Dost thou know any thing more respecting salvation?" His answer was, "What more should I know, when salvation is obtained by that faith alone?" Then the angel said, "Thou answerest like a musician who can sound but one note; I hear nothing but faith. If that is what thou knowest, and nothing more, thou knowest nothing. Depart hence and see thy companions." So he departed, and found them in a desert where there was no grass. He asked what was the reason of this; and was answered, "Because there is nothing of the church in them."

43. The angel thus spoke with him who was in faith not separated from charity:

"Friend, who art thou?" He answered, "I am a Christian of the Reformed Church." "What is thy doctrine and thence thy religion?" He replied, "Faith and charity." He said, "Are these two?" The answer was, "They cannot be separated." He said. "What is faith?" The other replied, "It is to believe what the Word teaches." He said, "What is charity?" The answer was, "It is to do what the Word teaches." He said, "Hast thou only believed these things, or hast thou also done them?" His answer was, "I have also done them."

The angel of heaven then looked at him, and said, "My friend, come along with me, and dwell with us."

---

## VI. ON THE NATURE OF FAITH SEPARATED FROM CHARITY.

44. That it may be seen what the nature of faith is, when separated from charity, I will shew it in its nakedness, as follows:

"That God the Father, being angry with mankind, rejected them from Him, and out of justice resolved to avenge Himself by their eternal damnation. And that he said to the Son, 'Descend; fulfil the law and take upon thyself the damnation destined for them; and then peradventure I shall be moved to compassion.' Wherefore He descended, and fulfilled the law, and suffered Himself to be hanged on the cross, and cruelly put to death. Which being done, He returned to the Father, and said, 'I have taken upon myself the damnation of mankind; therefore now be thou merciful;' thus interceding for them. But He had for answer, 'For their own sakes I cannot; however, as I saw thee on the cross, and beheld thy blood, I am moved to compassion. Still I will not pardon them; I will only impute unto them thy merit; and that, only to those who acknowledge this. This shall be the faith by which they may be saved.'"

45. Such is that faith exhibited in its nakedness. Who that has any enlightened reason does not see in it inconsistencies, which are contrary to the very Divine Essence? as, that God, who is love itself and mercy itself, could, out of anger and consequent vengeance, condemn men and devote them to hell? also, that He should desire to be moved to compassion by beholding the condemnation transferred to His Son; and by a view of His sufferings upon the cross and of His blood? Who possessing any enlightened reason does not see that one God could not say to another God, who was His equal, "I do

not pardon them, but I impute to them thy merit?" as well as also, "Now let them live as they please; only let them believe this, and they shall be saved?" Not to mention other absurdities.

46. But the reason why these things are not seen, is, because they have induced a blind faith, and thereby have shut people's eyes and stopped their ears. Shut people's eyes, and stop their ears, that is, cause them not to think from any understanding, and then tell those who are impressed with any idea of life eternal whatever you will, and they will believe it: yea, though you should tell them that God can be angry and breathe vengeance; that God can inflict eternal damnation upon any one; that God requires to be moved to compassion by His Son's blood: that he will impute and attribute that to man as a merit of his own, and will save him by his barely thinking so; as well as also, that one God could stipulate and enjoin such things to another God of one essence with Himself; with any other extravagances of a similar kind. But open your eyes and unstop your ears, that is, think of the above notions from your understanding; and you will see their utter disagreement with truth itself.

47. Shut people's eyes, stop their ears, and cause them not to think from any understanding; then might you not induce them to believe that God has given all His power to a man [the Pope], that he might be as God upon earth? Might you not induce them to believe that dead men ought to be invoked? that people ought to uncover their heads, and fall upon their knees, before their images? and that their carcases, bones, and sepulchres, are holy and ought to be venerated? But if you open your eyes, and unstop your ears, that is, if you think of these things from any understanding, will you not view them as enormities which human reason must abominate?

48. When these things, and the like, are received by a man whose understanding is shut up from a principle of religion, may not the temple in which he performs divine worship be then compared to a den or cavern under ground, where he does not know what the objects are which he sees? And may not his religion be compared to an apartment in a house in which there are no windows? And his voice, when worshipping, to sound, and not to speech? With such a man an angel of heaven cannot converse, because the one does not understand the language of the other.

---

## VII. THAT THOSE WHO ARE IN FAITH SEPARATED FROM CHARITY, ARE REPRESENTED IN THE WORD BY THE PHILISTINES.

49. In the Word, by all the names of nations and people, as also of persons and places, are signified things relating to the church; the church itself by Israel and Judah, because it was established among them, and various religious opinions [religiosa] by the nations and people round about them; religious opinions which accorded with the truth by the good nations, and discordant religious opinions by the wicked nations. There are two evil religious opinions into which every church degenerates in process of time: the one consists in adulterating its goods, and the other in falsifying its truths. That religious principle which adulterates the goods of the church, derives its origin from the love of rule; and the other religious principle which falsifies the truths of the church, derives its origin from the pride of self-derived intelligence. The religious principle which takes its origin from the love of rule, is meant in the Word by Babylon; and that which takes its origin from the pride of self-derived intelligence, is meant in the Word by Philistæa. It is well known who those of Babylon are at this day; but it is not known who those of Philistæa are. Those are of Philistæa who are in faith and not in charity.

50. That those are of Philistæa who are in faith and not in charity, may appear from various things which are said of them in the Word, when understood in the spiritual sense; as well from their disputes with the servants of Abraham and Isaac, as recorded in Gen. xxi. and xxvi., as from their wars with the children of Israel, related in the book of Judges, and in the books of Samuel and of Kings; for all the wars described in the Word, involve and signify, in the spiritual sense, spiritual wars. And because this religious principle, which consists in faith separated from charity, continually desires to invade the church, therefore the Philistines remained in the land of Canaan, and frequently infested the children of Israel.

51. Because the Philistines represented those who are in faith separated from charity, therefore they were called the *uncircumcised*, and by the uncircumcised are meant those who are without spiritual love, and thence are only in natural love: spiritual love is charity. The reason why these are called the *uncircumcised*, is, because by the circumcised are meant those who are in spiritual love. That the Philistines are called the *uncircumcised*, may be seen 1 Sam. xvii. 26, 36; 2 Sam. i. 20; and in other places.

52. That those who are in faith separated from charity were represented by the Philistines, is manifest not only from their

wars with the children of Israel, but also from many other circumstances which are recorded of them in the Word; as from those which are related of Dagon their idol; as of the hæmorrhoids and mice with which they were smitten and infested for placing the ark in the temple of their idol; and from the other things which occurred at the same time, and are mentioned 1 Sam. chap. v. and vi.; likewise from the history of Goliath, who was a Philistine, and was slain by David, as related 1 Sam. chap. xvii. For Dagon, their idol, was above like a man, and below like a fish; by which was represented their religion, which, by reason of faith, was as it were spiritual, but, from having no charity, was merely natural. By the emerods, or hæmorrhoids, with which they were smitten, were signified their filthy loves. By the mice with which they were infested, was signified the devastation of the church by falsifications of the truth. And by Goliath, who was slain by David, was represented the pride of their self-derived intelligence.

53. That those who are in faith separated from charity were represented by the Philistines, appears also from the prophetic parts of the Word, where they are treated of; as from these following. In Jeremiah: "Against the Philistines:—Behold, waters rise up out of the north, and shall be an overflowing flood, and shall overflow the land and all that is therein: the city, and them that dwell therein: so that the men shall cry, and every inhabitant of the land shall howl: Jehovah shall spoil [vastate] all the Philistines" (xlvii. 1, 2, 4). Waters rising up out of the north are falses from hell; which shall be an overflowing flood, and shall overflow the land and all that is therein, signifies the devastation by them of all things of the church; the city, and them that dwell therein, signifies the devastation of all its truths of doctrine; so that the men shall cry, and every inhabitant of the earth shall howl, signifies a want of all truth and goodness in the church; Jehovah shall spoil [vastate] all the Philistines, signifies their destruction. In Isaiah: "Rejoice not thou, whole Philistæa, because the rod that smote thee is broken; for out of the serpent's root shall come forth a cockatrice, and his fruit shall be a fiery flying serpent" (xiv. 29). Rejoice not thou, whole Philistæa, signifies let not them who are in faith separated from charity rejoice that they still remain; for out of the serpent's root shall come forth a cockatrice, signifies that from the pride of self-derived intelligence will proceed the destruction of all truth among them; and his fruit shall be a fiery flying serpent, signifies reasonings from false principles originating in evil, against the truths and goods of the church.

54. That by circumcision is represented purification from the evils of love merely natural, appears from these passages: "Circumcise yourselves to Jehovah, and take away the fore-

skins of your heart,—lest my fury come forth,—because of the evil of your doings" (Jer. iv. 4). "Circumcise the foreskin of your heart, and be no more stiff-necked" (Deut. x. 16). To circumcise the heart, or the foreskin of the heart, is to purify themselves from evils. Hence, on the contrary, by the uncircumcised are meant those who are not purified from the evils of love merely natural, thus who are not in charity. And because the unclean at heart is meant by the uncircumcised, it is said, "No stranger that is uncircumcised in heart, or uncircumcised in flesh, shall enter into my sanctuary" (Ezek. xliv. 9). "None that is uncircumcised shall eat the passover" (Exod. xii. 48). And that such are condemned, is declared in Ezek. xxviii. 10; xxxi. 18; xxxii. 19.

---

## VIII. THAT THOSE WHO ARE IN FAITH SEPARATED FROM CHARITY, ARE MEANT BY THE DRAGON IN THE APOCALYPSE.

55. It was said above, that every church in process of time declines into two common evil religious states, into one from the love of rule, and into the other from the pride of its own intelligence; and that in the Word the former is understood and described by Babylon, and the latter by Philistæa. Now inasmuch as the Apocalypse treats of the state of the Christian church, especially what that is at its end; therefore these two evil religious states are therein treated of, both generally and specifically. The religious state, which is meant by Babylon, is described in chap. xvii. xviii. xix., and is the harlot sitting upon the scarlet beast: and the religious state, which is understood by Philistæa, is described in chap. xii. xiii., and is represented there by the dragon, by the beast that rose out of the sea, and by the beast that rose out of the earth. That this religious state is meant by the dragon and his two beasts, could not heretofore be known; the reason is, because the spiritual sense of the Word was not before opened, and hence the Apocalypse was not understood; and especially, because the religious opinion of faith separated from charity was so prevalent in the Christian world, that nobody could see that it was there described; for every evil religious opinion blinds the eyes.

56. That the religious tenet of faith separated from charity is meant and described in the Apocalypse by the dragon and his two beasts, has not only been told me from heaven, but also shewn me in the world of spirits which is under heaven. Those who were in faith separated from charity, were seen by me assembled in a large company, like a great dragon with his tail extended towards heaven: and others of the same per-

suasion have been seen by me, separately, like dragons in appearance. For in that world such appearances take place from the correspondence which subsists between things spiritual and natural. On account of their so appearing, the angels of heaven call them dragonists. Moreover, there are several kinds of them: some of them constitute the head of the dragon, some his body, and some his tail. Those who constitute his tail, are those who have falsified all the truths of the Word; wherefore it is said of the dragon in the Apocalypse, that with his tail he drew down a third part of the stars of heaven; by the stars of heaven are signified the knowledges of truth, and by a third part, all.

57. Since then, by the dragon in the Apocalypse, are meant those who are in faith separated from charity; and this heretofore has not been known, and has also been hid for want of a knowledge of the spiritual sense of the Word; therefore a general explanation shall here be given of what is said concerning the dragon, in chap. xii.

58. In the twelfth chapter of the Apocalypse these things are recorded of the dragon: "And there was seen a great sign in heaven; a woman clothed with the sun, and the moon under her feet, and upon her head a crown of twelve stars. And she being with child, cried, travailing in birth, and pained to be delivered. And there was seen another sign in heaven; and behold, a great red dragon, having seven heads and ten horns, and seven crowns upon his heads. And his tail drew the third part of the stars of heaven, and cast them to the earth. And the dragon stood before the woman who was ready to be delivered, to devour her child as soon as it was born. And she brought forth a man child, who was to rule all nations with a rod of iron: and her child was caught up unto God, and his throne. And the woman fled into the wilderness, where she hath a place prepared of God, that they should feed her there a thousand two hundred and threescore days. And there was war in heaven: Michael and his angels fought with the dragon: and the dragon fought and his angels, and prevailed not; neither was their place found any more in heaven.—And when the dragon saw that he was cast unto the earth, he persecuted the woman who brought forth the man child. And unto the woman were given two wings of a great eagle, that she might fly into the wilderness, into her place, where she would be nourished for a time, and times, and half a time, from the face of the serpent. And the serpent cast out of his mouth water as a flood after the woman, that he might cause her to be carried away of the flood. And the earth helped the woman, and the earth opened her mouth, and swallowed up the flood which the dragon cast out of his mouth. And the dragon was wroth with the woman and went to make war with the remnant of her

seed, who keep the commandments of God, and have the testimony of Jesus Christ."

59. This is the explanation of these things: "And there was seen a great sign in heaven," signifies a revelation from the Lord respecting the future church, and respecting the reception of its doctrine and those by whom it would be impugned. "A woman clothed with the sun, and the moon under her feet," signifies the church which, from the Lord, is principled in love and in faith: "and upon her head a crown of twelve stars," signifies the wisdom and intelligence of its members originating in divine truths. "And she being with child," signifies the birth of doctrine: "cried, travailing in birth, and pained to be delivered," signifies resistance from those who are in faith separated from charity. "And there was seen another sign in heaven," signifies a further revelation. "And behold, a great red dragon," signifies faith separated from charity, which is called red from love merely natural: "having seven heads," signifies the false understanding of the Word: "and ten horns," signifies power in consequence of reception by many. "And seven crowns upon his heads," signifies falsified truths of the Word. "And his tail drew a third part of the stars of heaven, and cast them to the earth," signifies the destruction of all the knowledges of truth. "And the dragon stood before the woman who was ready to be delivered, to devour her child as soon as it was born," signifies their hatred of, and desire to destroy, the doctrine of the church at its birth. "And she brought forth a man child," signifies doctrine: "who was to rule all nations with a rod of iron," signifies which will convince from the power of natural truth originating in spiritual truth. "And her child was caught up unto God and his throne," signifies the protection thereof by the Lord out of heaven. "And the woman fled into the wilderness," signifies the church as existing amongst a few: "where she hath a place prepared of God," signifies its state in the meantime until it is provided that its numbers increase: "that they should feed her there a thousand two hundred and threescore days," signifies even until it increases to its appointed fulness. "And there was war in heaven; Michael and his angels fought with the dragon; and the dragon fought, and his angels," signifies the dissention and conflict of such as are in faith separated from charity against those who are in the doctrine of the church concerning the Lord and the life of charity: "and prevailed not," signifies that they fell: "neither was their place found any more in heaven," signifies that they were cast down. "And when the dragon saw that he was cast unto the earth, he persecuted the woman who brought forth the man child," signifies the infestation of the church by those who are in faith separated from charity, on account of its doctrine.

"And unto the woman were given two wings of a great eagle, that she might fly into the wilderness into her place," signifies circumspection while the church as yet is confined to a few: "where she would be nourished for a time, and times, and half a time, from the face of the serpent," signifies until the church grows to its appointed fulness. "And the serpent cast out of his mouth water as a flood after the woman, that he might cause her to be carried away of the flood," signifies their abundant reasonings, founded in false principles, with intent to destroy the church. "And the earth helped the woman; and the earth opened her mouth, and swallowed up the flood which the dragon cast out of his mouth," signifies that their reasonings, because they were grounded in falses, fell to the ground of themselves. "And the dragon was wroth with the woman, and went to make war with the remnant of her seed," signifies their continued hatred: "who keep the commandments of God, and have the testimony of Jesus Christ," signifies against those who live a life of charity, and believe in the Lord.

60. The thirteenth, or following chapter in the Apocalypse, treats of the dragon's two beasts; one of which was seen to rise out of the sea, and the other out of the earth: the former is treated of from the first verse to the tenth, and the latter from the eleventh verse to the eighteenth. That they are the dragon's beasts, appears from the second, fourth, and eleventh verses. By the first beast is signified faith separated from charity as to its confirmations from the natural man; and by the second is signified faith separated from charity as to its confirmations from the Word, which also are falsifications of the truth. But I pass over the explanation of these passages (because they contain their argumentations, which it would be necessary to draw out at some length), except the last: "Let him that hath understanding count the number of the beast, for it is the number of a man; and his number is six hundred sixty and six" (verse 18). "Let him that hath understanding count the number of the beast," signifies, let those who are in illumination inquire into the nature of the confirmations of that faith drawn from the Word: "for it is the number of a man," signifies that its quality is that of self-derived intelligence: "and its number is six hundred sixty and six," signifies every truth of the Word falsified.

---

## IX. THAT THOSE WHO ARE IN FAITH SEPARATED FROM CHARITY, ARE MEANT BY THE GOATS IN DANIEL AND IN MATTHEW.

61. THAT by the he-goat in the eighth chapter of Daniel,

and by the goats in the twenty-fifth chapter of Matthew, are meant those who are in faith separated from charity, is demonstrable from this circumstance, that they are opposed to the ram and to the sheep there mentioned. By the ram and by the sheep are denoted those who are in charity; for the Lord in the Word is called the shepherd; the church the sheep-fold; and the men of the church in general are called the flock, and specifically sheep. And since the sheep are those who are in charity, therefore the goats are those who are not in charity.

62. That those who are in faith separated from charity, are meant by he-goats [hirci], shall be demonstrated: I. From experience in the spiritual world. II. From the last judgment and those upon whom it was executed. III. From the description of the combat between the ram and the he-goat in Daniel. IV. And lastly, from the omission of charity by those of whom mention is made in Matthew.

63. I. *That those who are in faith separated from charity, are meant in the Word by he-goats; shewn from experience in the spiritual world.* In the spiritual world there appear all the things which are in the natural world: there appear houses and palaces; there appear paradises and gardens, and in them trees of every kind; there appear fields and ploughed lands; also plains and meadows; and likewise herds and flocks: all exactly resembling those which are seen upon our earth. Nor is there any difference between them, except that the latter are from a natural origin, and the former from a spiritual origin; wherefore the angels, who are spiritual, see those objects which are of a spiritual origin, just as men see those which are of a natural origin. All the things which appear in the spiritual world are correspondences; for they correspond to the affections of the angels and spirits. This is the reason why those who are in the affection of goodness and truth, and thence in wisdom and intelligence, dwell in magnificent palaces; about which there are paradises full of trees, which correspond; and these again are surrounded by fields and meadows, in which there repose flocks, which are appearances. But among those who are in evil affections the correspondences are opposite. These are either in the hells, where they are confined in workhouses which are without windows, but in which nevertheless there is light like an *ignis fatuus;* or they are in deserts, and live in huts, about which all things are barren, and where there are serpents, dragons, owls, and many other objects, which correspond with their evils. Between heaven and hell there is an intermediate place, which is called the world of spirits: into this every man comes immediately after death; and there also is an intercourse of one with another, similar to that of men with each other upon earth. All things which appear there also are correspondences. There appear there, likewise, gardens, groves, woods with trees

and shrubs, also green and flourishing fields; and at the same time various kinds of beasts, tame and wild; all according to correspondence with the affections of the spirits. There I have often seen sheep and he-goats, and likewise combats between them, similar to the combat which is described in Daniel, chap. viii. I have seen he-goats with horns bent forwards, and bent backwards; and I have seen them rush furiously upon the sheep. I have seen he-goats with two horns, with which they struck the sheep with great vehemence; and when I drew near to see what was the matter, I found spirits disputing with one another about faith and charity: from which it was plain, that faith separated from charity was what appeared like a he-goat, and that charity from which proceeds faith was what appeared like a sheep. Inasmuch as I have seen such scenes frequently, it is given me to know for certain, that those who are in faith separated from charity are meant in the Word by he-goats.

64. II. *That those who are in faith separated from charity are meant in the Word by he-goats, appears from the last judgment, and those upon whom it was executed.* The last judgment was executed upon no others than such as in externals were moral, and in internals not spirituals, or but little spiritual. Those who, as well in externals as in internals, were evil, were cast into hell long before the last judgment; and those who in externals and at the same time in internals were spiritual, were taken up into heaven long before the last judgment. For the judgment was not executed upon those who were in heaven, nor upon those who were in hell; but upon those who were in the midst between heaven and hell, and had there made to themselves pretended heavens. That the last judgment was executed opon them, and no others, may be seen in the small work on the LAST JUDGMENT, n. 59 and 70; and in the CONTINUATION RESPECTING THE LAST JUDGMENT: particularly in what there relates to the Reformed. At that time, those who were in faith separated from charity, not only in doctrine, but also in life, were cast into hell; and those who were in the same faith as to doctrine only, but yet were in charity as to life, were taken up into heaven. From which it was evident, that no others are meant by the he-goats and the sheep mentioned by the Lord in Matthew (chap. xxv.), where He speaks of the last judgment.

65. III. *That those who are in faith separated from charity, are meant in the Word by the he-goats, appears from the description of the combat between the ram and the he-goat in Daniel.* All the book of Daniel treats in a spiritual sense of subjects relating to heaven and the church; as does every other part of the Sacred Scripture, as is shewn in the DOCTRINE OF THE NEW JERUSALEM CONCERNING THE SACRED SCRIPTURE, n. 5—26: consequently this must be the case, in what is said in Daniel respecting the combat of the ram and the he-goat

which is as follows: "I saw in a vision—a ram, which had twc high horns—and the higher came up last: and that he with the horn pushed westward, and northward, and southward; and made himself great. Afterwards I saw a he-goat coming from the west on the face of the whole earth, which had a horn between his eyes, and that he ran to the ram in the fury of his power, and brake his two horns, and cast him to the ground, and stamped upon him. But the great horn of the he-goat was broken; and in its place came up four horns, and that out of one of them came forth a little horn, which waxed exceeding great towards the south, toward the east, and towards the pleasant (land),—and even to the host of heaven: and it cast down of the host, and of the stars, to the ground, and stamped upon them. Yea, he magnified himself even to the prince of the host; and from him the daily sacrifice was taken away, and the place of his sanctuary was cast down,—because he had cast down the truth to the ground. And I heard one saint saying, How long shall be the vision concerning the daily sacrifice and the transgression of desolation, to give both the sanctuary and the host to be trodden under foot? And he said, Until the evening and the morning; then shall the sanctuary be justified." (chap. viii. 2—14).

66. That this vision foretels future states of the church, appears manifestly: for it is said that the daily sacrifice was taken away from the prince of the host, the habitation of his sanctuary cast down, and that the he-goat cast down the truth to the ground; also, that the saint said, How long shall be the vision, concerning the daily sacrifice, and the transgression of desolation, to give the sanctuary and the host to be trodden under foot? and that it was until the evening and the morning, when the sanctuary will be justified. By evening is meant the end of the church, when there will be a new one. The same is meant afterwards in that chapter by the kings of Media and Persia as by the ram; and the same by the king of Greece as by the he-goat. For the names of kingdoms, nations, and peoples, as well as of persons and places, in the Word, signify thing appertaining to heaven and the church.

67. The explanation thereof is this: *The ram which had the two high horns, of which the higher came up last*, signifies those who are in faith originating in charity: *his pushing west ward, and northward, and southward*, signifies the dispersion of evil and falsity: *his becoming great*, signifies increase: *the he-goat which came from the west over the face of the whole earth*, signifies those who are in faith separated from charity, and the invasion of the church by them: *the west*, denotes the evil of the natural man: *which had a horn between his eyes*, signifies self-derived intelligence: *his running at the ram with the fury of his power*, signifies that he vehemently impugned charity and

its faith: *his breaking his two horns, throwing him to the ground, and stamping upon him*, signifies that he entirely dispersed both charity and faith; for he who disperses the one disperses the other also, because they form a one. That *the great horn of the he-goat was broken*, signifies the non-appearance of self-derived intelligence: *the coming up of four horns in the place of it*, signifies applications of the literal sense of the Word in confirmation: *the coming forth of a little horn out of one of them*, signifies reasoning that no one can fulfil the law, and do good of himself: *the growing of that horn towards the south, and towards the east, and towards the pleasant (land)*, signifies insurrection thereby against all things of the church: *and even to the host of heaven; and he cast down of the host and of the stars, and stamped upon them*, signifies destruction thus effected of all the knowledges of good and truth, which belonged to charity and faith: *that he magnified himself to the prince of the host, and from him was taken away the daily sacrifice, and the place of his sanctuary*, signifies that thus he desolated all things belonging to the worship of the Lord, and of his church: *that he cast the truth to the ground*, signifies that he falsified the truths of the Word: *by evening and morning, when the sanctuary will be justified*, is signified the end of that church, and the beginning of a new one.

68. IV. That those who are in faith separated from charity, are meant by the he-goats, appears from the omission of charity by them in Matthew. That no others are meant by the he-goats and the sheep in Matthew (chap. xxv. 31—46) than those who are meant by the he-goat and the ram in Daniel, is plain from this circumstance, that unto the sheep are enumerated the works of charity, and it is said, that they did them; and that unto the goats are enumerated the same works of charity, and it is said, that they did them not: and that the latter were therefore condemned. For with those who are in faith, separated from charity, there is an omission of works, in consequence of their denying that there is anything of salvation and of the church in them: and when charity, which consists in works, is thus removed, faith also falls to the ground, because faith originates in charity, and when there is no charity and faith, there is condemnation. If all the wicked had been meant there by the he-goats, the works of charity which they did not do would not have been enumerated, but the evils which they did do. The same is also meant by the he-goats in Zechariah: "Mine anger was kindled against the shepherds, and I punished the he-goats" (x. 3). And in Ezekiel: "Behold, I am judging between cattle and cattle, between the rams and the he-goats. Is it a small thing for you to have eaten up the good pasture, but ye must tread down with your feet the residue of the pastures? Ye have pushed all the diseased sheep with

your horns, till ye have scattered them abroad: therefore will I save my flock, and they shall no more be a prey" (xxxiv. 17, 18, 21, 22).

---

## X. THAT FAITH SEPARATED FROM CHARITY IS DESTRUCTIVE OF THE CHURCH, AND OF ALL THINGS APPERTAINING TO IT.

69. FAITH separated from charity is no faith, because charity is the life of faith, is its soul, and is its essence. And where there is no faith because there is no charity, there is no church. For which reason the Lord says, "When the Son of Man cometh, shall he find faith on the earth?" (Luke xviii. 8).

70. I have sometimes heard the he-goats and the sheep disputing upon this point, Whether those who have confirmed themselves in faith separated from charity, are in possession of any truth: and as the former declared they were in possession of much truth, the matter was examined into. They were questioned, Whether they knew what love is? what charity is? and what good is? And because these were what they had separated, they could not but make answer that they did not know. They were asked, "What is sin? what is repentance? and what is the remission of sins?" and because they answered, That those who are justified by faith have their sins remitted, so that they no longer appear; they were told, that this is not the truth. Being asked, "What is regeneration?" they replied, "That it is either baptism, or the remission of sins through faith." But they were told, that that is not the truth. When asked, "What the spiritual man is?" they replied, "He is one who is justified by the faith which we profess." But they were told that this is not the truth. Being questioned about redemption, the Lord's union with the Father, and the unity of God: they gave answers which were not truths: not to mention other particulars. After these questions and replies, a judgment was given upon the matter in debate, which was, That those who have confirmed themselves in faith separated from charity, have not any truth.

71. That this is the case, cannot be credited by them whilst in the world; because those who are in falses, see no other than that falses are truths; and think it is of no consequence to know any thing more than the particulars of their own faith. Their faith also is separated from the understanding, for it is a blind faith, and therefore they do not inquire. This, moreover, can only be inquired into by means of an understanding illuminated from the Word, wherefore the truths which are in the Word they convert into falses, thinking of faith when they

see mention made of love, repentance, remission of sins, and many other things which relate to a man's actions.

72. Moreover, it is to be well observed, that such are those who have confirmed themselves in faith alone, both in doctrine and life; but not of those who, although they have heard and believed that faith alone saves, have nevertheless shunned evils as sins.

THE END.

THE

# DOCTRINE OF LIFE

FOR THE

# NEW JERUSALEM,

FROM THE

# COMMANDMENTS OF THE DECALOGUE.

---

BY EMANUEL SWEDENBORG,

*Servant of the Lord Jesus Christ.*

---

BEING A TRANSLATION OF HIS WORK ENTITLED

"**DOCTRINA VITÆ** pro Nova Hierosolyma ex Præceptis Decalogi."

Amstelodami, 1763.

NEW YORK:

AMERICAN SWEDENBORG PRINTING AND PUBLISHING SOCIETY.

1873.

# THE DOCTRINE OF LIFE

FOR THE

# NEW JERUSALEM.

## I. ALL RELIGION HAS RELATION TO LIFE, AND THE LIFE OF RELIGION IS TO DO GOOD.

I. EVERY one who has any religion knows and acknowledges that whosoever lives well will be saved, and that whosoever lives wickedly will be condemned; for he knows and acknowledges, that whosoever lives well, thinks well, not only concerning God, but also concerning his neighbour; whereas it is otherwise with him who lives wickedly. The life of man is his love, and what a man loves, he not only does willingly, but also thinks willingly. The reason, therefore, why it is said that the life of religion is to do good, is, because doing good and thinking good form a one, and unless they do form a one with man, they do not belong to his life. But these things are to be proved in what follows.

2. That religion has relation to life, and that the life thereof is to do good, is manifest to every one who reads the Word, and is acknowledged by every one whilst he is reading it. It is written in the Word, "Whosoever shall break one of these least commandments, and shall teach men so, he shall be called the least in the kingdom of heaven; but whosoever shall do and teach them, the same shall be called great in the kingdom of heaven. For I say unto you, that except your righteousness shall exceed the righteousness of the scribes and pharisees, ye shall in no case enter into the kingdom of heaven." (Matt. v. 19, 20). "Every tree that bringeth not forth good fruit, is hewn down and cast into the fire; wherefore by their fruits ye shall know them" (Matt. vii. 19, 20). "Not every one that saith unto me, Lord, Lord, shall enter into the kingdom of heaven, but he that doeth the will of my Father who is in heaven" (Matt. vii. 21). "Many will say to me in that day, Lord, Lord, have we not prophesied in thy name? and in thy name

done many wonderful works? but then I will profess to them, I never knew you: depart from me, ye that work iniquity" (Matt. vii. 22, 23). "Whosoever heareth these sayings of mine and doeth them, I will liken him unto a wise man which built his house upon a rock; but every one that heareth these sayings of mine and doeth them not, shall be likened unto a foolish man which built his house upon the sand" (Matt. vii. 24, 26). Jesus said, a sower went forth to sow;—and some seed fell by the way side;—some fell upon stony places;—Some fell among thorns:—and some on good ground. That which fell on good ground is he that heareth the Word and understandeth it; which also beareth fruit, and bringeth forth, some a hundred fold, some sixty, and some thirty. When Jesus said these words, he cried out saying, He that hath ears to hear, let him hear (Matt. xiii. 3—9, 23). "The Son of Man shall come in the glory of his Father,—and then shall he reward every man according to his works" (Matt. xvi. 27). "The kingdom of God shall be taken from you, and given to a nation bringing forth the fruits thereof" (Matt. xxi. 43). "When the Son of Man shall come in his glory,—then shall he sit upon the throne of his glory;" and he shall say to the sheep on the right hand, "Come, ye blessed of my Father, inherit the kingdom prepared for you from the foundation of the world: for I was a hungered, and ye gave me meat: I was thirsty, and ye gave me drink: I was a stranger, and ye took me in: naked, and ye clothed me: I was sick, and ye visited me: I was in prison, and ye came unto me. Then shall the righteous answer, When saw we thee so? And the King shall answer and say unto them, Verily, I say unto you, inasmuch as ye have done it to one of the least of these my brethren, ye have done it unto me." And the King shall speak in like manner to the goats on the left, and inasmuch as they have not done such things, he shall say, "Depart from me, ye cursed, into everlasting fire, prepared for the devil and his angels" (Matt. xxv. 31—46). "Bring forth fruits worthy of repentance,—and now also the axe is laid unto the root of the trees; every tree, therefore, which bringeth not forth good fruit, is hewn down and cast into the fire" (Luke iii. 8, 9). Jesus said, "Why call ye me, Lord, Lord, and no not the things which I say? Whosoever cometh to me, and heareth my sayings, and doeth them,—is like a man which built a house,—and laid the foundation on a rock;—but he that heareth and doeth not, is like a man that without a foundation built a house upon the earth" (Luke vi. 46—49). Jesus said, "My mother and my brethren are these, who hear the word of God and do it" (Luke viii. 21). "When ye begin to stand without, and to knock at the door, saying, Lord, Lord, open unto us;—he shall—say unto you I know not whence ye are:—depart from me, all ye workers of iniquity" (Luke xiii. 25, 27). "This is the condemnation, that light is come into the world, and men loved darkness rather than light, because their deeds were evil; for every one that doeth evil hateth the light,—lest his deeds should be reproved; but he who doeth truth cometh to the light, that his deeds may be made manifest, that they are wrought in God" (John iii. 19—21). "They that have done good shall come forth to the resurrection of life" (John v. 29). "We know that God heareth not sinners, but if any man be a worshipper of God, and doeth his will, him he heareth" (John ix. 31). "If ye know these things, happy are ye if ye do them" (John xiii. 17). He that hath my commandments and keepeth them, he it is that loveth me,—and I will love him, and will manifest myself to him;—and I will come to him, and make my abode with him. He that loveth me not, keepeth not my sayings (John xiv. 21, 23, 24). Jesus said, "I am the true vine, and my Father is the husbandman; every branch in me that beareth not fruit, he taketh away; and every branch that beareth fruit, he purgeth it, that it may bring forth more fruit" (John xv. 1, 2). "Herein is my Father glorified, that ye bear much fruit; so shall ye be my disciples" (John xv. 8). "Ye are my friends, if ye do whatsoever I command you;—I have chosen you, that you should go and bring forth fruit, and that your fruit should remain" (John xv. 14, 16). The Lord said to John, "Unto the angel of the church of Ephesus write—I know thy works:—I have somewhat against thee, because thou hast left thy first love;—repent, and do the first works: or else I will—remove thy candlestick out of his place" (Rev. ii. 1, 2, 4, 5). "To the angel of the church of Smyrna write,—I know thy works" (Rev. ii. 7—9). "To the angel of the church in Pergamos write,—I know thy works;—repent" (Rev. ii. 12, 13, 16). "To the angel of the church in Thyatira write, I know thy works and charity,—and thy latter works to be more than the first" (Rev. ii. 19). "To the angel of the church in Sardis write—I know thy works; that thou hast a name that thou livest, and art dead;—I have not found thy works perfect before God:—repent" (Rev. iii. 1, 2, 3). "To the angel of the church in Philadelphia write,—I know thy works" (Rev. iii. 7, 8). "To the angel of the church of the Laodiceans write, —I know thy works;—repent" (Rev. iii. 14, 15, 19). "I heard a voice from heaven, saying,—Blessed are the dead which die in the Lord from henceforth;—yea, saith the Spirit, that they may rest from their labours, and their works do follow them" (Rev. xiv. 13). "A book was opened, which is the book of life, and the dead were judged out of those things which were written in the books, according to their works" (Rev. xx. 12). "Behold, I come quickly, and my reward is with me, to give every man according as his work shall be" (Rev. xxii. 12). In like manner it is written in the Old Testament: "Recompense them according to their deeds, and according to the works of their own hands" (Jerem. xxv. 14). Jehovah, whose "eyes are open upon all the ways of men, to give every one according to his ways, and according to the fruit of his doings" (Jerem. xxxii. 19). "I will punish them for their ways, and reward them their doings" (Hosea iv. 9). Jehovah hath dwelt with us "according to our ways and according to our doings" (Zech. i. 6). So there are many places in which it is required that men should do the statutes, commandments, and laws; as in the following; "Ye shall keep my statutes and my judgments, which if a man do, he shall live in them" (Levit. xviii. 5). "Ye shall observe all my statutes and all my judgments, and do them" (Levit. xix. 37; xx. 8; xxii. 31). Blessings are pronounced, if they do the commandments, and curses if they do them not (Levit. xxvi. 4—46). The children of Israel were commanded to make to themselves a fringe on the borders of their garments, that they might remember all the precepts of Jehovah to do them (Deut. xxii. 12): not to mention a thousand other passages to the same purport. That works are what constitute man a member of the church, and that he is saved according thereto, the Lord also teaches in his parables, several of which imply, that they who do good are accepted, and that they who do evil are rejected; as in the parable concerning the husbandmen in the vineyard (Matt. xxi. 33—44); and concerning the fig-tree which did not yield fruit (Luke xiii. 6, 9); and concerning the talents and pounds given to trade with (Matt. xxv. 14—31; Luke xix. 13—25); and concerning the Samaritan who bound up the wounds of him that fell among thieves (Luke x. 30—37); and concerning the rich man and Lazarus (Luke xvi. 19—31); and concerning the ten virgins (Matt. xxv. 1—12).

3. The true reason why every one, who has any religion, knows and acknowledges that he who lives well will be saved, and that he who lives ill will be condemned, is grounded in the conjunction of heaven with the man who is acquainted by the Word that there is a God, that there is a heaven and a hell, and that there is a life after death: hence is derived that general perception. Wherefore in the doctrine of the Athanasian Creed, which is universally received throughout all Christendom, what is said in the conclusion is universally received also, viz. "Jesus Christ, who suffered for our salvation, ascended into heaven, and sitteth at the right hand of the Father Almighty, whence he shall come to judge the quick and the dead; and then they who have done good shall enter into life eternal, and they who have done evil into everlasting fire."

4. There are many nevertheless in Christian churches, who teach that faith alone is saving, and not any good of life, or good work; they add also, that evil of life or evil work does not condemn those who are justified by faith alone, because

they are in God and in Grace. But it is extraordinary, that although they teach such doctrines, still they acknowledge,—in consequence of a general perception derived from heaven,—that those are saved who live well, and those are condemned who live ill. That they acknowledge this, is evident from the *Exhortation* which is publicly read in all churches, as well in England as in Germany, Sweden, and Denmark, previously to the celebration of the Holy Supper. That in those kingdoms there are some who teach the doctrine of faith alone, is well known. The *Exhortation* which is publicly read in England previous to the celebration of the sacrament of the Lord's Supper, is as follows.

5. "The way and means thereto (to be received as worthy partakers of that holy table,) is, first, to examine your lives and conversations by the rule of God's commandments, and whereinsoever ye shall perceive yourselves to have offended either by will, word, or deed, there to bewail your own sinfulness, and to confess yourselves to Almighty God, with full purpose of amendment of life; and if ye shall perceive your offences to be such as are not only against God, but also against your neighbours, then ye shall reconcile yourselves unto them, being ready to make restitution and satisfaction, according to the uttermost of your powers, for all injuries and wrongs done by you to any other, and being likewise ready to forgive others that have offended you, as ye would have forgiveness of your offences at God's hand; for otherwise the receiving of the holy communion doth nothing else but increase your damnation. Therefore if any of you be a blasphemer of God, a hinderer or slanderer of his Word, an adulterer, or be in malice or envy, or in any other grievous crime, repent you of your sins, or else come not to that holy table: lest after the taking of that holy sacrament the devil enter into you, as he entered into Judas, and fill you full of all iniquities, and bring you to destruction both of body and soul."

* 7. It was given me to ask some of the English clergy who professed and preached the doctrine of faith alone (which was done in the spiritual world), whether, whilst they were reading in their churches the above exhortation, in which faith is not even mentioned, they believed what is there asserted, that if any do evil, and do not repent, the devil will enter into them, as he entered into Judas, and destroy both body and soul? They replied, that in the state in which they were, whilst reading the exhortation, they knew and thought no other than that what they read was the truth and essence of religion; but that, when they began to conceive and compose their discourses or

* This paragraph is n. 7, and the preceding one is n. 5; the reason of which is, that in n. 5 of the original the exhortation to the sacrament is quoted in English as above, and n. 6 is merely occupied by a translation of the same into Latin.

sermons, they thought differently, because they then thought of faith as the only means of salvation, and of the good of life as being only accessory thereto in promoting the public good. But still it was proved to conviction, that they also had a general perception that whosoever lives well is saved, and whosoever lives ill is condemned, and that they had this perception when they were not under the influence of their own *proprium*, or selfhood.

8. The reason why all religion has relation to life, is, because every one after death is his own life; for it remains the same as it was in the world and is in no respect changed; inasmuch as an evil life cannot be converted into a good life, nor a good life into an evil life, these being opposites, and conversion into an opposite is extinction. It is on account of this opposition that a good life is called life, and an evil life is called death. Hence it is that religion has relation to life, and that the life thereof is to do good. That man after death is such as his life has been in the world, may be seen in the treatise concerning *Heaven and Hell*, n. 470—484

## II. NO ONE CAN DO GOOD, WHICH IS REALLY GOOD, FROM HIMSELF.

9. At this day scarcely any one knows, whether the good which he does be from himself or from God; the reason is, because the church has separated faith from charity, and good relates to charity. A man gives to the poor, relieves the needy, endows churches and hospitals, promotes the good of the church, of his country, and of his fellow-citizens, frequents places of public worship, listens attentively to what is said there, and is devout in his prayers, reads the Word and books of piety, and thinks about salvation; and yet knows not whether he does such things from himself or from God. It is possible he may do them from God, and it is possible he may do them from himself: if he does them from God, they are good; if from himself, they are not good. Yea, good deeds of a like nature may be done by man from himself, which yet are actually evil: as is the case with such as are hypocritical, which are grounded in deceit and artifice.

10. Good deeds done from God and from man's self, may be compared with gold. Gold, which is real gold from its inmost ground, and is called sterling gold, is good gold: gold mixed with silver, is also gold, but its goodness is according to the mixture: it is still less gold, when mixed with copper; but gold artificially made, and only resembling gold in colour, is not good, inasmuch as the substance of good is not in it. There are also articles; as gilded silver, copper, iron, tin, lead; and also gilded wood, and gilded stone; which superficially may appear as gold, but as they are not gold, they are either valued

according to the excellence of the workmanship, or according to the value of the gilded material, or according to the value of the gold which may be scraped off. These differ in goodness from real gold, as a man's clothes differ from the man himself. It is possible also that rotten wood, and dross, yea, and even dung, may be overlaid with gold: such apparent gold may be compared with pharisaical good.

11. Man has the skill to discern whether gold be substantially good, whether it be mixed and counterfeit, and whether it be only a covering of gold; but he has not the skill to discern whether the good which he does be in itself good. He knows only this: that good from God is good, and that good from man is not good. Wherefore, it being of importance to salvation to know whether the good which he does be from God, or whether it be not from God, it is expedient that it should be revealed. But before it is revealed, it may be necessary to speak concerning the various kinds of good.

12. There is civil* good, moral good, and spiritual good. Civil good is that which a man does whilst acting under the influence of the law of the land; and by this good, and according to it, he is a citizen in the natural world. Moral good is that which a man does whilst acting under the influence of the law of reason; and by this good, and according to it, he is a man. Spiritual good is what a man does whilst acting under the influence of a spiritual law; and by this good, and according to it, he is a citizen in the spiritual world. These three kinds of good follow in this order; spiritual good is the supreme, moral good is the middle, and civil good is the ultimate or lowest.

13. The man who is principled in spiritual good, is a moral man, and also a civil man; whereas the man who is not principled in spiritual good, appears as if he were a moral and civil man, but still he is not so in reality. The reason why the man who is principled in spiritual good is a moral and civil man, is, because spiritual good has the essence of good in it, and consequently includes moral and civil good also. The essence of good cannot possibly originate in any other but in Him who is Good Itself. Give to thought its utmost range, call forth all its powers, and inquire whence it is that good is good, and you will perceive that it is from its *esse*,† and that that is good which

* The term *civil* is here used to denote what appertains to the state, or the community, to which man belongs here on earth; according to which sense, *civil* good is that, which is connected with, and conducive to, the common good of the state, or community, and is regulated by the laws thereof. According to the same sense, a *civil* man (see n. 13), is one, who consults the good of the state or community to which he belongs, by submitting his conduct to the regulation of its laws.

† It is not possible to express by any single word in our language, the precise idea which the author here means to convey by the word *esse*. The reader, who is acquainted with the Latin tongue, will readily apprehend the full meaning of the

has in it the *esse* of good, consequently, that that is good which is from good itself, that is, from God; consequently that good not from God, but from man, is not good.

14. From what is said in the *Doctrine concerning the Sacred Scripture*, n. 27, 28, 38, it may be seen that the supreme, the middle, and the ultimate, make a one, like end, cause, and effect, and that in consequence of making a one, the end itself is called the primary end, the cause the mediate end, and the effect the ultimate end. Hence it will be evident, that in the case of the man who is principled in spiritual good, moral good with him is middle spiritual good, and civil good is ultimate spiritual good. Hence then it is, as already observed, that the man who is principled in spiritual good, is a moral man, and a civil man; and that the man who is not principled in spiritual good, is neither a moral nor a civil man, but only appears to be so. He appears to be so both to himself and to others.

15. The reason why a man who is not spiritual can still think and thence discourse rationally, like a spiritual man, is, because the understanding of man is capable of being elevated into the light of heaven, which is truth, and of seeing by that light; but it is possible for the will of man not to be elevated in like manner into the heat of heaven, which is love, and not to act under its influence. Hence it is, that truth and love do not make a one with man, unless he is spiritual: hence also it is that man can exercise his faculty of speech: this likewise forms a ground of distinction between man and beast. It is owing to the understanding's being capable of elevation to heaven without an elevation of the will at the same time, that man has the capacity of being reformed, and of becoming spiritual: but he never is reformed and rendered spiritual, until the will is elevated also. By virtue of this faculty enjoyed by the understanding above that of the will, man is capable of thinking rationally, and thence of discoursing rationally, like one who is spiritual, whatsoever be his nature and quality, even although he be principled in evil. Nevertheless it does not hence follow that he is rational; and the reason is, because the understanding does not lead the will, but the will the understanding, the latter only teaching and pointing out the way; as is observed in the *Doctrine concerning the Sacred Scripture*, n. 115; and so long as the will is not, with the understanding, in heaven, the man is not spiritual, and consequently not rational; for when he is left to

term; it may be expedient however, in order to assist the conception of the unlearned, to observe, that by the term *esse* is expressed the inmost ground or principle of a thing's existence; and when applied here to good, it signifies good in its inmost ground or principle, which is God; and that nothing therefore is really good, but what has its ground or principle of goodness in God. The same term *esse* is applied below, n. 43 and 48, to the human will, to distinguish it from the understanding, the understanding being only an existence, whose *esse*, or ground of being, is in the will.

his own will, or to his own love, then he rejects the rational conclusions of his understanding concerning God, heaven, and eternal life; and he assumes in their place, such conclusions as are in agreement with the love of his will, and calls them rational. This subject is entered into more at length, in the work entitled *Angelic Wisdom concerning the Divine Love and Wisdom.*

16. In the following pages those who do good from themselves will be called natural men, inasmuch as what is moral and civil with them, is, as to its essence, natural: but those who do good from the Lord will be called spiritual men, inasmuch as what is moral and civil with them, is, as to its essence spiritual.

17. That no one can do any good, which is really good, from himself, the Lord teaches in John: "A man can receive nothing, except it be given him from heaven" (iii. 27). And again: "He that abideth in me, and I in him, the same bringeth forth much fruit; for without me ye can do nothing" (xv. 5). "He that abideth in me, and I in him, the same bringeth forth much fruit," signifies, that all good is from the Lord; fruit signifying good: "without me ye can do nothing," signifies, that no one can do good from himself. Those who believe in the Lord, and do good from him, are called the children of light (John xii. 36; Luke xvi. 8); and children of the bridechamber (Mark ii. 19); and children of the resurrection (Luke xx. 36); and sons of God (Luke xx. 36; John i. 12); and born of God (John i. 13); and it is said of such, that they shall see God (Matt. v. 8); and that the Lord will make his abode with them (John xiv. 23); and that they have the faith of God (Mark xi. 22); and that their works are done from God (John iii. 21). This is summed up in these words, "As many as received him, to them gave he power to become the sons of God, even to them that believe on his name, who were born, not of blood, nor of the will of the flesh, nor of the will of man, but of God" (John i. 12, 13). To believe in the name of the Son of God, is to believe the Word, and to live according thereto; the will of the flesh is the *proprium* or selfhood of man's will, which in itself is evil; and the will of man is the *proprium* of his understanding, which in itself is falsity derived from evil: those who are born thereof, are such as will and act, and think and speak, from their *proprium*: those who are born of God, are such as will and act, and think and speak, from the Lord. In short, that is not good which is from man, but that which is from the Lord.

## III. SO FAR AS MAN SHUNS EVILS AS SINS SO FAR HE DOES WHAT IS GOOD, NOT FROM HIMSELF, BUT FROM THE LORD.

18. Who does not know, or may know, that evils prevent the Lord's entrance into man? For evil is hell, and the Lord i

heaven; and hell and heaven are opposites; so far, therefore, as man is in the one, so far it is not possible for him to be in the other; for one acts against and destroys the other.

19. Man, during his abode in the world, is in the midst between hell and heaven; beneath is hell, and above is heaven; and he is kept in the liberty of turning himself either to hell or to heaven; if he turns himself to hell, he averts himself from heaven; but if he turns himself to heaven, he averts himself from hell. Or, what amounts to the same, man, during his abode in the world, is in the midst between the Lord and the devil, and is kept in the liberty of turning himself either to the one or to the other: if he turns himself to the devil, he averts himself from the Lord; but if he turns himself to the Lord, he averts himself from the devil. Or, what is the same thing, man during his abode in the world, is in the midst between evil and good, and is kept in the liberty of turning himself either to the one or to the other: if he turns himself to evil, he averts himself from good; but if he turns himself to good, he averts himself from evil.

20. It has just been asserted, that man is kept in the liberty of turning himself this way or that: but it is to be observed, that every man has this liberty, not from himself, but from the Lord; wherefore it is said that he is *kept* in it. Concerning the equilibrium between heaven and hell, and man's being therein, and thence in freedom, see the treatise on *Heaven and Hell*, n. 589—596, and n. 597—603. That every man is kept in freedom, and that freedom is never taken away from any one, will be shewn in its proper place.

21. From these considerations it is manifest, that so far as man shuns evils, so far he is with the Lord, and in the Lord; and so far as he is in the Lord, so far he does good, not from himself but from the Lord. Hence results this general law: *That so far as any one shuns what is evil, so far he does what is good.*

22. But herein two things are required: the first is, that a man ought to shun evils because they are sins, that is, because they are infernal and diabolical, consequently opposed to the Lord and the divine laws. The second is, that a man ought to shun evils as sins, as from himself, but to know and believe that he does so from the Lord. But these two requisites will be treated of in the following articles.

23. From what has been said these three consequences follow, I. That if a man wills and does what is good, before he shuns evils as sins, the good things which he wills and does are not good. II. That if a man thinks and speaks such things as are pious, and does not shun evils as sins, the pious things which he thinks and speaks are not pious. III. That if a man knows and is wise about many things, and does not shun evils as sins, he has no wisdom.

24. I. The reason why the good things which a man wills and does are not good, before he shuns evils as sins, is, because, before this, he is not in the Lord: as was said above. As for example, if he gives alms to the poor, relieves the needy, endows churches and hospitals, does good to the church, to his country, and to his fellow-citizens; teaches the Gospel and converts souls, discharges his duty as a judge with justice, as a trader with sincerity, and as a citizen with uprightness; and yet makes light of evils as sins,—as the evils of fraud, of adultery, of hatred, of blasphemy, and such like: in this case, it is not possible he can do any good but such as is inwardly evil, inasmuch as he does it from himself and not from the Lord; consequently, he himself is in it, and not the Lord; and the good actions in which man himself is, are all defiled with his evils, and regard himself and the world. Nevertheless, those same actions above enumerated are inwardly good, if a man shuns evils as sins;—as the evils of fraud, of adultery, of hatred, of blasphemy, and such like: for in this case he does them from the Lord, and they are said to be wrought in God (John iii. 19, 20, 21).

25. II. The reason why the pious things which a man thinks and speaks before he shuns evils as sins, are not pious, is, because, he is not in the Lord. As for example: if he frequents places of public worship, attends devoutly to what is there preached, reads the Word and books of piety, partakes of the sacrament of the Lord's supper, offers up daily prayer; yea, if he even thinks much concerning God and salvation; and yet makes light of evils which are sins, as the evils of fraud, of adultery, of hatred, of blasphemy and such like: in this case the pious things which he thinks and speaks are inwardly not pious, inasmuch as the man himself with his evils is in them. He indeed at such time is ignorant of this; but nevertheless those evils are within, and escape his observation: for he is as a fountain whose water is impure, by reason of the impurity of its source. His religious exercises, therefore, are either the effect of habit only, or they are meritorious, or they are hypocritical; they ascend indeed towards heaven, but, like smoke in the air, change their course, and fall down again.

26. It has been given me to hear and see many after death who were enumerating their good works and exercises of piety, such as are mentioned above, n. 24, 25, and others beside. Amongst them I saw also some who had lamps and no oil, and inquiry was made whether they had shunned evils as sins, and it was found that they had not; wherefore it was declared to them that they were evil. They were also seen afterwards to enter into caverns inhabited by similar evil spirits.

27. III. The reason why man has no wisdom, unless he shuns evils as sins, notwithstanding his being skilful and wise

in many things, is, because his wisdom is from himself, and not from the Lord. As for example, if he is skilful in the doctrines of his church, and has a perfect knowledge of whatever relates thereto; if he knows how to confirm such doctrines by the Word, and by reasonings; if he is versed in the doctrines of all former churches, and at the same time in the decrees of all councils; nay, if he even knows truths, and also sees and understands them, so as to be perfectly acquainted with the nature of faith, of charity, of piety, of repentance and the remission of sins, of regeneration, of baptism and the holy Supper of the Lord, and of redemption and salvation; still he is not wise unless he shuns evils as sins. For until evils are so shunned, knowledges are without life,—appertaining to the understanding only, and not to the will: which in time perish, for the reason given above, n. 15; and after death the man himself casts them off, because they do not agree with the love of his will. Still, however, knowledges are highly necessary, because they teach how a man ought to act, and when he brings them into act, then they live with him;—not before.

28. All that has been said above is taught in many passages of the Word, of which it may suffice to adduce the following. The Word teaches that no one can be in good, and, at the same time, in evil; or, what is the same, that no one can, as to his soul, be in heaven, and at the same time, in hell. This is taught in the following passages: "No man can serve two masters: for either he will hate the one and love the other: or else he will hold to the one and despise the other; ye cannot serve God and mammon" (Matt. vi. 24). "How can ye, being evil, speak good things? for out of the abundance of the heart the mouth speaketh. A good man out of the good treasure of the heart, bringeth forth good things, and an evil man out of the evil treasure bringeth forth evil things" (Matt. xii. 34, 35). "A good tree bringeth not forth corrupt fruit, neither doth a corrupt tree bring forth good fruit: every tree is known by its fruit: for of thorns men do not gather figs, nor of a bramble-bush gather they grapes" (Luke vi. 43, 44).

29. The Word teaches also that no one can do good from himself, but from the Lord: Jesus said, "I am the true vine and my Father is the husbandman; every branch in me that beareth not fruit he taketh away; and every branch that beareth fruit he purgeth it, that it may bring forth more fruit.—Abide in me, and I in you, as the branch cannot bear fruit of itself, except it abide in the vine, no more can ye, except ye abide in me. I am the vine, ye are the branches: he that abideth in me, and I in him, the same bringeth forth much fruit; for without me ye can do nothing. If a man abide not in me, he is cast forth as a branch, and is withered, and men

gather them, and cast them into the fire, and they are burned" (John xv. 1, 2, 4—6).

30. The Word teaches also, that so far as man is not purified from evils, his good deeds are not good, nor are his pious acts pious, neither is he wise; and *vice versa*. This is taught in the following passages: "Woe unto you, Scribes and Pharisees, hypocrites! for ye make clean the outside of the cup and platter, but within they are full of extortion and excess. Thou blind Pharisee! cleanse first that which is within the cup and platter, that the outside of them may be clean also. Woe unto you, Scribes and Pharisees, hypocrites! for ye are like unto whited sepulchres, which indeed appear beautiful outward, but are within full of dead men's bones, and of all uncleanness: even so ye also outwardly appear righteous unto men, but within ye are full of hypocrisy and iniquity" (Matt. xxiii. 25—28). And also from these words in Isaiah: "Hear the words of Jehovah, ye rulers of Sodom, give ear unto the law of our God, ye people of Gomorrah: To what purpose is the multitude of your sacrifices unto me?—Bring no more vain oblations; incense is an abomination unto me, the new moons and the sabbaths, —I cannot away with it, it is iniquity.—Your new moons and your appointed feasts my soul hateth.—When ye spread forth your hands, I will hide mine eyes from you; yea, when ye make many prayers, I will not hear; your hands are full of bloods. Wash you, make you clean; put away the evil of your doings from before mine eyes; cease to do evil:—though your sins be as scarlet, they shall be as white as snow; though they be red like crimson, they shall be as wool" (i. 10, 11, 13,—18): the summary sense of which words is, that unless a man shuns evils, all his acts of worship and all his works likewise, are void of good, for it is said, I cannot bear iniquity, make you clean, put away the evil of your doings, cease to do evil. So in Jeremiah: "Return ye every man from his evil way, and amend your doings" (xxxv. 15).

That such persons are not wise, appears also from Isaiah: "Woe unto them that are wise in their own eyes, and prudent in their own sight" (v. 21). And again: "The wisdom of their wise men shall perish, and the understanding of their prudent men shall be hid. Woe unto them that seek deep to hide their counsel from the Lord, and their works are in the dark" (xxix. 14, 15). And again: "Woe unto them that go down to Egypt for help, and stay on horses, and trust in chariots, because they are many, and in horsemen, because they are very strong; but they look not into the Holy One of Israel, neither seek Jehovah! But he will arise against the house of the evil doers, and against the help of them that work iniquity. Now the Egyptians are men, and not God; and their horses are flesh, and not spirit" (xxxi. 1, 2, 3). Man's own intelligence is thus described: Egypt denotes science; the horse understanding thence derived; the chariot denotes doctrine and the horseman intelligence from the same origin; of all which it is said, Woe unto them who do not look to the Holy One of Israel, and do not seek Jehovah. Their destruction by evils, is meant by his arising against the house of the evil doers, and against the help of them that work iniquity: that the above things originate in man's *proprium*, and consequently have no life in them, is meant by the Egyptians being men and not God, and by their horses being flesh and not spirit. Man and flesh denote man's *proprium;* God and spirit are life from the Lord; the horses of the Egyptians are man's own intelligence. There are many other passages in the Word, which thus describe intelligence self-derived, and intelligence from the Lord; which are to be understood only by means of the spiritual sense.

That no one will be saved by the good deeds which proceed from self, because they are not good, appears from the following passages: "Not every man that saith unto me, Lord, Lord, shall enter into the kingdom of heaven, but he that doeth the will of my Father.—Many will say unto me in that day, Lord, Lord, have we not prophesied in thy name, and in thy name cast out devils, and in thy name done many wonderful works? But then will I profess unto them, I never knew you; depart from me, *ye that work iniquity*" (Matt. vii. 21—23). And in another place: "And ye begin to stand without, and to knock at the door, saying, Lord, Lord, open unto us.—Then shall ye begin to say, We have eaten and drunk in thy presence, and thou hast taught in our streets. But he shall say, I tell you, I know you not whence you are; depart from me, all ye *workers of iniquity*" (Luke xiii. 25—27). For all such are like unto the Pharisee, who "stood and prayed" [in the temple], saying, "I am not as other men, extortioners, unjust, adulterers; I fast twice in the week, I give tithes of all that I possess" (Luke xviii. 11—14). They are also those who are called "unprofitable servants" (Luke xvii. 10).

31. It is a truth that no man can do good, which is really good, from himself: but so to apply this truth as to destroy every good of charity performed by the man who shuns evils as sins, is an enormous perversion, for it is diametrically contrary to the Word, which enjoins man to do good;—it is contrary to the precepts of love towards God and our neighbour, on which hang all the law and the prophets, and it undermines and overturns the whole of religion; for every one knows that religion consists in doing good, and that every one will be judged according to his deeds. Man is so constituted that he is enabled to shun evils as of himself by power derived from the Lord, if he implore it; and what he does after this is good from the Lord.

## IV. SO FAR AS ANY ONE SHUNS EVILS AS SINS, SO FAR HE LOVES TRUTHS.

32. THERE are two universals which proceed from the Lord, divine good and divine truth: divine good is of his divine love, and divine truth is of his divine wisdom. Those two in the Lord are a one, and thence proceed as a one from him; but they are not received as a one by the angels in heaven, and by men on earth. There are angels and men who receive more of divine truth than of divine good, and there are others who receive more of divine good than of divine truth; hence it is that the heavens are distinguished into two kingdoms, one of which is called the celestial kingdom, the other the spiritual kingdom: the heavens which receive more of the divine good, constitute the celestial kingdom, but those which receive more of the divine truth constitute the spiritual kingdom. Concerning these two kingdoms, into which the heavens are distinguished, see the *Treatise on Heaven and Hell*, n. 20—28. But still the angels of all the heavens are so far in wisdom and intelligence, as good with them makes a one with truth; the good which does not make a one with truth, is to them not good: and the truth which does not make a one with good, is to them not truth. Hence it appears that good conjoined with truth constitutes love and wisdom with an angel and with man: and whereas an angel is an angel from the love and wisdom which he has, and in like manner man is man, it is evident, that good conjoined with truth causes an angel to be an angel of heaven, and a man to be a man of the church.

33. Inasmuch as good and truth are a one in the Lord, and proceed as a one from him, it follows, that good loves truth, and truth loves good, and that they desire to be a one. The like is true of their opposites: evil loves falsity, and falsity loves evil, and they are desirous of being a one. In the following pages we will call the conjunction of good and truth the celestial marriage, and the conjunction of evil and falsity the infernal marriage.

34. It is a consequence of what has been said, that so far as any one shuns evils as sins, so far he loves truths, for so far he is principled in good; according to what was shown in the foregoing article. And on the other hand, so far as any one does not shun evils as sins, so far he does not love truths, because so far he is not principled in good.

35. A man who does not shun evils as sins, may indeed love truths, but then he does not love them because they are truths, but because they serve to extend his reputation, whence he derives honour or gain; wherefore, when they are no longer subservient to this end, he ceases to love them.

36. Good relates to the will, truth to the understanding

From the love of good in the will, proceeds the love of truth in the understanding; from the love of truth proceeds the perception of truth; from the perception of truth, the thought of truth; and from these comes the acknowledment of truth, which is faith in its genuine sense. That this is the order of progression from the love of good to faith, is proved in the *Treatise concerning the Divine Love and the Divine Wisdom.*

37. Inasmuch as good is not good, as was above observed, unless it be conjoined with truth, it follows that good cannot be said to exist until it is so conjoined: nevertheless it continually wills to exist; wherefore, in order to its existence, it desires and procures to itself truths, from whence it derives its nourishment and formation. This is the reason that, so far as any one is principled in good, so far he loves truths; consequently, he so far loves truths as he shuns evils as sins; for so far he is principled in good.

38. So far as any one is principled in good, and by virtue of good loves truths, so far he loves the Lord, inasmuch as the the Lord is Good Itself and Truth Itself; wherefore the Lord is with man in good and in truth. If the latter be loved by virtue of the former, then the Lord is loved; and not otherwise. This the Lord teaches in John: "He that hath my *precepts* and keepeth them, he it is that loveth me;—he that loveth me not, keepeth not my words" (xiv. 21, 24). And in another place: "If ye keep my commandments, ye shall abide in my love" (John xv. 10). The precepts, words, and commandments of the Lord are truths.

39. That good loves truth, may be illustrated by application to the several cases of a priest, of a soldier, of a merchant, and of an artificer. And first of a *priest:* If he be principled in the good of the priesthood, which consists in providing for the salvation of souls, in teaching the way to heaven, and in leading those whom he teaches; so far as he is principled in that good, so far from the love and desire thereof, he procures for himself those truths in abundance, in proportion to the influence of the delight which constitutes his good. So if a *soldier* be principled in the love of a military life, and is sensible of good arising either from the protection of the state, or, from the advancement of his own reputation; he also, by virtue of that good, and according to it, procures to himself military science; and in case he be advanced to a post of command, military intelligence: these things are as truths, whereby the delight of his love, which is his good, is nourished and formed. So if a *merchant* be engaged in trading from the love thereof, he imbibes with pleasure all those things, which, as means, enter into and compose that love: these also are as truths, whilst trading is the good thereof. Lastly, if an *artificer* apply in good earnest to his business, and love it as the good of his life, he purchases

instruments, and perfects himself in such things as relate to the science of his particular employment, and thereby he causes his work to be good. From these cases it is evident, that truths are the means whereby the good of the love-principle exists, and acquires reality: consequently, that good loves truths in order to its existence. Hence, in the Word, by doing the truth is meant the causing good to exist: as by doing the truth (John iii. 21): by doing the Lord's sayings (Luke vi. 47): by keeping his precepts (John xiv. 21): by doing his words (Matt. vii. 24): by doing the word of God (Luke viii. 21): and by doing the statutes and judgments (Levit. xviii. 5). This also is meant by doing good and bearing fruit, for good or fruit is that which exists.

40. That good loves truth, and wills to be conjoined with it may be illustrated, also, by comparison with meat and water, or with bread and wine, which ought to be taken together, inasmuch as meat or bread alone does not suffice for nourishment without water or wine: wherefore the one seeks and desires the other. By meat and bread also in the Word, in its spiritual sense, is meant good, and by water and wine is meant truth.

41. From what has been said, it may now appear, that he who shuns evils as sins, loves truths and desires them; and that the more he shuns evils as sins, so much the more he loves and desires truths, because he is so much the more principled in good. Hence he comes into the heavenly marriage, which is the marriage of good and truth, in which heaven is, and in which the church will be.

## V. SO FAR AS ANY ONE SHUNS EVILS AS SINS, SO FAR HE HAS FAITH, AND IS A SPIRITUAL MAN.

42. FAITH and life are distinct from each other, like thinking and doing; and as thinking has relation to the understanding, and doing has relation to the will, it follows, that faith and life are distinct from each other, like the understanding and will. He who knows the distinction between these latter, may know also the distinction between the former; and he who knows the conjunction of the latter, may also know the conjunction of the former; wherefore something concerning the understanding and will shall be premised.

43. Man has two faculties, of which one is called the *will*, and the other the *understanding*. These faculties are distinct from each other, but are so created, that they may become a one; and when they are a one, they are called *the mind*: wherefore they constitute the human mind, and all the life of man therein. As all things in the universe, which are according to divine order, have relation to good and truth, so all things with man have relation to the will and the understanding: for good

with man is of his will, and truth with him is of his understanding; for these two faculties are the receptacles and subjects of those things, the will being the receptacle and subject of all things of good, and the understanding the receptacle and subject of all things of truth. Goods and truths have no other abiding place with man; nor, consequently have love and faith; inasmuch as love is of good, and good is of love, and faith is of truth, and truth is of faith. Nothing more important can be known, than how the will and understanding form one mind: they form one mind as good and truth make a one; for a similar marriage exists between the will and the understanding, as between good and truth. The nature of this latter marriage was, in some degree, shewn in the preceding article; to which we will now add, that as good is the very *esse* of a thing, and truth is the *existere* of a thing thence derived, so the will, with man, is the very *esse* of his life, and the understanding is the *existere* of his life, thence derived: for good, which is of the will, forms itself in the understanding, and, in a certain manner, renders itself visible.

44. That a man may know, think, and understand many things, and yet not be wise, was shewn above; n. 27, 28: and since it is [the office] of faith to know and to think, and still more to understand that a thing is, so it is possible for a man to believe that he has faith, and yet have it not. The reason of his not having it, is, because he is in the evil of life, and the evil of life and the truth of faith can never act as a one. The evil of life destroys the truth of faith; because the evil of life is of the will, and the truth of faith is of the understanding; and the will leads the understanding, and causes it to act as a one with itself; wherefore, should there be anything in the understanding which does not agree with the will, when man is left to himself, or thinks under the influence of his evil and the love thereof, then he either casts out the truth which is in the understanding, or by falsification forces it in to unity. It is otherwise with those who are in the good of life; for they, when left to themselves, think under the influence of good, and love the truth which is in the understanding, because it agrees therewith. Thus there is effected a conjunction of faith and of life, like the conjunction of truth and of good, each resembling the conjunction of the understanding and the will.

45. Hence then it follows, that in proportion as man shuns evils as sins, in the same proportion he has faith, because in the same proportion he is principled in good, as was shewn above. This is confirmed also by its contrary, that whosoever does not shun evils as sins, has not faith, because he is in evil, and evil has an inward hatred against truth; outwardly indeed, it can put on a friendly appearance, and endure, yea, love, that truth should be in the understanding; but when the exterior is put

off, as is the case after death, then truth, which was thus for wordly reasons received in a friendly manner, is first cast off, afterwards is denied to be truth, and finally is held in aversion.

46. The faith of a wicked man is intellectual faith, in which there is no good from the will; consequently, it is a dead faith, which is like the respiration of the lungs without its animation from the heart: the understanding also corresponds to the lungs, and the will to the heart. It may be compared likewise with a beautiful harlot, adorned with purple and gold, who is inwardly infected with a malignant disease; a harlot also corresponds to the falsification of truth, and hence, in the Word, is mentioned to signify such falsification. It is also like a tree abounding with leaves and yielding no fruit, which the gardener cuts down: a tree likewise signifies man, its leaves and blossoms the truths of faith, and its fruit the good of love. But it is otherwise with faith in the understanding, in which there is good from the will. This faith is alive, and is like the respiration of the lungs in which there is animation from the heart: and it is like a beautiful wife, whom chastity endears to her husband: it is also like a tree that bears fruit.

47. There are many [truths] which appear to belong to faith only,—as that God is—that the Lord, who is God, is the Redeemer and Saviour,—that there is a heaven and a hell—that there is a life after death; and many others of a similar nature, of which it is not said, that they are to be done, but that they are to be believed. These [truths] of faith are also dead with the man who is principled in evil, but alive with him who is in good. The reason is, because the man who is in good, not only does well from the will, but also thinks well from the understanding, not merely before the world, but also when he is left to himself in private. It is otherwise with him who is in evil.

48. It was observed, that those [truths] appear to be of faith only: but the thought of the understanding derives its *existere* from the love of the will, which is the *esse* of the thought in the understanding, as was said above (n. 43): for whatsoever any one wills from love, that he wills to do, to think, to understand, and to speak; or, what is the same thing, whatsoever any one loves from the will, that he loves to do, to think, to understand, and to speak. When a man shuns evil as sin, then he is in the Lord, as was shewn above, and the Lord operates all things: wherefore to those who asked him, "What shall we do, that we might work the works of God?" he replied, "This is the work of God, that ye believe on him whom he hath sent" (John vi. 28, 29). To believe on the Lord, is not only to think that he is, but also to do his words as he elsewhere teaches.

49. That those who are in evils have no faith, however they may suppose that they have, has been shewn by instances of such in the spiritual world. They were conducted to a heavenly

society, whence the spiritual principle of the faith of the angels entered into the interiors of the faith of those who were thus conducted, whereby they perceived themselves to have only a natural or external principle of faith, and not its spiritual or internal principle; wherefore they themselves confessed that they had no faith, and that they had persuaded themselves in the world, that to believe, or to have faith, consisted in thinking a thing to be this or that, for any reason. But it was perceived to be otherwise with the faith of those who were not in evil.

50. Hence it may be seen what spiritual faith is, and what the faith is which is not spiritual. Spiritual faith is with those who do not commit sin: for those who do not commit sin, do good, not from themselves but from the Lord, as was shewn above (n. 18—31), and by faith become spiritual. Faith with such is truth. This is what the Lord teaches in John: "This is the condemnation, that light has come into the world, and men love darkness rather than light, because their deeds were evil. For every one that doeth evil hateth the light, neither cometh to the light, lest his deeds should be reproved: but he that doeth truth, cometh to the light, that his deeds may be made manifest, that they are wrought in God" (iii. 19—21)

51. What has been said above is confirmed by the following passages from the Word: "A good man, out of the good treasure of his heart, bringeth forth that which is good; and an evil man, out of the evil treasure of his heart, bringeth forth that which is evil: for of the abundance of the heart, his mouth speaketh" (Luke vi. 45.; Matt. xii. 35). By the heart in the Word, is meant the will of man; and inasmuch as man's thoughts and speech originate in the will, it is said, out of the abundance of the heart the mouth speaketh. Again: "Not that which goeth into the mouth defileth a man, but that which cometh out of the mouth, this defileth the man" (Matt. xv. 11): by the heart is here also meant the will. Again: Jesus said concerning the women who washed his feet with ointment, "Her sins—are forgiven—for she loved much;" and afterwards he said, "Thy faith hath saved thee" (Luke vii. 47—50): whence it is evident, that when sins are remitted, that is, when they cease, faith saves. That those are called sons of God, and born of God, who are not in the *proprium* of their own will, and thereby not in the *proprium* of their own understanding, that is, who are not in evil, and thence in the false, and that these are such as believe on the Lord, he himself teaches in John i. 12, 13; which passage may be seen explained above, n. 17, towards the end.

52. From these considerations it results, that man is not endowed with a grain of truth more than he has of good; consequently, not with a grain of faith, except so far as it is conjoined with life. The thought may be, that a thing is in the understanding; but there cannot be an acknowledgment amounting

to faith, unless there be consent in the will. Thus faith and life march on with equal step. From these observations it is now evident, that so far as any one shuns evils as sins, so far he has faith, and becomes spiritual.

## VI. THE DECALOGUE TEACHES WHAT EVILS ARE SINS.

53. WHAT nation on earth does not know that it is evil to steal, to commit adultery, to commit murder, and to bear false witness? Unless this were known, and unless the prevention of such evils were effected by laws, mankind must inevitably perish; for no society, commonwealth, or kingdom, could subsist without them. Who can conceive that the Israelitish nation was so much more ignorant than others as not to know this? It must needs therefore be matter of surprise to some, that those laws, so universally known throughout the earth, should be promulgated from Mount Sinai, by Jehovah himself, in so miraculous a manner. But listen [for a moment]. The miraculous promulgation of those laws was designed to shew, that they are not only civil and moral laws, but also spiritual laws, and that to act contrary to them is not only to do evil to a fellow-citizen and society, but is also to sin against God: wherefore those laws, in consequence of their promulgation from Mount Sinai by Jehovah, were made laws of religious obligation; for it is evident that whatever Jehovah God commands must be with a view to stamp such religious obligation upon the thing commanded, and to shew that it ought to be done for his sake, and for the sake of man's salvation.

54. Inasmuch as those laws were the first-fruits of the Word, and consequently the first-fruits of the church which was about to be established by the Lord amongst the people of Israel; and inasmuch as they contained a brief summary of all things relating to religion, whereby the conjunction of the Lord with man, and of man with the Lord, is effected; therefore they were so holy that nothing could be more so.

55. That they were most holy may appear from the fact that Jehovah himself, that is, the Lord, descended upon Mount Sinai, in fire, and attended by angels, and thence promulgated them with a loud voice; and that the people prepared themselves for three days to see and hear:—that the mountain was fenced about lest any one should approach and die:—that neither the priests nor the elders were to approach it, but Moses only:—that those laws were written on two tables of stone by the finger of God: that the face of Moses shone, when he brought them down a second time from the mountain:—that they were afterwards deposited in the ark, and the ark in the inmost part of the tabernacle; and that over the ark was set the mercy-seat, and over the mercy-seat cherubs of gold;—that this inmost part

of the tabernacle was accounted most holy, and was called the holy of holies:—that without the vail, within which was this most holy place, were arranged the things which represented the holy things of heaven and of the church; as the candlestick with the seven sconces of gold, the golden altar of incense, and the table overlaid with gold, on which was the shew-bread, with the curtains of fine linen, purple, and scarlet. The sanctity of the whole tabernacle originated solely in the law which was in the ark. By reason of the sanctity of the tabernacle thus originating from the law in the ark, it was enjoined that all the people of Israel should encamp around it in order according to their tribes, and should journey in order after it; at which times there was over it a cloud by day, and a fire by night. By reason of the sanctity of that law, and the presence of the Lord therein, the Lord discoursed with Moses from over the mercy-seat between the cherubs: and the ark was called "Jehovah-There." For the same reason, also, it was not lawful for Aaron to enter within the vail, except with sacrifices and incense. Inasmuch as that law was the essential sanctity of the church, therefore the ark was introduced into Zion by David; and was afterwards deposited in the midst of the temple of Jerusalem, and constituted its most sacred place. By reason of the Lord's presence in that law, and around it, miracles were always wrought by the ark in which that law was contained; as when the waters of Jordan were divided, and whilst the ark rested in the middle, the people passed over on dry ground;—also as when the walls of Jericho fell down in consequence of carrying the ark about them; also as when Dagon, the god of the Philistines, fell down before it, and afterwards was found lying at the threshold of the temple, with his head separated from the trunk;—and as when the Bethshemites were smitten because of the ark, to the number of several thousands, besides other miracles; all of which were in consequence of the Lord's presence in his ten words, which are the commandments of the decalogue.

56. A further ground of the great power and sanctity of that law, was, because it was the complex of all things appertaining to religion; for it consisted of two tables, one of which contains all things which are on God's part, and the other all things in one complex which are on the part of man: therefore, the precepts of that law are called the ten words or commandments, because ten signify all. But how that law is the complex of all things of religion, will be seen in the following article.

57. Inasmuch as the conjunction of the Lord with man, and of man with the Lord, is effected by that law, therefore it is called the *Covenant* and the *Testimony;* the covenant because it conjoins, and the testimony because it testifies; for a covenant signifies conjunction, and a testimony the testification [or witnessing] thereof. It was for this reason that there were two

tables, one for the Lord, the other for man. Conjunction is effected by and from the Lord; but only when man does those things which are written in his table: for the Lord is continually present, and operative, and desirous to enter, but it is for man in the exercise of the freedom which he enjoys from the Lord, to open the door; for he says. "Behold, I stand at the door and knock: if any man hear my voice, and open the door, I will come in to him, and will sup with him, and he with me" (Rev. iii. 20).

58. In the other table, which is for man, it is not said that he should do this or that good, it is said that he should not do this or that evil; as—that he should not kill;—that he should not commit adultery;—that he should not steal;—that he should not bear false witness;—that he should not covet: the reason is, because man cannot do anything good from himself, but when he ceases to do evils, then he does good, not from himself, but from the Lord. That man is able to shun evils as from himself, by virtue of the Lord's power, if he implore it, will be seen in what follows.

59. What was stated above, n. 55, concerning the promulgation, sanctity, and power of this law, is proved by the following passages in the Word.

That Jehovah descended upon Mount Sinai in fire, and that the mount then smoked and quaked; and that there were thunderings, lightnings, a thick cloud, and the voice of a trumpet, Exod. xix. 16, 18; Deut. iv. 11; v. 19—22.

That the people prepared and sanctified themselves for three days previous to the descent of Jehovah, Exod. xix. 10, 11, 15.

That the mountain was fenced about, to prevent any one from approaching to the foot of it, lest he should die; and that not even the priests, but Moses alone, was to approach, Exod. xix. 12, 13, 20—23; xxiv. 1, 2.

The law itself, as promulgated from Mount Sinai, Exod. xx. 2—17: Deut. v. 6—22.

That the law was written on two tables of stone with the finger of God, Exod. xxxi. 18; xxxii. 15, 16; Deut. ix. 10.

That the face of Moses shone when he brought the tables down from the mount the second time, Exod. xxxiv. 29—35.

That the tables were laid up in an ark, Exod. xxv. 16; xl. 20; Deut. x. 5; 1 Kings viii. 9.

That over the ark was set the mercy-seat, and over the mercy-seat cherubs of gold, Exod. xxxv. 17—21.

That the ark, with the mercy-seat and cherubs, constituted the inmost of the tabernacle; and that the golden candlestick, the golden altar of incense, and the table overlaid with gold on which was the shew-bread, constituted the exterior part of the tabernacle; and that the ten curtains of fine linen, purple, and scarlet, constituted its outermost part; Exod. xxv. 1 to the end; xxvi. 1 to the end; xl. 17—28.

That the place where the ark was, was called the holy of holies, Exod. xxvi. 33.

That all the people of Israel encamped around the tabernacle in order according to their tribes, and journeyed in order after it, Numbers ii. 1 to the end.

That at such times there was over the tabernacle a cloud by day, and fire by night, Exod. xl. 38; Numb. ix. 15, 16 to the end; xiv. 14; Deut. i. 33.

That the Lord discoursed with Moses from over the ark, between the cherubs, Exod. xv. 22; Numb. vii. 89.

That the ark, by reason of the law contained in it, was called "Jehovah-There;" for Moses said, when the ark went forward, "Arise Jehovah;" and when it rested, "Return Jehovah," Numb. x. 35, 36; 2 Sam. vi. 2; Psalm cxxxii. 8.

That by reason of the sanctity of that law, it was not lawful for Aaron to enter within the vail, except with sacrifies and incense, Levit. xvi. 2—14.

That the ark was introduced into Zion by David with sacrificing and rejoicing, 2 Sam. vi. 1—19; and that Uzzah died, because he touched it, verses 6, 7, of the same chapter.

That the ark was placed in the midst of the temple at Jerusalem, where it constuted the most holy place, 1 Kings vi. 19; viii. 3—9.

That by reason of the Lord's presence and power in the law which was in the ark, the waters of Jordan were divided, and, whilst the ark rested in the midst, the people passed over on dry ground, Josh. iii. 1—17; iv. 5—20.

That the walls of Jericho fell down in consequence of carrying the ark about them, Josh. vi. 1—20.

That Dagon the God of the Philistines fell to the earth before the ark, and afterwards was found lying on the threshold of the temple with his head separated from the trunk, 1 Sam. v. 3, 4.

That the Bethshemites, by reason of the ark, were smitten to the number of several thousands, 1 Sam. vi. 19.

60. That the tables of stone on which the law was written were called the tables of the covenant; and that the ark, by reason thereof, was called the ark of the covenant, and the law itself was called the covenant; Numb. x. 33; Deut. iv. 13, 23; v. 2, 3; ix. 9; Josh. iii. 11; 1 Kings viii. 21; Rev. xi. 19; and in many other places. The reason why the law was called the covenant, is, because a covenant signifies conjunction; wherefore it is said of the Lord, that he should be "for a covenant of the people" (Isaiah xlii. 6; xlix. 8); and he is called "the messenger of the covenant" (Mal. iii. 1); and his blood "the blood of the covenant" (Matt. xxvi. 28; Zech. ix. 11; Exod. xxiv. 4—10); and for the same reason the Word is called the Old Covenant and the New Covenant. Covenants also are made for the sake

of love, friendship, and consociation,—consequently conjunction.

61. That the precepts of that law were called the ten words, Exod. xxxiv. 28; Deut. iv. 13; x. 4;* they are so called, because ten signifies all, and words signify truths; for there were more than ten. Inasmuch as ten signifies all, therefore the curtains of the tabernacle were ten (Exod xxvi.1); and therefore the Lord said, that a man about to receive a kingdom, called ten servants, and gave them ten pounds to trade with (Luke xix. 13): therefore he likened the kingdom of the heavens to ten virgins (Matt. xxv. 1): for the same reason the dragon is described as having ten horns, and upon his horns ten diadems (Rev. xii. 3): Likewise the beast coming up out of the sea (Rev. xiii. 1); and also another beast (Rev. xvii. 3, 7); as well as the beast in Daniel (vii. 7, 20, 24). The like is signified by ten, (Levit. xxvi. 26; Zech. viii. 23); and in other places. Hence come tenths, or tithes, by which is signified something from all.

VII. MURDERS, ADULTERIES, THEFTS, AND FALSE WITNESS, OF EVERY KIND, WITH THE CONCUPISCENCES PROMPTING THERETO, ARE EVILS WHICH OUGHT TO BE SHUNNED AS SINS.

62. It is well known, that the law of Sinai was written on two tables, and that the first table contains those things which relate to God, and the second, those which relate to man. That the first table contains all things relating to God, and the second, all things relating to man, does not appear in the letter; nevertheless all things are therein, and therefore they are called the ten words, by which are signified all truths in the complex, as may be seen above, n. 61. But in what manner all things are therein, cannot be explained in a few words: it may, however be comprehended from what was adduced in the *Doctrine concerning the Sacred Scripture*, n. 67. Hence it is, that it is said, murders, adulteries, thefts, and false witness, of every kind.

63. A religious persuasion has prevailed, that no one can fulfil the law; and the law is, not to kill, not to commit adultery, not to steal, and not to bear false witness. It is admitted that every civil and moral man may, in his civil and moral life, fulfil these precepts of the law; but to fulfil them from a principle of spiritual life, is supposed, according to the above persuasion, to be impossible. From this it follows, that the motive to the obedience of those precepts, is only to avoid punishment and loss in this word, and not to avoid punishment and loss in the next: hence it is that the man with whom the above per-

* See the margin of the English Bible.

suasion prevails, thinks those evils lawful in the sight of God, but unlawful in the sight of the world. It is owing to this religious persuasion, that man remains in the concupiscence of all the above evils, and is only restrained from the outward commission of them by worldly considerations; wherefore such a person after death, although he had not committed murder, adultery, theft, and false witness, is still in the concupiscence to commit them, and also does commit them, when the external, which he had in the world, is removed from him; for all concupiscence remains with man after death. On this account it is, that such persons act in unity with hell, and cannot but have their lot with those who are in hell. The lot of those, however, is different who do not wish to commit murder, adultery, theft, and to bear false witness, because so to act is contrary to [the law of] God. These, after enduring some combat against the forbidden evil, lose at length all inclination, consequently all concupiscence leading to the commission of it; saying in their hearts that it is sin, and in its essence infernal and diabolical. These, after death, when the external, which they had in the world, is removed, act in unity with heaven; and because they are in the Lord, are also admitted into heaven.

64. It is a common maxim in every religion, that man ought to examine himself, to do the work of repentance, and to desist from sins; and that in case he does not, he remains in a state of condemnation. That this is a maxim common to every religion, may be seen above, n. 4—8. It is also a universal maxim prevailing throughout the Christian world, that the decalogue ought to be taught, and that children should be initiated thereby into the Christian religion; for it is put into the hands of all young children. They are also taught by their parents and masters, that to do the evils forbiden in the decalogue is to sin against God; yea, the parents and masters are convinced thereof whilst they are instructing their children. How surprising then it is that these same [parents and masters], and also the children when they grow up, should think that they are not under that law, and that they cannot do the things prescribed in that law! Can there be any other reason that they should learn thus to think, than because they love the forbidden evils, and consequently the falses which favour them? These therefore are those who do not make the precepts of the decalogue precepts of religion. That the same persons live without religion, may be seen in the *Doctrine of Faith.*

65. All nations on the face of the earth, who have any religion, are in possession of precepts similar to those contained in the decalogue; and all those who live according thereto, from a religious principle, are saved; but all who do not live according thereto, from a religious principle, are condemned. Those who live according thereto, from a religious principle, being instructed

after death by angels, receive truths, and acknowledge the Lord ; the reason is, because they shun evils as sins, and hence are principled in good, and good loves truth, and receives it from the desire of its love, as was shewn above, n. 32—41. This is meant by the Lord's words to the Jews: "The kingdom of God shall be taken from you, and given to a nation bringing forth the fruits thereof" (Matt. xxi. 43); and also by these words: "When the Lord of the vineyard cometh—he will miserably destroy those wicked men, and will let out his vineyard unto other husbandmen, who shall render him the fruits in their season" (Matt. xxi. 40, 41); and by these: "I say unto you, that many shall come from the east and the west, and from the north and the south, and shall sit down—in the kingdom of God; but the children of the kingdom shall be cast out into outer darkness" (Matt. viii. 11, 12; Luke xiii. 29).

66. We read in Mark, that a certain rich man came to Jesus, and asked him, What he should do to inherit eternal life? To whom Jesus replied, "Thou knowest the commandments: Thou shalt not commit adultery; thou shalt not kill; thou shalt not bear false witness; thou shalt not steal; honour thy father and mother." He answering said, "All these have I kept from my youth." Jesus looked at him and loved him ; yet he said, "One thing thou lackest; go thy way, sell whatsoever thou hast, and give to the poor, and thou shalt have treasure in heaven; and come, take up the cross, and follow me" (x. 17—22). It is said that Jesus loved him, and this, because he said he had kept those commandments from his youth; but whereas he lacked these three things, he had not removed his heart from riches, he had not fought against concupiscences and he had not as yet acknowledged the Lord to be God; therefore the Lord said unto him that he should sell all that he had, whereby is meant, that he should remove his heart from riches;—that he should take up the cross, whereby is meant, that he should fight against concupiscences;—and that he should follow him, by which is meant, that he should acknowledge the Lord to be God. The Lord here spake, as in all other cases, by correspondences. See the *Doctrine respecting the Sacred Scripture*, n. 17. No one can shun evils as sins unless he acknowledge the Lord, and approach him, and unless he fight against evils, and thus remove concupiscences. But more will be said on this subject in the article concerning combats against evils.

### VIII. SO FAR AS ANY ONE SHUNS MURDERS OF EVERY KIND AS SINS SO FAR HE HAS LOVE TOWARDS HIS NEIGHBOUR.

67. By murders of every kind are understood also enmities, hatreds, and revenge, of every kind, which breathe a murderous purpose; for therein murder lies hid, as fire in wood beneath

the ashes. Infernal fire is nothing else, and it is from this ground that men are said to burn with hatred and revenge, which are murders in a natural sense. But by murders, in a spiritual sense, are meant all modes of killing and destroying the souls of men, which are various and manifold; and by murder, in a supreme sense, is meant to hate the Lord. These three kinds of murder make a one, and cohere together; for whosoever is disposed to kill the body of man in this world, is also disposed after death to kill the soul of man, and even to destroy the Lord; for he burns with anger against him, and wills to put out his name.

68. These kinds of murder lie concealed inwardly with man from his birth; but still he learns from his infancy to cover them over with civil and moral conduct, which he must needs practise in his intercourse with mankind; and so far as he loves honor or gain, so far he is watchful over himself lest his murderous inclinations should appear. This man does with his external, whilst those things are of his internal: such is man in himself. Now as he lays aside his external with the body when he dies, and retains his internal, it is evident what a devil he must become unless he be reformed.

69. Inasmuch as the above-mentioned kinds of murder lie inwardly concealed in man from birth, as has been said, and at the same time thefts of every kind, and false witness of every kind, with the concupiscences prompting thereto (concerning which more will be said presently); it is evident, that unless the Lord had provided the means of reformation, man must needs have perished eternally. The means of reformation which the Lord has provided are these:—that man is born in mere ignorance;—that whilst an infant he is kept in a state of external innocence;—soon after in a state of external charity; and then in a state of external friendship: but as he comes into the exercise of thought, by virtue of his understanding, he is kept in a certain freedom of acting according to reason. This is the state which was described above, n. 19; and which we shall here transcribe with a view to what follows: it runs thus:

"Man, during his abode in the world, is in the midst between hell and heaven; beneath is hell, and above is heaven: and he is kept in the liberty of turning himself either to hell or heaven; if he turns himself to hell, he averts himself from heaven, but if he turns himself to heaven, he averts himself from hell. Or, what amounts to the same, man, during his abode in the world, is in the midst between the Lord and the devil, and is kept in the liberty of turning himself either to the one or to the other: if he turns himself to the devil, he averts himself from the Lord, but if he turns himself to the Lord, he averts himself from the devil. Or, what is the same thing, man, during his abode in the world, is in the midst between evil and good, and is kept in the liberty of turning himself either to the one or to the other: if he turns himself to evil he averts himself from good, but if he turns himself to good, he averts himself from evil." See the same above, n. 19; see also n. 20—22.

70. Now, as evil and good are two opposites, in all respects like hell and heaven, or like the devil and the Lord, it follows, that if man shuns evil as sin, he comes into the good that is opposite to the evil. The good opposite to the evil which is meant by murder, is the good of neighbourly love.

71. Inasmuch as this good and that evil are opposites, it follows, that the latter is removed by the former. Two opposites cannot abide together, as heaven and hell cannot abide together: supposing them to be together, there would result that lukewarm state, of which it is written in the Revelation, "I know thy works, that thou art neither cold or hot; I would thou wert cold or hot; so then because thou art lukewarm and neither cold nor hot, I will spue thee out of my mouth" (iii. 15, 16).

72. When man is no longer in the evil of murder, but in the good of love towards his neighbour, then whatsoever he does is the good of that love, consequently, is a good work. A priest, who is in that good, as often as he teaches and leads his flock, does a good work, because he acts from the love of saving souls. A magistrate, who is in that good, as often as he executes the laws of order and justice, does a good work, because he acts from the love of his country, of society, and of his fellow-citizens. A merchant, likewise, if he be in that good, does a good work in every negotiation. He is in the love of his neighbour and his country; society, his fellow-citizens, and also his domestics, are his neighbour, for whose good he provides whilst providing for his own. An operative, also, who is in that good, labours faithfully under its influence, for others as for himself, fearing his neighbour's loss as his own. The reason why all the deeds done by such are good works, is, because so far as any one shuns evils, so far he does good, according to the general law above stated, n. 21; and he who shuns evil as sin, does good, not from himself, but from the Lord (n. 18—31). It is otherwise with him who does not regard murders of every kind, which are enmities, hatreds, revenge, and the like, as sins; whether be he a priest, magistrate, merchant, or operative, what he does is not a good work, because his every work partakes of the evil which is within him; for his internal is what produces; his external may be good, but only as to others, not as to himself.

73. The Lord inculcates the good of love in many passages in the Word; and teaches it particularly in Matthew by reconciliation with our neighbour, in these words: "If thou bring thy gift to the altar, and there remember that thy brother hath ought against thee, leave there thy gift before the altar,

and go thy way: first be reconciled to thy brother; and then come and offer thy gift. Agree with thine adversary quickly, whilst thou art in the way with him; lest—the adversary deliver thee to the judge, and the judge deliver thee to the officer, and thou be cast into prison: verily, I say unto thee, thou shalt by no means come out thence, until thou hast paid the uttermost farthing" (v. 23—26): that to be reconciled to a brother is to shun enmity, hatred, and revenge; that is, to shun such evils as sins, is evident. The Lord also teaches, in Matthew, "Whatsoever ye would that men should do to you, do ye even so to them, for this is the law and the prophets" (vii. 12): consequently evil should not be done to him. Not to mention many other passages to the same purport. The Lord also teaches, that murder consists in being angry with a brother or a neighbour without a cause, and in accounting him as an enemy (Matt. v. 21, 22).

## IX. SO FAR AS ANY ONE SHUNS ADULTERIES OF EVERY KIND AS SINS, SO FAR HE LOVES CHASTITY.

74. By adultery, in the sixth commandment of the decalogue, in a natural sense, is not only meant to commit fornication, but also to act obscenely, to discourse lasciviously, and to think filthily. But by committing adultery, in a spiritual sense, is meant, to adulterate the goods of the Word, and to falsify its truths: and, in a supreme sense, by committing adultery is meant to deny the Lord's divinity and to profane the Word. These are the several kinds of adultery. The natural man, by means of his rational light, may know that by adultery is meant to act obscenely, to discourse lasciviously, and to think filthily; but he does not know, that by committing adultery is also meant, to adulterate the goods of the Word, and to falsify its truths; and still less that it means to deny the Lord's divinity and to profane the Word. Hence he does not know, that adultery is so great an evil, as that it may be called essentially diabolical; for whosoever is [principled] in natural adultery is also in spiritual adultery, and *vice versa*. That this is the case will be demonstrated in a particular treatise concerning *Conjugal Love*. But those are simultaneously in adulteries of every kind, who do not regard adulteries as sins, both in faith and life.

75. The reason why so far as any one shuns adultery, so far he loves marriage; or, what is the same thing, so far as any one shuns the lasciviousness of adultery, so far he loves the chastity of marriage; is, because the lasciviousness of adultery and the chastity of marriage are two opposites; wherefore so far as man is not in the one, so far he is in the other. The case in this respect is as was described above, n. 70.

76. It is impossible for any one to know what the chastity

of marriage is, unless he shuns the lasciviousness of adultery as sin. A man may know that in which he is, but he cannot know that in which he is not: if he know anything in which he is not by description, or by thinking about it, still he only knows it obscurely, and as involved in doubt; wherefore he does not see it in a clear light, and free from doubt, until he is in it: in the latter case therefore he knows, but in the former case he may be said to know and not to know. The truth is, that the lasciviousness of adultery and the chastity of marriage, compared with each other, are like hell and heaven compared with each other; and that the lasciviousness of adultery makes hell with man, and the chastity of marriage makes heaven with him. The chastity of marriage, however, abides only with those who shun the lasciviousness of adultery as sin; see n. 111, below.

77. From what has been said it may without ambiguity be concluded and seen, whether a man be a Christian or not, yea, whether he has any religion or not: for whosoever does not regard adulteries as sins, in faith and life, is not a Christian, neither has he any religion. But, on the other hand, whosoever shuns adulteries as sins, especially if he hold them in aversion, by reason of their being sins, and still more, if he abominate them on that account, has religion, and if he be in the Christian Church, is a Christian. But more will be seen on this subject in the *Treatise concerning Conjugal Love:* in the mean time, see what is said upon it in the *Treatise on Heaven and Hell*, n. 366—386.

78. That to commit adultery is also meant to act obscenely, to speak obscenely, and to think filthily, is manifest from the Lord's words in Matthew: "Ye have heard that it was said by them of olden time, thou shalt not *commit adultery;* but I say unto you that whosoever looketh on a woman to lust after her, hath *committed adultery* with her already in his heart" (v. 27, 28).

79. That by committing adultery in a spiritual sense, is meant to adulterate the good of the Word, and to falsify its truth, is evident from the following passages; "Babylon—hath made all nations drink of the wine of her *fornication*" (Rev. xiv. 8). The angel said, "I will shew thee the judgment of the great whore that sitteth upon many waters, with whom the kings of the earth have committed *fornication*" (Rev. xvii. 1, 2). "All nations have drunk of the wine of the wrath of her *fornication*, and the kings of the earth have committed *fornication* with her" (Rev. xviii. 3). God "hath judged the great whore which did corrupt the earth with her *fornication*" (Rev. xix. 2). Fornication is spoken of in regard to Babylon, because by Babylon are meant those who arrogate to themselves the divine power of the Lord, and profane the Word by adulter

ating and falsifying it; wherefore also Babylon is called "the mother of harlots and abominations of the earth" (Rev. xvii 5). The same is signified by whoredom in the prophets; as in Jeremiah: "I have seen also in the prophets of Jerusalem a horrible thing; they *commit adultery* and walk in lies" (xxiii. 14). So in Ezekiel: "Two women the daughters of one mother, —committed *whoredoms* in Egypt, they committed *whoredom* in their youth;—one played the harlot when she was mine; she doted on her lovers, on the Assyrians her neighbours;—she committed her *whoredoms* with them;—yet she forsook not her *whoredoms* from Egypt.—The other was more corrupt in her inordinate love than the former, and in her *whoredoms* more than her sister in her *whoredoms;* she increased her *whoredoms,* she loved the Chaldeans; the Babylonians came to her into the bed of love, and defiled her by their *whoredom*" (xxiii. 2—17): these words relate to the Israelitish and Jewish church, which are called the daughters of one mother: by their whoredoms are meant the adulterations and falsifications of the Word; and whereas, in the Word, by Egypt is signified science, by Assyria reasoning, by Chaldea the profanation of truth, and by Babylon the profanation of good, therefore it is said that they committed whoredom with them. The like is said in Ezekiel concerning Jerusalem, whereby is signified the church as to doctrine: "Thou didst trust in thine own beauty, and playedst the harlot because of thy renown, and pouredst out thy *fornications* on every one that passed by:—Thou hast also committed *fornication* with the Egyptians thy neighbours, great of flesh, and hast increased thy *whoredoms.*—Thou hast played the *whore* also with the Assyrians, because thou wast insatiable—and couldst not be satisfied. Thou hast moreover, multiplied thy *fornication*—unto Chaldea. Thou art a wife that committeth *adultery,* which taketh strangers instead of her husband: they give gifts to all whores, but thou givest gifts to all thy lovers, and hirest them that they may come unto thee on every side for thy whoredom. Wherefore, O harlot, hear the word of Jehovah" (xvi. 15, 26, 28, 29, 32, 33, 35). That by Jerusalem is meant the church, may be seen in the *Doctrine concerning the Lord,* n. 62, 63. The like is signified by whoredoms in Isaiah, xxiii. 17, 18; lvii. 3; and in Jeremiah iii. 2, 6, 8, 9; v. 7; xiii. 27; xxix. 23; and in Micah i. 7; and in Nahum iii. 4; and in Hosea iv. 10, 11; and in Levit. xx. 5; and in Numbers xiv. 33; xv. 39; and in other places. For the same reason also the Jewish nation was called by the Lord "an adulterous generation" (Matt. xii. 39; xvi. 4; Mark viii. 38.)

## X. SO FAR AS ANY ONE SHUNS THEFTS OF EVERY KIND AS SINS, SO FAR HE LOVES SINCERITY.

80. By to steal, in a natural sense, is not only meant to steal and to rob, but also to defraud, and under any pretence to take away the goods of another. But by to steal, in a spiritual sense, is meant, to deprive another of the truths of his faith, and of the goods of his charity: whereas by to steal, in the supreme sense, is meant to take away from the Lord what is his, and to attribute it to oneself, and thus to claim righteousness and merit. These are thefts of every kind; and they also make a one, as do adulteries of every kind, and murders of every kind, spoken of above. The reason why they make a one, is, because one kind is involved in the other.

81. The evil of theft enters deeper into man than any other evil, because it is conjoined with deceit and cunning, and deceit and cunning insinuate themselves even into the spiritual mind of man, which is the seat of his thought as grounded in understanding. That man has a spiritual mind and a natural mind, will be seen below.

82. The reason why man loves sincerity so far as he shuns theft as sin, is, because theft is also fraud, and fraud and sincerity are two opposites: wherefore so far as any one is not in fraud, so far he is in sincerity.

83. By sincerity is also meant integrity, justice, fidelity, and uprightness. Man cannot be principled in these virtues from himself, so as to love them by and for the sake of them; but whosoever shuns fraud, deceit, and cunning, as sins, thereby becomes principled in those virtues, not from himself but from the Lord, as was shewn above, n. 18—31. This is true in regard to every one in his station and office; whether he be a priest, magistrate, judge, merchant, or operative.

84. The same appears from many passages of the Word; as from the following: "He that walketh righteously, and speaketh uprightly; he that despiseth the gain of oppressions, that shaketh his hands from holding of bribes; that stoppeth his ears from hearing of blood, and shutteth his eyes from seeing evil; he shall dwell on high" (Isaiah xxxiii. 15, 16). "Jehovah, who shall abide in thy tabernacle, who shall dwell in thy holy hill? He that walketh uprightly and worketh righteousness,—he that backbiteth not with his tongue, nor doth evil to his neighbour" (Psalm xv. 1—3). "Mine eyes shall be upon the faithful of the land that they may dwell with me: he that walketh in a perfect way, he shall serve me. He that worketh deceit shall not dwell within my house; he that speaketh lies shall not tarry in my sight. I will early destroy all the wicked of the land, that I may cut off all wicked doers from the city" (Psalm ci. 6—8).

That he who is not inwardly sincere, just, faithful, and upright, remains in reality insincere, unjust, unfaithful, and devoid of uprightness, the Lord teaches in these words: "Except your righteousness shall exceed the righteousness of the scribes and Pharisees, ye shall in no case enter into the kingdom of heaven" (Matt. v. 20): by the righteousness which exceeds the righteousness of the scribes and Pharisees, is meant interior righteousness, in which the man is [principled] who is in the Lord. That man ought to be in the Lord, he himself teaches in John: "The glory which thou gavest me, I have given them, that they may be one even as we are one; I in them, and thou in me, that they may be perfect in one;—and that the love wherewith thou hast loved me may be in them, and I in them" (xvii. 22, 23, 26); from whence it is evident, that they are perfect when the Lord is in them. These are they who are called the pure in heart, who shall see God; and the perfect as their Father in the heavens (Matt. v. 8, 48.)

85. It was said above, n. 81, that the evil of theft enters more deeply with man than any other evil, because it is conjoined with deceit and cunning, and deceit and cunning insinuate themselves even into the mind of the spiritual man, where his thought is with the understanding; wherefore it may be expedient here to say something concerning the *mind* of man. That the mind of man is his understanding and will together, may be seen above, n. 43.

86. Man has a natural mind and a spiritual mind: the natural mind is beneath, and the spiritual mind is above; the natural mind is the mind of his world, and the spiritual mind is the mind of his heaven. The natural mind may be called the *animal* mind, but the spiritual mind the *human* mind. A man is also distinguished from an animal by this, that he has a spiritual mind, whereby he has a capacity of being in heaven during his abode in the world: by this also it is that man lives after death.

Man, as to his understanding, can be in his spiritual mind, and thence in heaven; but he cannot be as to his will in his spiritual mind, and thence in heaven, unless he shuns evils as sins; and unless he be in heaven as to his will also, he still is not in heaven; for the will draws the understanding downwards, and causes it to be alike animal and natural as itself.

Man may be compared to a garden,—the understanding to light, and the will to heat; a garden is in light and not at the same time in heat, during winter, but it is in light and heat together during summer: the man, therefore, who is in the light of the understanding alone, is as a garden in the time of winter; but he who is in the light of the understanding and at the same time in the warmth of the will, is as a garden in the time of summer. The understanding also is wise from spiritual light, and the will loves from spiritual heat; for spiritual light is the divine wisdom, and spiritual heat is the divine love.

So long as man does not shun evils as sins, the concupiscences of evils close up the interiors of the natural mind on the part of the will, being like a dense veil there, and as a black cloud beneath the spiritual mind, and prevent it from being opened: but as soon as man shuns evils as sins, then the Lord flows-in out of heaven, and removes the veil, and disperses the cloud, and opens the spiritual mind, and thus introduces him into heaven.

So long as the concupiscences of evils close up the interiors of the natural mind, as just observed, so long man is in hell; but as soon as those concupiscences are dispersed by the Lord, man is in heaven. Further, so long as the concupiscences of evils close up the interiors of the natural mind, so long he is a natural man; but as soon as those concupiscences are dispersd by the Lord, he becomes a spiritual man. Again, so long as the concupiscences of evils close up the interiors of the natural mind, so long man is an *animal*, differing only in this, that he can think and speak, even concerning such things as he does not see with his eyes, which he derives from the faculty of elevating his understanding into the light of heaven; but as soon as those concupiscences are dispersed by the Lord, man becomes truly a *man*, because he then thinks what is true, in the understanding, from good in the will. Lastly, so long as the concupiscences of evils close up the interiors of the natural mind, so long man is as a garden in the time of winter; but as soon as those concupiscences are dispersed by the Lord, he is like a garden in the time of summer.

The conjunction of the will and the understanding with man is meant in the Word by the heart and soul, and by the heart and spirit; as where it is said, that God should be loved with all the heart, and with all the soul (Matt. xxii. 37), and that God would give a new heart, and a new spirit (Ezek. xi. 19; xxxvi. 26, 27); by the heart is meant the will and its love, and by the soul and the spirit, the understanding and its wisdom.

## XI. SO FAR AS ANY ONE SHUNS FALSE WITNESS OF EVERY KIND AS SINS, SO FAR HE LOVES TRUTH.

87. By bearing false witness, in a natural sense, is not only meant to act in the character of a false witness, but also to lie and to defame. By bearing false witness, in a spiritual sense, is meant, to assert, and to persuade others, that what is false is true, and that what is evil is good, and *vice versâ:* but in the supreme sense, by bearing false witness, is meant to blaspheme the Lord and the Word. These are what constitute the bearing of false witness in a threefold sense; and they make a

one with the man who acts as a false witness, tells a lie, and defames his neighbour, as may appear from what was shewn in the *Doctrine concerning the Sacred Scripture*, in relation to the threefold sense of all that is contained in the Word, n. 5—7, &c., and n. 57.

88. Inasmuch as a lie and truth are two opposites, it follows, that so far as any one shuns a lie as sin, so far he loves truth.

89. So far as any one loves truth, so far he is desirous of knowing it, and so far he is affected when he finds it; nor can any other attain unto wisdom: and so far as he loves to do the truth, so far he is made sensible of the pleasantness [*amoenitas*] of the light in which the truth is. It is similar to the subjects spoken of above;—as with sincerity and justice with him who shuns thefts of every kind; with chastity and purity with him who shuns adulteries of every kind; and with love and charity with him who shuns murders of every kind, &c. But he who is in their opposites, knows nothing concerning them, although they contain every thing.

90. It is truth which is meant by the seed in the field, concerning which the Lord speaks in these words: "A sower went out to sow.—And as he sowed, some fell by the way-side, and it was trodden down, and the fowls of the air devoured it; and some fell upon a rock, and as soon as it was sprung up, it withered away, because it lacked moisture; and some fell among thorns, and the thorns sprang up with it and choked it; and other fell upon good ground, and sprang up, and bare fruit, a hundred fold" (Luke viii. 5—8; Matt. xiii. 3—8; Mark iv. 3—8). The sower here is the Lord, and the seed is his Word, consequently truth: the seed by the way-side is with those who care nothing about truths: the seed on a rock is with those who are concerned about truth, but not for its own sake,—thus not interiorly; the seed among thorns is with those who are in the concupiscences of evil; but the seed in the good ground is with those who from the Lord love the truths which are in the Word, and practise them in dependence on him,—thus bearing fruit. That this is the meaning of the parable appears from the Lord's explication of it (Matt. xiii. 19—23; Mark iv. 14—20; Luke viii. 11—15). Hence it is evident, that the truth of the Word cannot take root with those who care nothing about truth; nor with those who love truth outwardly and not inwardly; nor with those who are in the concupiscences of evil; but with those in whom the concupiscences of evil are dispersed by the Lord In these last, the seed, that is, the truth, is rooted in their spiritual mind. Concerning which, see above, n. 86.

91. It is a common opinion at this day, that salvation consists in believing this or that doctrine of the church, and not in doing the commandments of the decalogue (which are, not to kill, not to commit adultery, not to steal, not to bear false witness,

both in a confined and extended sense): for it is urged, that works are not regarded, but faith from God: when, in fact, so far as any one is in those evils, so far he is without faith. As was shewn above, n. 42—52. Consult your reason, and consider well, whether any murderer, adulterer, thief, and false witness, so long as he is in the concupiscence of such evils, can have faith; and further, whether the concupiscence of such evils can possibly be otherwise dispersed than by not willing to do them because they are sins, that is, because they are infernal and diabolical: wherefore, whosoever supposes, that salvation consists in believing this or that doctrine which the church teaches, and is still an evil-doer, must needs come under the description of that foolish one mentioned by the Lord in Matthew (vii. 26). Such a church is thus described in Jeremiah: "Stand in the gate of the house of Jehovah, and proclaim there this word:—Thus saith Jehovah of hosts the God of Israel, Amend your ways and your doings:—Trust ye not in lying words, saying, The temple of Jehovah, the temple of Jehovah, the temple of Jehovah, are these.—Will ye steal, murder, and commit adultery, and swear falsely,—and come and stand before me in this house, which is called by my name, and say, We are delivered, to do all these abominations? Is this house become a den of robbers?—Behold, even I have seen, saith Jehovah" (vii. 2-4, 9—11).

## XII. IT IS NOT POSSIBLE FOR ANY ONE TO SHUN EVILS AS SINS, SO AS TO HOLD THEM INWARDLY IN AVERSION, EXCEPT BY COMBATS AGAINST THEM.

92. Every one, may know from the Word and from doctrine thence derived, that the *proprium*, [or selfhood,] of man, is evil from his birth, and that it is in consequence of this that from an innate concupiscence, he loves evils, and is led into them, so that he wills to revenge, to defraud, to defame, and to commit adultery; and in case he does not think that they are sins, and resist them on that account, he commits them as often as opportunity offers, and when his interest and reputation are not endangered. Hence it is that man, does those things from delight, if destitute of religion.

93. Inasmuch as this *proprium*, [or selfhood,] of man, constitutes the first root of his life, it is evident what sort of a tree man would become, if that root were not extirpated, and a new one implanted: he would be a rotten tree, of which it is said, that it is to be cut down and cast into the fire (Matt. iii. 10; vii. 19). This root is not removed, and a new one implanted in its stead, unless man regards the evils, which constitute the root, as destructive to his soul, and wishes on that account to alienate himself from them: but inasmuch as they are of his *proprium*,

and consequently delightful, he cannot effect their removal but with a degree of unwillingness, and of struggle against them,—thus of combat.

94. Every one who believes that there is a hell and a heaven, and that heaven is eternal felicity, and that hell is eternal misery; and who further believes, that those who commit evil go to hell, and those who do good, to heaven,—is brought into a state of combat: and he who combats, acts from an interior principle, and in opposition to that concupiscence which constitutes the root of evil; for whosoever combats against any thing, does not will it,—and to have concupiscence is to will. Hence is it evident, that the root of evil can only be removed by combat against it.

95. So far, therefore, as any one fights against evil, and thereby removes it, so far good succeeds in its place, and from good only he looks evil in the face, and then sees it to be infernal and horrible; and because it is so, he not only shuns it, but also holds it in aversion, and at length abominates it.

96. The man who fights against evils, must needs combat as from himself; otherwise he does not fight, but stands like an automation, seeing nothing and doing nothing; and from the evil [in which he is] he continually thinks in favour of evil, and not against it. But still it is well to be known that the Lord alone fights in man against evils, and that it only appears to man as if he fought from himself, and that the Lord is willing it should so appear, inasmuch as without such appearance there could be no combat,—consequently no reformation.

97. Such combat is not grievous, except to those who have given up the reins to their concupiscences, and have deliberately indulged them, and also to those who have confirmed themselves in the rejection of the holy things of the Word and of the church. To others it is not grievous; and should they resist evils in intention only once in a week, or a fortnight, they will perceive a change.

98. The Christian church is called the church militant, and it cannot be called militant except as fighting against the devil, consequently against the evils which are from hell;—hell is the devil. This combat consists in the temptation which every member of the church endures.

99. The Word in many places treats of combats against evils, which are temptations; such are understood by these words of the Lord: "Verily, I say unto you, except a corn of wheat fall into the ground and die, it abideth alone, but if it die, it bringeth forth much fruit" (John xii. 24): and also by these: "Whosoever will come after me, let him deny himself, and take up his cross, and follow me. Whosoever will save his life shall lose it; but whosoever shall lose his life for my sake and the gospel's, the same shall save it" (Mark viii.

34, 35): by the cross is understood temptation; as also in Matt. x. 38; xvi. 24; Mark x. 21; Luke xiv. 27; by his life is meant the life of man's *proprium* or selfhood; as also in Matt. x. 39; xvi. 25; Luke ix. 24; and particularly John xii. 25; which is also the life of the flesh that "profiteth nothing" (John vi. 63). Concerning combats against evils, and victories over them, the Lord speaks to the churches in the Revelation; as to the *church in Ephesus:* "To him that overcometh will I give to eat of the tree of life, which is in the midst of the paradise of God" (Rev. ii. 7): to the *church in Smyrna:* "He that overcometh shall not be hurt of the second death" (Rev. ii. 11): to the *church in Pergamos:* "To him that overcometh will I give to eat of the hidden manna, and will give him a white stone, and in the stone a new name written, which no one knoweth, saving he that receiveth it" (Rev. ii. 17): to the *church in Thyatira:* "He that overcometh, and keepeth my works unto the end, to him will I give power over the nations, and I will give him the morning star" (Rev. ii. 26, 28): to the *church in Sardis:* "He that overcometh, the same shall be clothed in white raiment" (Rev. iii. 5): to the *church in Philadelphia:* "Him that overcometh will I make a pillar in the temple of my God,—and I will write upon him the name of my God, and the name of the city of my God, the New Jerusalem, which cometh down out of heaven from God—and my new name" (Rev. iii. 12): and to the *church in Laodicea:* "To him that overcometh, will I grant to sit with me in my throne" (Rev. iii. 21).

## XIII. MAN OUGHT TO SHUN EVILS AS SINS, AND TO COMBAT AGAINST THEM, AS FROM HIMSELF.

100. Those combats, which are temptations, may be seen particularly treated of in the work *On the New Jerusalem and its Heavenly Doctrine*, published in London in 1758 from n. 187—201. Whence they are, and their nature, may be seen, n. 196, 197. How and when they occur, n. 198. What good they effect, n. 199. That the Lord combats for man, n. 200. Concerning the Lord's combats or temptations, n. 201.

101. It is of divine order that man should act from freedom according to reason, since to act from freedom according to reason is to act from himself. Nevertheless, these two faculties, *freedom* and *reason*, are not of man's *proprium*, but are of the Lord within him: and so far as he is a man, they are not taken away from him, because without them he could not be reformed: for he could not do the work of repentance, he could not fight against evils, and afterwards bring forth fruits worthy of repentance. Now since freedom and reason are with man from the

Lord, and man acts from them, it follows, that he does not act from himself, but as from himself.*

102. The Lord loves man, and wills to dwell with him: yet he cannot love him and dwell with him, unless he is received and loved reciprocally;—thence, and not otherwise, there is conjunction. For this cause the Lord has given freedom and reason to man; freedom, to think and will as from himself, and reason, according to which [he may think and will]. It is not possible to love any one and to be conjoined with any one, with whom there is no reciprocation, neither is it possibe to enter into and remain with any one with whom there is no reception. Inasmuch as receptivity and reciprocality are in man from the Lord, therefore the Lord says, "Abide in me, and I in you" (John xv. 4). "He that abideth in me, and I in him, the same bringeth forth much fruit" (John xv. 5). "At that day ye shall know that—ye are in me, and I in you" (John xiv. 20). That the Lord is in the truths and in the goods which man receives, and which abide with him, he also teaches in these words: "If ye abide in me, and my words abide in you.—If ye keep my commandments, ye shall abide in my love" (John xv. 7, 10). "He that hath my commandments, and keepeth them, he it is that loveth me,—and I will love him,—and will make my abode with him" (John xix. 21, 23). Thus the Lord dwells in his own with man, and man in those things which are from the Lord, and thus in the Lord.

103. Now as there is with man, from the Lord, this power of yielding or withholding reciprocation and thence mutual [love], therefore the Lord directs, that man should repent; and this no one can do, but as from himself: "Jesus said, Except ye repent, ye shall all perish" (Luke xiii. 3, 5). Jesus said, "The kingdom of God is at hand; repent ye, and believe the Gospel" (Mark i. 15). Jesus said: "I come—to call sinners to repentance" (Luke v. 32). "Jesus said to the churches, Repent" (Rev. ii. 5, 16, 21, 22; iii. 3); also, "They repented not of their deeds" (Rev. xvi. 11).

104. Because there is with man from the Lord this power of yielding or withholding reciprocation, and thence mutual [love], therefore the Lord enjoins, that man should do the commandments, and should bring forth fruits; as in these words: "Why call ye me Lord, Lord, and do not the things that I say?" (Luke vi. 46—49). "If ye know these things, happy are ye if ye do them" (John xiii. 17). "Ye are my friends, if ye do whatsoever I command you" (John xv. 14). "Whosoever shall do and teach the same, shall be called great in the kingdom of the heavens" (Matt. v. 19). "Whosoever heareth these sayings

* That man has freedom from the Lord, may be seen above, n. 19, 20; and in the Treatise on *Heaven and Hell*, n. 589—596, 597—603. What freedom is, may be seen in the *New Jerusalem and its Heavenly Doctrine*, n. 141—149.

of mine and doeth them, I will liken him unto a wise man" (Matt. vii. 24). "bring forth fruits meet for repentance" (Matt. iii. 8). "Make the tree good and its fruit good" (Matt. xii. 33). "The kingdom shall be—given to a nation bringing forth the fruits thereof" (Matt. xxi. 43). "Every tree that bringeth not forth good fruit, is hewn down and cast into the fire" (Matt. vii. 19). Not to mention many other passages of a like nature; from which it is evident, that man ought to do good from himself, but by the Lord's power, which he should implore; and this is to do good as from himself.

105. Inasmuch as there is with man from the Lord this power of yielding or withholding reciprocation and thence mutual [love], therefore man will render an account of his works, and be recompensed according to them; for the Lord says, "The Son of Man shall come,—and reward every one according to his works" (Matt. xvi. 27). "They that have done good shall come forth to the resurrection of life, and they that have done evil to the resurrection of damnation" (John v. 29). "Their works do follow them" (Rev. xiv. 13). All were judged according to thir works (Rev. xx. 13). "Behold I come, and my reward is with me, to give to every one according as his work shall be" (Rev. xxii. 12). If there were no reciprocality with man, there could be no imputation.

106. Because reception and reciprocality are with man, therefore the church teaches, that man should examine himself, confess his sins before God, desist from them, and lead a new life. That this is taught by every church in Christendom, may be seen above, n. 3—8.

107. If man had not had receptivity and thence thought as from himself, nothing could have been said to him about faith, for neither is faith from man. Without these man would be like chaff in the wind, and would stand as though he were inanimate, with his mouth open and his hands hanging down waiting for influx, thinking nothing, and doing nothing in the things which concern his salvation. He has indeed no active power in those things from himself, but still he has a power of re-acting as from himself.

But these things will be placed in a still clearer light in the Treatises concerning *Angelic Wisdom.*

## XIV. IF ANY ONE SHUNS EVILS FOR ANY OTHER REASON THAN BECAUSE THEY ARE SINS, HE DOES NOT SHUN THEM, BUT ONLY PREVENTS THEIR APPEARING BEFORE THE EYES OF THE WORLD.

108. THERE are moral men who keep the commandments of the second table of the decalogue, being guilty neither of theft, nor of blasphemy, nor of revenge, nor of adultery; and

such of them as persuade themselves that such things are evil, because they are hurtful to the common good of the state, and thereby contrary to the laws of humanity, also live in the exercise of charity, sincerity, justice, and chastity. But if they practise these goods, and shun those evils, only because they are evils, and not at the same time because they are sins, they are still merely natural man, and with merely natural men the root of evil remains ingrafted, and is not removed; wherefore the good actions which they perform are not good, because they proceed from themselves.

109. A natural moral man may appear before men in the world altogether like the spiritual moral man, but not before the angels in heaven; for before the angels in heaven, if he be principled in what is good, he appears as an image of wood, and if he be principled in what is true, as an image of marble in which is no life:—it is otherwise with the spiritual moral man: for the natural moral man is externally moral, and the spiritual moral man is internally moral, and what is external without what is internal is not alive: it lives indeed, but not the life which is called *life*.

110. The concupiscences of evil, which form the interiors of man from his birth, are not removed except by the Lord alone: for the Lord flows in from what is spiritual into what is natural; whereas man of himself enters from what is natural into what is spiritual, and this influx is contrary to order, and does not operate upon concupiscences to the removal of them, but incloses them more and more closely in proportion as it confirms itself: and since hereditary evil thus lies concealed and shut up, after death, when man becomes a spirit, it bursts the covering within which it was concealed in the world, and breaks out, like the discharge from an ulcer which had been only superficially healed.

111. There are various and manifold causes operating to render man moral in an external form; but if he be not also moral in an internal form, he is still not moral. As for example: If any one abstain from adultery and fornication through fear of the civil law and its penalties;—through fear of the loss of reputation, and thence of honour;—through fear of diseases which may be thereby contracted;—through fear of family broils from his wife, and consequent disturbance of his tranquillity; —through fear of revenge from the husband or his connections; —from poverty or avarice;—from imbecility arising either from disease or abuse, or from age, or from impotence; yea, if he abstain from them from any natural or moral law, and not at the same time from a spiritual law, he is still inwardly an adulterer and fornicator: for he still believes that they are not sins, and consequently he does not make them unlawful in his spirit before God, and thus in spirit he commits them, although not before the world in the body; wherefore after death, when he becomes

a spirit, he speaks openly in favour of them. Hence it is evident, that a wicked person may shun evils as being hurtful, but that none but a Christian can shun evil as sins.

112. The case is similar in respect to thefts and frauds of every kind;—with every kind of murder and revenge, and with every kind of false witness and lies. No one can be cleansed and purified from them of himself: for there are infinite concupiscences inherent in every one of those evils, which man sees not but as one uncompounded thing, whereas the Lord sees the smallest unit [singularissima] in every series. In a word, man cannot regenerate himself, that is, form in himself a new heart and a new spirit, but the Lord alone [can do this]: who is himself the Reformer and Regenerator. Wherefore if man wills to make himself anew from his own prudence and intelligence, it is only like a covering deformed face with paint, and anointing a part affected with inward rottenness with a cleansing ointment.

113. Therefore the Lord says in Matthew, "Thou blind Pharisee, cleanse first that which is within the cup and platter, that the outside of them may be clean also" (xxiii. 26). And in Isaiah: "Wash you, make you clean, put away the evil of your doings from before mine eyes, cease to do evil:" and then "though your sins be as scarlet, they shall be white as snow; though they be red like crimson, they shall be as wool" (i. 16, 18).

114. To what has been said above, let these remarks be added: I. That Christian charity, with every one, consists in his performing faithfully the duties of his calling: for thus if, he shuns evils as sins, he daily does what is good, and is himself his own particular use in the common body: thus also the common good is provided for, and that of each individual in particular. II. That other works are not properly works of charity, but are either its signs, or benefits, or debts.

FINIS.

www.ingramcontent.com/pod-product-compliance
Lightning Source LLC
LaVergne TN
LVHW050514100826
845148LV00002B/335

* 9 7 8 1 4 2 5 5 2 1 8 6 8 *